MERLIN'S DAUGHTERS

MERLIN'S DAUGHTERS

CONTEMPORARY WOMEN WRITERS OF FANTASY

CHARLOTTE SPIVACK

Contributions to the Study of Science Fiction and Fantasy, Number 23

GREENWOOD PRESS
NEW YORK • WESTPORT, CONNECTICUT • LONDON

Library of Congress Cataloging-in-Publication Data

Spivack, Charlotte.
  Merlin's daughters.

  (Contributions to the study of science fiction and
fantasy, ISSN 0193-6875 ; no. 23)
  Bibliography: p.
  Includes index.
  1. Fantastic fiction, American—Women authors—
History and criticism. 2. American fiction—20th
century—History and criticism. 3. Women and literature
—United States. 4. Quests in literature. I. Title.
II. Series.
PS374.F27S65   1987   813'.0876'099287   86-12088
ISBN 0-313-24194-5 (lib. bdg. : alk. paper)

Library of Congress Catalog Card Number: 86-12088
ISBN: 0-313-24194-5
ISSN: 0193-6875

First published in 1987

Greenwood Press, Inc.
88 Post Road West, Westport, Connecticut 06881

Printed in the United States of America

∞

The paper used in this book complies with the
Permanent Paper Standard issued by the National
Information Standards Organization (Z39.48-1984).

10 9 8 7 6 5 4 3 2 1

To my brother Charles,
who remembers

CONTENTS

PREFACE

FANTASY FICTION IN AMERICA has suffered from a persistent critical ambivalence.[1] Unlike England, where writers like J. R. R. Tolkien and C. S. Lewis receive serious critical attention from critics and reviewers, America has tended to repress fantasy as the shadow side of popular literature. Even while science fiction and detective novels have become academically acceptable as worthy of intellectual analysis, fantasy is often rejected as frivolous (what one science-fiction writer called "cute stories about unicorns") or categorically relegated to the juvenile shelves. In a travesty of literary judgment, such works as Patricia McKillip's brilliant *Riddle of the Stars* trilogy are reviewed only in children's literature journals, where they are solemnly condemned for their unseemly depth and difficulty. What accounts for this disparity between attitudes toward fantasy, lauded by its most famous practitioner, Tolkien, as a godlike activity of "subcreation," and scorned by some reviewers as juvenile cuteness?[2] Brian Attebury suggests as reasons for the prevailing American hostility to fantasy our double inheritance from the Puritans and the Enlightenment, combined with our national devotion to pragmatism and materialism.[3] Ursula K. Le Guin, posing the question of why Americans are afraid of dragons, also attributes the fear in part to Puritanism, the work ethic, and profit-mindedness.[4] She further suggests that our sexual mores are also partly to blame, for Americans tend to regard reading (and writing) fantasy fiction as effeminate. This provocative insight into a possible relationship between fantasy and the feminine provided the inspiration for this book.

Is there then an element of gender discrimination in our haste to classify fantasy as juvenile? Is there also perhaps an underlying fear of this particular genre which is receptive to dreams, to the dark, to the unconscious, which tends to subvert science and technology and to reject limits imposed by the rational mind? Is there perhaps even a suspicion that fantasy literature with its otherworldly landscapes, its mythic monsters, and its magical spells, represents escape reading in its most dangerous sense by suggesting preferable modes of reality? These questions underlie my text.

Essentially my purpose is twofold. The first is simply to demonstrate the literary quality of ten representative female fantasists. In this I address the general reader whom I wish to make aware of this neglected body of authentic literature. My method here is necessarily synoptic and evaluative as well as interpretive. The second is addressed to the specialist as well as to the general reader. This concerns the feminist perspective in these works. While studying these women writers (and others), I discovered an underlying thematic pattern common to their fiction that is directly relevant to the fear and hostility aroused by fantasy. These women have found the fantasy novel a congenial medium for certain ideas that clash with the dominant culture and ideology of our still largely patriarchal society. Through these writers the metaphorical fantasy quest takes on a new dimension of political and social meaning. Just as women writers have modified and expanded the scope of science fiction, they have also revisioned the nature of conventional fantasy. The new "enchanted quest" is distinctively feminine.

As I attempt to elucidate this feminist perspective, which has enriched fantasy through its prevailing undercurrent of suggestive, often subversive, commentary on our cultural milieu, I shall also try to clarify if not precisely define my elusive key words "fantasy" and "feminine." My approach to "fantasy" is inductive. I agree with Attebury that it is easier to place a group of books on a shelf and call them fantasy than it is to arrive at an acceptable definition.[5] I shall briefly survey recent theory of fantasy in my opening chapter, then turn my attention to that particular *kind* of fantasy exemplified in the Earthsea trilogy and *The Lord of the Rings.* My use of the terms "feminine" and "masculine" refers to cultural constructs and psychic components, not to biological women and men. Whether or not men really *are* more aggressive than women is not the issue; culturally the masculine is perceived as aggressive.

My choice of these particular ten authors is admittedly personal, conditioned in part by my preference for certain features such as the

Arthurian mythos. I have omitted both Gothic or horror fantasy and sword and sorcery or epic fantasy. I have also omitted science-fiction/fantasy hybrids as well as lost-world fantasy. My overall organization is simply chronological, based on the date of the first published work of fantasy. The paucity of footnotes in several chapters is a matter of realism, not fantasy. Nothing has been written about these authors, not even substantive reviews. Critical neglect has in fact been another criterion for inclusion. With the exception of Le Guin, the authors under consideration here have been woefully neglected, not by readers but by critics.

Implicit in my aims and in my choice of authors is an ultimate desire to modify the canon. I wish to challenge the politics of exclusion that has kept works of fantasy, particularly those written by contemporary women fantasists, in the dark or, worse, in the playroom. On a more positive note, I wish to acknowledge the enthusiasm of the twelve hundred or so students who have taken my course in Masterpieces of Modern Phantasy these last few years. *They* are not afraid of dragons.

MERLIN'S DAUGHTERS

1.

FANTASY AND THE FEMININE

IN SPITE OF THE PERVASIVE CRITICAL AMBIVALENCE toward individual works of fantasy, the theory of fantasy literature has attracted much critical attention in recent years. Pioneering attempts to define the nature of "the fantastic" were Harvey Cox's *The Feast of Fools* (1969), which stressed the element of festive release in the impulse to fantasy, and Tzvetan Todorov's *The Fantastic: A Structural Approach to a Literary Genre* (1970, tr. 1973), which narrowly perceived fantasy as a moment of hesitation experienced in the presence of an apparently supernatural event.[1] More recently, W. R. Irwin and Eric Rabkin have also dealt with fantasy theory, stressing respectively "the impossible" (*The Game of the Impossible: A Rhetoric of Fantasy* [1976]) and the reversal of the ground rules of narrative (*The Fantastic in Literature* [1976]).[2] All of these studies are essentially concerned with "the fantastic" as an element in much of the world's literature rather than with a specific kind of literature that is popularly recognized as "fantasy." Colin Manlove rightly noted that most definitions of fantasy are either too broad or too narrow, "too inclusive to be definite or too definite to include very much."[3] In Manlove's own attempt to delimit fantasy he defines it as "a fiction evoking wonder and containing a substantive and irreducible element of supernatural or impossible worlds."[4] I have argued elsewhere that the word "fantasy" is so diversely and diffusely used as to preclude definition, suggesting that a strictly literary genre or subgenre might usefully (and on solid historical and etymological grounds) be distinguished as "phantasy."[5] My own emphasis is on the psychological dimension of fantasy fiction, consonant with Ursula K. Le Guin's observation that fantasy deals with the journey to self-knowledge, speaking "to the unconscious, from the unconscious, in the language of the unconscious, symbol and archetype."[6]

For this reason I must reject the notion of "the impossible" as a logical starting point for dealing with fantasy. To define fantasy in terms of the impossible is to define possibility in terms of scientific realism. The events in fantasy fiction may be physically impossible, but they are not psychologically impossible. Like the content of dreams, they have psychic validity. Contrast with realism may indeed be a helpful approach to fantasy but not based on the expectations of realism, i.e., whether a given event can or cannot happen in the physical world. *Dr. Jekyll and Mr. Hyde* may be a fantasy, but schizophrenia is a real phenomenon.

A better starting point is the recognition of the symbolic nature of fantasy as opposed to the representational nature of realism. Plato long ago distinguished between art produced by fantasy (a mental faculty) as symbolic and art produced by the imagination (a different mental faculty) as representative of images existing in the real world.[7] In contemporary critical terminology, realistic fiction is essentially metonomy, the part signifying the whole. The story of a child growing up in a New York ghetto, for example, is paradigmatic of the lives of all urban minority children. Fantasy fiction, on the other hand, is essentially metaphor, based on implied resemblance between two basically unlike things. The fantasy quest for a magic talisman, for example, does not imply a whole of which it is a part, but rather it constitutes a totally symbolic action. The quest for an object symbolizes a quest for meaning on the nonmaterial level of experience. Similarly, magic as means to fulfill the quest serves as a symbolic action. The transformation of a person into a dragon is not paradigmatic of whole populations in the process of literal change to reptilian form. Instead, it functions as metaphor, indicating that a person who behaves monstrously is inwardly dragonish.

The two most central and significant symbols in most contemporary fantasy, through which both narrative form and thematic content are articulated, are the quest and magic. As Jane Mobley perceptively notes, "Magic is the informing principle in fantasy."[8] The quest—not surprising—implies a question. Just as the detective novel asks "Whodunit," so the fantasy novel asks "What do I seek?" The former question is directed outward, the latter inward. The mode by which the detective novel answers its outward question is rational deduction from given evidence. The mode by which the fantasy quest is identified inwardly and fulfilled is magic. Whereas the conundrum of the mystery novel is literal, the quest in the fantasy novel is symbolic. It is a metaphor of the search for meaning, for identity.

Magic must also be viewed as metaphorical rather than literal. Mobley precisely defines magic as "a creative power capable of actualizing itself in form."[9] This actualization is transformational: Magic changes the appearance of things. Magic in fantasy functions as both impersonal force at work in the world and as personal directed use of power by a gifted individual. As Peter Beagle's bumbling magician Schmendrick (*The Last Unicorn*) puts it, everything is crouching in readiness to become something else. Magic as an elemental force in nature brings about changes: the cocoon turns into a butterfly. Magic in the individual is creativity. As Le Guin observes, "Wizardry is artistry."[10] The creative power of the imagination transforms reality by actualizing itself in form: notes into music, the alphabet into poetry, the child into a hero. In fantasy, then, magic serves as a metaphor of the creative power of the imagination. The fantasy fiction under consideration in this book may thus be perceived as an "enchanted quest," an inner journey informed by magic.

This kind of fantasy is a modern, i.e., postmedieval genre. The Middle Ages did not develop fantasy as a separate form since the medieval mind perceived the world "with an all-inclusive awareness of simultaneous realities."[11] The medieval romance, the ancestor of fantasy, combined the mundane and the magical, the picaresque and the numinous, the physical and the supernatural. To an age that lovingly and repeatedly depicted the ascent of the Virgin to heaven, a flying dragon posed no problem in credibility. For the Middle Ages, however, the dynamic of magic was sacred. God the ultimate wizard was the source of all creative transformation that occurred vertically, down from and upward toward the divine. The secular movement of the Renaissance opened the possibility through science of horizontal transformation, in effect bringing about both fantasy and science fiction. Like Lord Dunsany's Elfland drifting away from the fields we know, the newly divided psyche of Western culture split off conscious from unconscious, rational from irrational, spirit from matter.[12] Magic, no longer permeating the primary world, retreated to the secondary world of the imagination. In literature this split led to science fiction as the extrapolation of the rational and to fantasy as the extrapolation of the nonrational. Early science fiction experimented with voyages to the moon, while fantasy delved into the dark forest of the unconscious, home of the vampire and dragon. From a materialist perspective one might call the science-fiction speculation realistic—people have traveled to the moon—but although the vampire and dragon are not materially real, they are real elements in the psyche and as such are symbolic of human problems, projections, dreams, and nightmares.

The earliest fantasy in English, Edmund Spenser's *The Faerie Queene*, offers a symbolic quest narrative in an imagined or secondary world where magic is operative. Each of its six books features a knight's quest for perfection in a given virtue, with the entire work, which was never finished, aimed at representing the total person perfect in all the moral virtues. (What do I seek? Moral perfection.) The dynamic of transformation is magic, but *The Faerie Queene* is a transcendental fantasy, with magic both vertical and horizontal, a product of intervention by supernatural powers as well as by wizards. A moral allegory as well as a fantasy, *The Faerie Queene* seeks to change the individual but otherwise functions conservatively to confirm the established value of its religious and political milieu. It is not, as many later fantasies were to be, subversive.

Fantasy over the next two centuries following Spenser will not concern us here, for in its escape from mimetic realism English popular literature for the most part diverged either into hyperrational science fiction or antirational Gothic. Horror fiction proliferated in the eighteenth century, with chilling tales of ghosts and monsters, haunted castles and decayed ruins, asserting a need for sexual and instinctual freedom through voicing the repressed and ghoulish underside of a society totally dedicated to rationality. Rosemary Jackson has demonstrated the connection between Gothic fantasy and cultural taboo in her study of fantasy as subversion from a psychoanalytical perspective.[13]

It is not until the nineteenth century that we see a resurgence in England of the Spenserian secondary-world model of fantasy fiction. William Morris, an ardent medievalist and social reformer, wrote several long fantasy novels structured as quests and moved by magic. Also in the nineteenth century a new religious focus was introduced into fantasy by George MacDonald, a devout Scottish minister. MacDonald's adult works *Lilith* and *Phantastes* (named for a character in Spenser) are transcendental fantasies positing a specifically Christian quest for rebirth.

Several fantasists in the twentieth century have continued the tradition of the transcendental mode, the most important being the Inklings: C. S. Lewis, J. R. R. Tolkien, and Charles Williams. Williams's fantasies are overtly theological, set in the primary world which is spiritually invaded by supernatural forces. In one novel the Holy Grail reappears in rural England; in another the two protagonists are dead, returning to London to fulfill a spiritual mission. Lewis's Narnia stories for children and space trilogy for adults are symbolically Christian. Neither Aslan the Narnian lion nor Ransome the new Pendragon is Christ but both are metaphors of the self-sacrificial redeemer. Tolkien's *Lord of the Rings* is neither theological nor overtly Christian, but the morality of his Middle Earth is clearly symbolic of Christian dualism, with evil represented in terms of darkness and his wizard Gandalf reborn and garbed in white after his return from the dead. All three are transcendental fantasists with immortality as one goal of the quest and with magic emanating from above through supernatural intervention.

Several modern fantasists, including the Inklings, have also turned to the Arthurian mythos for the material of the fantasy quest. For most of these writers the Arthurian realm, although ostensibly medieval and European, is symbolically a secondary world not based on historical accuracy. One well-known example is T. H. White who in the opening volume of his four-novel series deliberately uses anachronisms to alienate his setting from realistic reader expectations, although he also incorporates authentic detail concerning medieval life on such matters as falconry and castle architecture. Since White's *The Once and Future King* Arthurian fantasy has proliferated so as to become a veritable subgenre.[14] Five of the ten authors I discuss have written Arthurian fantasy.

Many fantasy writers have created wholly original secondary worlds. Of these the most phenomenally successful is J. R. R. Tolkien whose trilogy achieved a remarkable readership especially in this country in the 1960s. Much more than a mere best seller, *The Lord of the Rings* was a spiritual construct for our materialistic time, a powerfully evocative symbol of what seemed to be wrong and what should be done about it. For the younger generation who read it twenty times, who memorized genealogies and learned to write Elvish, it had the force of a sacred text. Tolkien is significant for introducing a new element into fantasy fiction, i.e., political subversion.[15] Tolkien converted the quest to *find* something into a quest to *destroy* something. As metaphor Frodo's quest to destroy the ring of power signaled a protest against the establishment: antiwar, antitechnology, antipower politics. Those rational adults who viewed the Middle Earth mania as mere adolescent escapism missed the point of this devastatingly imaginative critique of our society. It is no coincidence that its popularity peaked during the Vietnam era. Since the force of its protest was symbolic rather than literal, its message was lost to the "realists." Frodo is still not recognized for the significant twentieth-century hero that he is. This self-effacing hobbit undermines two major mythic role models of Western patriarchal society, Faust and Prometheus. Frodo is an anti-Faust, committed to destroying power, not in its manifestations but at its source, and an anti-Prometheus, distrustful of the potentially destructive uses of that stolen fire of technology. In this sense, although Tolkien's trilogy is notoriously lacking in female characters, the work exhibits decidedly "feminine" themes.

Fantasy has flourished since Tolkien. At the moment it is burgeoning, with several new writers exemplifying the literary potential inherent in the genre. At this point I must return to my given subject, women fantasists. I must address the question of whether there is a distinctively feminine—or even feminist—fantasy or whether the top women writers of fantasy simply prove their ability to write superior versions of the traditional genre. I should also ask whether the genre itself is perhaps "feminine" as opposed to, at the extreme, hard-core "masculine" science fiction. I have already suggested that the women writers discussed here have indeed modified the genre in significant ways, as they have also influenced and changed science fiction. To varying degrees the work of these ten writers does represent a feminine revisioning of the fantasy quest and its heroes, the fantasy world and its occupants, and, above all, the meaning of magic at the heart of fantasy. This is not to say that all of these writers are feminists, nor is it to suggest that all of them are consciously committed to rejecting the models of past fantasy masterpieces. To a substantial degree, however, a feminine perspective on plot, character, theme, structure, and imagery is pervasive in the novels of these writers. Furthermore, as I hope to demonstrate, these writers are, unlike Spenser and rather more like Tolkien, only much more so, ultimately and profoundly subversive.

First let us look at the most obvious ways in which fantasy by female writers is different. The most immediately evident distinction is the choice of female protagonists. Andre Norton's Witch World series is about women; the trilogies of Ursula K. Le Guin and Patricia McKillip feature both female and male protagonists; Evangeline Walton, Vera Chapman, and Marion Zimmer Bradley all focus on female protagonists. Even more important than the mere choice of women as leading characters, however, is the concept of hero that underlies the choice. In much sword and sorcery written by women, for example, female heroes play conventional male roles as warriors. Their emphasis is on physical strength, courage, and aggressive behavior. In the fantasy novels the female protagonists also demonstrate physical courage and resourcefulness, but they are not committed to male goals. Whether warriors or wizards, and there are both, their aim is not power or domination, but rather self-fulfillment and protection of the community.

Furthermore, just as major women characters are often both masculine and feminine in their abilities, both expert with swords and devoted to peace, so male characters are also complex, with their aggressive natures modified by sensitivity. At the same time, those traditionally male traits of pride, sexual prowess, and desire for domination are often subjected to negative scrutiny. In short, the traditional roles of both men and women are reevaluated and recreated in these works. Probably the best examples of the modified male are found in the fantasies of Mary Stewart and Katharine Kurtz, which at first appear simply masculine in approach. Stewart's trilogy is devoted to the life of Merlin, the archetypal male wizard, but his intuitiveness, his sensitivity to nature, his minimizing of power, all seem feminine, permitting him in effect to function as the feminine side of his king. Kurtz's heroes in her two trilogies play traditional male roles, as warriors, priests, and politicians, but their conduct is by no means traditional. In her pseudomedieval fantasy world the male heroes exhibit traits usually associated with and often repressed as feminine.

Another overtly feminist strategy in these novels is the assumption of a female point of view on conventionally masculine subjects. Several women writers have turned to the Arthurian legend, which they have not dealt with in conventional ways. Instead, they offer a feminine perspective on the legendary events. Vera Chapman, for example, in her Arthurian trilogy, creates a new character to narrate part of the old story—King Arthur's daughter—and endows minor characters with strong personalities to narrate the rest—Bertilak's wife and Lynette. Both Marion Zimmer Bradley and Gillian Bradshaw retell events from the point of view of major female characters. Bradshaw makes Gwynhwyfar a first-person narrative voice, thereby reconceiving the role of the much maligned queen as a sympathetic woman. Bradley focuses on Morgan le Fay, recreating her role as a complex and positive character, far removed from the villainous part she plays in the original. Through these women narrators the events also shift in importance, with battles and politics losing emphasis in favor of human relationships and reactions.

A further narrative device favored by women fantasy writers is the circular as opposed to the linear plot.[16] As Le Guin succinctly states it in her Earthsea trilogy, "To go is to return."[17] Both Le Guin and Patricia McKillip in their trilogies put an emphasis on the second half of the traditional quest, the return, culminating in rebirth. The paradigm of the mythic hero, followed at least in part by most fantasists, includes eight stages from miraculous birth and inspired childhood through a period of meditation, the undertaking of a quest, a literal or symbolic death, journey to the underworld, and ultimately rebirth and apotheosis. Most, however, concentrate on the first half, with emphasis on the climactic nature of the quest. This heroic outward movement, responding to the call to adventure, is aimed at establishing the ego, as Joseph Campbell and others have pointed out, but the total self is not achieved until after the symbolic death, descent, and rebirth, followed by a return to the starting place. Le Guin's and McKillip's heroes return to their place of birth, as does Mary Stewart's Merlin, whose final enchanted sleep takes place in the very cave wherein he was conceived.[18]

Another recurring feature in fantasy by women writers is the return to the matriarchal society of the ancient Celtic world. The traditional late medieval setting, with the panoply of chivalric knighthood, is rejected in favor of the very early or premedieval, before the worship of the goddess has given way to Christianity. The Grail as motif is thus often replaced by the sacred cauldron. Evangeline Walton's translation and adaptation of the Welsh epic *The Mabinogion* is a convincing depiction of life in ancient Dyved where the mother goddess was worshipped.

Bradley also chooses a Celtic setting, with a plot stressing the conflict between the established matriarchy and the threatening new patriarchy introduced by Christianity. Andre Norton, on the other hand, creates her own original matriarchal society in her futuristic Witch World.

All of these techniques are clearly and readily apparent as feminist in focus: the emphasis on female protagonists, the preference for a matriarchal society as setting, the use of a circular rather than linear plot structure, and the assumption of a feminine point of view on subject matter traditionally presented from a male perspective. What more deeply distinguishes these fantasies by women writers is something much less obvious but ultimately much more significant. These works, which employ the fantasy quest as metaphor for the search for meaning through magic as metaphor for the transforming power of the creative imagination, are subtly but forcefully subversive of certain key concepts in the mainstream traditions of Western civilization. Much more than Tolkien, whose hobbits quietly prodded American youth into opposing the war in Vietnam, these fantasies are quietly undermining the foundations of capitalism, power politics, and Christian dualism. As Michael Butor points out in his study of the fairy tale, "[f]airyland is a criticism of ossified reality. It does not remain side by side with the latter; it reacts upon it; it suggests that we transform it, that we reinstate what is out of place."[19] Similarly, in the secondary worlds of fantasy the wizard's spell and the dragon's flame are metaphorically endeavoring to transform society in the direction of feminist values.

The first of these subversive motifs is the renunciation of the power principle in politics. As we have seen, Tolkien also introduces this theme but in a much more limited way. Frodo undertakes a quest to destroy the ring of power because the ring has been forged by a quintessentially evil figure. Power is the legitimate aim of other major figures representing the good. The aims of power-seeking are fulfilled in several ways that are positive in context: the dragon is slain, the war is fought and won, the king is restored to the throne. These goals are regarded as good ones. In contrast, in many of the fantasies written by women, the *desire* for power is denounced as a principle. It is not a matter of the good guys exerting power in order to crush the power-seeking of the bad guys. Instead, power-seeking as such is rejected. The goal in these quests is to *not* slay the dragon, to *not* take the treasure, to *not* seize the throne, to *not* dominate the Other.

In Andre Norton's Witch World, for example, the group of characters with potentially the greatest power is the Council of Witches. These gifted women have innate spiritual strength that enables them to perform magic. They use their skills in magic, however, only to negate or avert aggressive actions on the part of their power-hungry neighbors. The psychic power of these witches is superior to the steel weapons used by men. These wise women are committed to protecting their own free society and to maintaining the balance in nature. They use their magic to avert the threat of rape, war, and other forms of male domination, but when the threat is dispelled they do not establish their own political system. They retire to their own inner spiritual development. Their major antagonist is a technologically advanced society that they are forced to repel for the sake of remaining free. In so doing they do not adopt the technology that they see as a potentially dangerous base of tyrannical power.

Le Guin's Earthsea trilogy traces the career of a wizard from boyhood through maturity when he becomes an archmage. The major lesson he learns from his training is *not* to use the magical powers he possesses. Eager to perform impressive deeds of magic, he violates the stricture with disastrous consequences to himself and others. Through the course of the trilogy he gains maturity as he becomes able to manifest his wizardry through renouncing its usage except when absolutely necessary. He does not even kill the dragon but rather negotiates with it for future peaceful coexistence. The highest aim of wizardry is *being*, not *doing*.

The hero of McKillip's trilogy, *Riddle of the Stars,* is also faced with the challenge of accepting power, but he wishes to reject it from the start. The thoughtful, introspective type, he is part farmer, part student. His dearest wish is to marry his fiancée and settle down on his farm, spending his leisure in solving riddles, his favorite intellectual occupation. When he learns that it is his destiny to play an important role in the fate of the world, he desperately resists. Although the need to assume power is thrust upon him by the pressure of events, he never surrenders his desire for a quiet life of hard work and contemplation, without political involvement. He is by temperament what Le Guin's hero strives to become.

In her Arthurian trilogy, Gillian Bradshaw depicts the thrust for both military and political power as destructive of nature. More heroic than either the warriors or the leaders are the women who give birth, who heal, who suffer to maintain their families and households in the violent context of war and strife. Power comes and goes, passing through bloodstained hands, but the distaff world provides continuity through nurture. To the young mother whose husband is killed in battle the cause of empire is ill-conceived and meaningless. Even the death of King Arthur is shown to be the senseless result of a vain power struggle. What finally establishes Gawain as a member of the inner Arthurian circle is not his battle prowess, which he has demonstrated repeatedly to the point of madness, but rather his kindness to a fatally wounded soldier. Easing the pain of a dying man without any hope of reward or recognition is the highest kind of heroism.

In feminist fantasy, then, power for the sake of power is denounced in favor of living and letting live. The code of the warrior and the ruler is deglorified and exposed as negative and destructive, while the role of the wizard is exalted for its perceptive passivity.

A second subversive theme in fantasies by women writers is the vindication of mortality. Contrary to accepted tradition, immortality, whether assumed as a literal afterlife or sought as a lasting fame in this life, is not aspired to. As Le Guin's hero explains, "Death is the price we pay for our life" (*FS*, p. 180). Her trilogy offers a vehement protest against a misguided desire for immortality. The concluding novel concerns the need to free Earthsea from the malignant influence of a sorcerer who has opened the gate between life and death in order to gain immortality for himself and, with it, power over others. All of the light, the color, and the joy have left the world since movement between life and death has become possible. Magic no longer works, for the loss of distinction has killed the imagination. The living exist in a shadowy way, resembling the world of the dead, the Dry Land, for without death, life has no meaning.

Susan Cooper's novels also incorporate the theme of rejecting immortality. She focuses on individual choice, presenting one character who opts for immortal life and one who refuses it. The unfortunate man who takes on the burden of immortality illustrates the dire consequences of everlasting life. He is a wanderer who has survived for centuries and longs to be freed from his endless existence. For him death will be a relief. The other character is a young man who discovers his identity as the son of King Arthur. Transposed to the modern age, he must choose between joining his legendary father in immortality or staying on the farm in Wales where he has been brought up by the rural couple whom he had thought were his parents. For him the immediate loving bonds of family are more important than the immortal role as Pendragon.

Evangeline Walton's handling of the same theme in her fantasy based on *the Mabinogion* shifts attention from the desire for immortality to the vindication of mortality. In the ancient Celtic world depicted in these works, desire for immortality on the part of an individual seems egoistically defiant of nature, for in the natural scheme of life all are reborn into higher levels of being. Death is therefore but a gateway to rebirth on a higher plane. The newly introduced Christian idea of eternal reward or punishment conflicts with belief in the goddess who claims both Time and Death as her children, and from whose womb will come rebirth as well as birth. The notion of an eternal afterlife imposes a moral structure on an inevitable natural process that is inherently evolutionary.

In dealing with Arthurian themes, both Bradshaw and Stewart stress acceptance of mortality in the context of the renewal of nature.

Bradshaw's Gwynhwyfar will not accept the tale that Arthur will come again, preferring the consolation of spring, when life is naturally reborn. Stewart's Merlin retires to his cave, but not for an eternity.

A third subversive theme is the depolarization of values. Nothing has been more central to fiction in the Western world than the depiction of conflict between right and wrong, hero and villain. The clarity and vehemence of the conflict have pervaded popular literature in particular, because of its generally diminished regard for moral and aesthetic ambiguity. But even allowing for the greater ambiguity inherent in major fiction, the lines of force are even there clearly drawn: Raskolnikov was wrong to murder the pawnbroker; Scrooge should not have fired Bob Cratchett; Huck Finn was right to defend Jim, even at peril to his own soul. In the case of the women fantasy writers, however, these lines dissolve. One major example is the fiction of Le Guin, which is informed by Taoism in its moral structure. Unlike Christianity, Taoism rejects the polarization of opposites. Living well according to Taoism means living in harmony with nature, thereby maintaining a balance between natural opposites. In Earthsea good and evil do not exist as moral constructs, and light and dark are of equal value. Of the many elements held in binary suspension none is more basic than life and death, each of which requires the other.

In Norton's Witch World series, earthly standards of good and evil and moral judgments about reward and punishment become totally extrinsic and irrelevant on other planets. The hero of the first work is an army deserter in this world, but his humane sensitivity helps him become a savior in another. In McKillip's riddling world good and evil do not exist as concepts. By implication identity (more precisely, the search for identity) is valorized through the premium set on the ability to answer riddles, but truth remains the elusive ultimate riddle. In her narrative such modes of behavior as shape-changing function creatively or destructively, resisting ethical categorization. Furthermore, the omnipresent figure of Deth the harpist is both lauded and condemned, both accepted and rejected, emerging as a strong and essential presence but beyond moral judgment.

In the Arthurian and Celtic fantasies the depolarization of values is most evident in connection with sexuality. In the works of both Walton and Bradley sexuality is regarded as natural and blameless. In the absence of concepts of marriage, paternity, and legitimacy, the sexual act is free and fertility welcome. Sexual union is regarded as initiatory rather than possessive. Even incest is not prohibited, and Arthur's sense of guilt over the incestuous birth of Mordred is seen as a product of arbitrary Christian legalism.

In Bradshaw's Arthurian trilogy valorization is treated as a theme in itself. Her characters are concerned with the contrary forces of Dark and Light but find these opposites coexisting in every human being. Several who are devoted to serving the Light find themselves caught up in destructive behavior patterns that aid the Dark. Well-meaning characters perform actions that have negative consequences, but not out of malice or turpitude. Since things go both right and wrong in this world, moral blame is often essentially irrelevant. To condemn Gwynhwyfar's adultery as morally evil, then, is to misinterpret the act and misrepresent human reality.

The depolarization of values in feminist fantasy involves more than the rejection of moral dualism. One of the most profound and fundamental polarities is that of Self and Other. Much of human history has been characterized by political and religious intolerance of the Other. And in much literature male authors have posited the female as Other. Contrary to the long-established literary tradition of subduing or eliminating the Other as undesirable alien (or even of forcefully converting this alien presence, as in the case of Shylock), several women writers of fantasy direct their narratives toward acceptance of the Other, not merely dealienating it (and themselves) but actually integrating Self and Other.

Katharine Kurtz's double trilogy offers a striking illustration of this attitude. She is concerned with a gifted alien race, who are for centuries rejected as Other and mistreated for their giftedness. In these novels the perspective on discrimination is heightened through the fact that the difference—the Otherness—is one of superiority, not supposed inferiority. Fear motivates the prejudice of the establishment in the absence of any antisocial behavior on the part of those discriminated against. Andre Norton's novels concentrate on the integration of Otherness. In her elaborately imaginative other worlds, rational races exist in a multitude of forms. Wisdom of the scientific, philosophical, and mystical varieties exists in serpentine, winged, furred, and scaled as well as two-legged species. Similarly in McKillip's world, although the races are all human, the deeply engrained provincialism of the peoples from differing areas is unsullied by the aggressiveness of zenophobia. Otherness is an uncontested fact of life, a feature lending variety, amusement, and endless conversational possibilities.

Also implicit in depolarization is the rejection of transcendence in favor of immanence, a feature that sharply differentiates the fantasy worlds of the women writers from those of the Christian school, including the Inklings. One of the most elegantly detailed and pervasively immanent worlds is Le Guin's Earthsea. Although there is reference to a creator, clearly all is immanent within the creation. The highest wisdom available to the wizard is knowledge of the true names of things. These names are not imposed but derived, as the wizard finds Logos a process not unrelated to his own becoming. McKillip's world in its sly and subtle way is also an attack on transcendence. Much of her trilogy concerns the search for the so-called High One, who may or may not exist. Transcendence has been inherited in this world as an hypothesis but not wholly believed in and vulnerable to disproof. Here, as in Earthsea, understanding a thing is based on knowing its name, but here it is carried further to the point of transformation. Knowing about trees enables one ultimately to become a tree. Needless to say, tapping that deep-down sense of identity with trees in oneself is not easy.

Inherent in the theme of immanence is the stress on the importance of the natural environment. These fantasies are ecology-minded, often with an attendant bias against technology which is usually regarded as exploitative. Earthsea is totally without modern technology, and the heart of the ethical dictum is maintaining the balance in nature. In the Witch World, the enemies of nature as well as of human peace are the technological societies. In Walton's series the earth is worshipped as a manifestation of the mother goddess. To neglect the needs of the earth or to endanger its fruitfulness is to strike at the heart of life, all life. In Bradley's Celtic world the sacred places are those in nature. Worship must take place out of doors, not in a building, which is a human structure. Trees and waters are sacred. One social dimension of this attitude toward fecund nature is sexual permissiveness. Cutting down trees and prohibiting sex are both violations of nature.

In the fantasy fiction of contemporary women writers, then, certain patriarchal systems prevalent in our time are quietly being questioned, subverted, and revisioned. Far from being cute stories about unicorns written for juveniles, these mature, thought-provoking novels represent an intellectual and imaginative rebellion against the status quo. Through their prevailing metaphor of magic, they seek to transform society through the creative power of the imagination. The quest is a fantasy metaphor, but the transformation is a real goal. As Terry Eagleton points out, it "is not just that women should have equality of power and status with men; it is a questioning of all such power and status. It is not that the world will be better off with more female participation in it; it is that without the 'feminization' of human history, the world is unlikely to survive."[20]

2.

ANDRE NORTON

ONE OF THE MOST POPULAR CONTEMPORARY WRITERS of fantasy and science fiction, several of whose books have sold over a million copies, Andre Norton has been singularly lacking in critical acclaim. Several reasons have been suggested for the neglect of this writer of over ninety books, whose works also include Gothics, adventure stories, westerns, and mysteries. To some extent she has suffered from her own reticence, not being the kind of author to self-advertise before fans at national conferences. Perhaps she too has been mistakenly labeled as a writer for juveniles.[1] These factors are relevant, but the critical neglect lies also in part within the very fact of her popularity. Her wide reading public has simply taken Andre Norton for granted, not as the author of a single masterpiece but rather as a steadily dependable writer who is always there with a couple of entertaining new paperbacks every year. The would-be critic, on the other hand, is likely to be intimidated by the vast output and remarkable variety of this prolific writer. Whatever the reasons, the neglect is not justified in terms of overall quality, for in spite of her long list of titles Norton has written several excellent books, and the consistently high level of her work deserves serious consideration. She may be prolific and popular, but she is no hack. Her steady flow of quality writing without achieving a single masterpiece is reflected in the fact that she has received only one award nomination for a single book—*Witch World* (1963) was a Hugo nominee—but she was the first woman writer (and the fourth writer) to win the coveted Gandalf award for lifetime achievement in fantasy.

Born in Ohio of pioneer stock with an Indian strain in the family line, Mary Alice Norton was a solitary, bookish child, greatly influenced by her literary-minded mother and very interested in family history, a rich subject that inspired her first historical novels. As a child she spent much time playing with the collection of miniature animals in the household, a hobby later reflected in her sympathetic treatment of the animal world. When the depression interrupted her college career, she became a librarian, specializing for a time in children's literature. Her library work also gave her the opportunity for research, which in turn provided material for later novels. After almost twenty years as a librarian, she went to work as a reader for Gnome Press for a few years, then retired in 1966 to devote herself to full-time writing. Because of her poor health she moved to Florida, where she now resides in her house with the miniature animal collection, several feline companions, and a huge library reflecting her research interests in anthropology, history, folklore, witchcraft, cats, Victorian architecture, and Icelandic and Anglo-Saxon sagas. Of course she still writes. Andre Norton is not her pseudonym, as many readers think, but her real name. She changed her name from Mary Alice to Andre very early in her career when she was writing boys' adventure stories and realized that the feminine name would alienate her audience.

Andre Norton describes herself as a "staid teller of old-fashioned stories with firm plots and morals."[2] An admirer of eighteenth-century novelists Fielding and Smollett as well as of contemporary fantasists Piper, Mundy, and Hodgson, she professes an aesthetic commitment to a clear, strong, fast-moving narrative. She believes in a tightly woven pattern of action that does not indulge in wasted words or digress into irrelevant description. Her own novels fulfill what she regards as the legitimate purpose of fiction, i.e., to tell an entertaining story. In her fantasy novels the strong plot line offers a series of variations on what Joseph Campbell called the monomyth, in which the lowly hero, in Norton's case usually a misfit, moves through a series of ordeals to self-realization. The hero's journey is thus ultimately inward.

Norton's fantasy worlds are populated with a variety of species, alien and animal as well as human. Her rational beings appear in many shapes, including avian, reptilian, feline, and hybrid. Frequently her animal characters are superior telepathic beings. Her protagonists, of whatever shape and size, tend to be outcasts of society, isolated but sustained by a strong conviction of personal ethics. Often they possess psychic powers. At odds with their worlds, they fear loss of selfhood more than physical danger.

In Norton's novels the heroic quest for self-realization ends typically in union with another. The resolution of inner conflict is androgynous. For Norton the integration of Self and Other is of supreme importance, whether the Other is gender or species. This central and pervasive theme is a feminist concern closely related to her emphasis on the freedom and integrity of the individual.

In her emphasis on the sanctity of the individual, Norton is also antitechnological.[3] Close in spirit to Tolkien and White, she feels that the Industrial Revolution represents a loss rather than a gain for the human race, and in her books the villains are usually people who exploit science for personal ends. In the Witch World series, for example, the enemy are the Kolder, a technologically advanced and cruel race from a parallel universe. Even when her settings are futuristic, she favors the traditional values of the past which confer dignity and meaning on the individual.

In contrast to the machine, which she sees as a threat, Norton emphasizes the jewel or talisman as object of power. Her recurring use of this motif results from her long interest in psychometry. Serving as a link between history and speculative archeology, psychometry involves the presence of a spiritual residue in an artifact that has been handled by people throughout ages of time. These residual events, emotions, and experiences from the past can be evoked to confer power on an adept who is able to tap them. A jewel, precious stone, or a crafted object may possess such age-old historical impressions, but only the psychically sensitive person can discover this inherent power. The ability to divine the properties of an object through touch, to contact its latent spiritual content is largely but not exclusively attributed to women and to children of both sexes in Norton's work. Jewels of power are especially important in the Witch World series, where they are primarily used by witches. In the Magic series, written for juveniles, several artifacts function to produce magical effects for the young protagonists. And in *Merlin's Mirror* (1975) Norton's fictionalized treatment of the Arthurian wizard's career, both the titular mirror and several other items possess such magical properties.

Norton is above all committed to telling a story, and she tells it in clear, effective prose. Not given to metaphors or lyricism, her style is focused on narrative movement, dialogue, and descriptive foreground. Episodes are precisely delineated with the larger surrounding world left only as an impression. In this respect Norton is quite unlike Tolkien and White, who draw their worlds with minute, painstaking detail. But her scenes are moving and vivid, and both the outward action and inward growth are drawn convincingly and absorbingly.

Norton's greatest achievement is her widely acclaimed Witch World series. The original volume, *Witch World,* was initially based on research into the subject of the medieval crusaders' overseas kingdoms. Although sometimes labeled science fiction, the work is definitely fantasy, for on the alien planet where the action takes place magic is operative, and the only technology present is depicted as a threat to survival. Entrance to this unnamed planet is possible through interdimensional gates. Past entries through the centuries have peopled the Witch World (not a name but a descriptive label) with a variety of human cultures, ranging from primitive tribes, like the Falconers and the Vupsall, through the pseudomedieval societies of Alizon, Karsten, and Estcarp, to the modernistic, highly technological Kolder. The power of magic rests essentially in the Council of Witches, who reside in Estcarp. The witches are an esoteric group who subject their initiates to long years of hard training and who maintain their virginity as the source of their power. The most mysterious section of the planet is Escore, home of the original Old Race and also a variety of other races, including the Green People who control vegetation, the amphibious Krogan, the reptilian Vrang, the avian Fianna, the subterranean Thas, the cervine Benthan, the lupine Gray Ones, and the semiarboreal Mosswives.

As explained in Sandra Miesel's helpful introduction to the Gregg Press edition of *Witch World,* the influence of British myth and folklore is evident in the quests and journeys, the charms and superstitions, the landscape with its towers and megaliths.[4] Miesel also suggests that Norton's idea of magical power resembles the Melanesian concept of *Mana,* an essence present in everything but especially strong in certain places and things capable of releasing that power for the gifted person who can tap it. Such endowed individuals can weave illusions, heal injuries, and read minds by establishing contact with this resident essence. This idea is akin to but more universal than the idea of psychometry, which is focused on specific talismans.

Witch World begins with an account of Simon Tregarth, a disgraced American army officer after World War II, who escapes death by passing through an interdimensional gate, the Arthurian Siege Perilous, to an unnamed planet. In this strange world he comes to the aid of a young witch, Jaelithe, through whom he becomes aware of the struggle between the powerful but embattled witch race, the Estcarpians, and both the savage races of Alizon and Karsten and the technologically superior alien race, the Kolder. Simon is uniquely endowed to help because of his combined understanding of technology, learned on earth, and latent talent for magic, a product of his Cornish ancestry.

Web of the Witch World (1964) continues the struggles of the witches against the Kolder and introduces the theme of marriage. Simon and Jaelithe come to love each other and decide to marry although in so doing she must break her vow as a witch and lose her jewel of power. Much to her astonishment, however, her magical powers do not fade after marriage. Instead, she and Simon learn how to exercise a new and even stronger magical power together, which they will pass on to their children, whose adventures are told in the remaining works in the series.

In *Witch World* and *Web of the Witch World* Norton parallels the story of Simon and Jaelithe with that of their friends Koris, an exiled lord, and Loyse, an escaped heiress. Whereas Simon was rejected by his world for breaking its laws, Koris is rejected by his as an ugly, misshapen misfit. Both Jaelithe and Loyse are strong females, heroic, daring, and resourceful. Although lacking Jaelithe's psychic power, Loyse equals her in physical courage. An unwilling heiress of a brutal father and a victim of a forced marriage, Loyse becomes totally self-reliant in order to escape. Insulted by her father, who despises her pale, drab appearance, she disciplines herself in body and mind in preparation for the moment of running away from her wretched life. She cuts her long hair, rubs soot over her face, dons mail, and arms herself with a sword. Even before she gets safely out of the household, she finds an opportunity to save a captured young witch from rape. After her escape, and after many dangerous encounters, she meets and forms a relationship with Koris. The two couples—alien and witch, exile and runaway—gain strength from each other as well as from within their own natures. Together they succeed in destroying the Kolder menace.

The three remaining volumes in the Tregarth series are told by the three children of Simon and Jaelithe. They are triplets, two boys and a girl, with a close psychic bond among them. Each can feel the others' experiences, and all can communicate mentally with one another even over long distances. Jaelithe remarks in *Witch World* that a human being is actually threefold: a body to act, a mind to think, and a spirit to feel. From this perspective the triplets constitute the three parts of a total person. Kyllan is the warrior, a body to act; Kemoc is a seer, a mind to think; and Kaththea is a sorceress, a spirit to feel. This technique of splitting a personality into separate components is a feature of characterization in fairy tales, here successfully adapted to Norton's fantasy world where the typical quest is for individual wholeness. It is also a technique reflecting the feminine theme of integration and dealienation.

Three Against the Witch World (1965) is narrated by Kyllan the warrior. Through his account the reader learns that Simon and Jaelithe disappeared while the triplets were yet young, never returning from an expedition to investigate further threats against Estcarp. The three have been raised by foster parents. The immediate danger is for Kaththea, who has been kidnapped into the witches' keep where she is held captive. The rescue mission succeeds largely because of the strong psychic bond that permits the brothers to communicate with their sister from her prison. The warrior's exciting tale is told in less laconic language than he avows (fortunately), for the adventures take place in mysterious Escore, land of legend, with its strange mythic races, such as the Green People who take on the coloring of their surroundings and who use for their magic the rhythm and flow of nature.

Warlock of the Witch World (1967) is related by Kemoc, the seer. Like his brother, he is called upon to rescue his sister, this time from an evil wizard, Dinzil, who holds her in submission to his will. Often regarded as the finest of the Tregarth series, this work is highly imaginative, with its account of the legendary races of Escore. One such race is the amphibious Krogan, one of whom, a young woman named Orsya, comes to the aid of Kemoc, implementing his rescue of Kaththea. The reptilian Vrang are respected for their ancient wisdom, and the Marfay are one of the most unusual, with scaled skin, webbed feet, hands, and with back and front covered with a wedge-shaped shell.

One of the most delightful of these alien races is the seemingly all-female Mosswives. Shy but willing to be friendly, they are uncouth in appearance. The Mosswife whom Kemoc meets is gray as a tree, stumpy of frame, with a wrinkled, withered face, flat nose, and long hair much resembling tree moss, which can be gathered about her body like a mantle. Legend has it that Mosswives like to have their children fostered by humans, but since no one has ever sighted a Mossman, that part of the legend may be mere rumor. (The reader cannot help recalling the counterpart in Tolkien's ents, whose entwives are missing.) One of the Mosswives directs Kemoc to Loskeetha, famed as one who can read the future. Loskeetha lives in a cave, a solitary wise being who somewhat recalls Yoda from the *Star Wars* film series. A slight person, fragile and ancient, Loskeetha does not look a bit like a Mosswife, for she has very little hair. She wears bracelets of polished bone about her wrists and ankles. Her vision is not of the definite future but of possible futures. From her Kemoc learns of alternatives, not of predestined events.

One of the most powerful episodes occurs near the end when Kemoc becomes ensorcelled. His body is metamorphosed into that of a gray-green toad, his hands and feet webbed but with thick paws. His human mind continues to function within this monstrous toadlike form. His efforts to save his sister, who has become an arrogant accomplice of her captor, are complicated by this transformation, but he succeeds only to find that she has lost both her powers as a witch and her sense of her own identity. But he succeeds.

Kaththea is the narrator of the last volume, *Sorceress of the Witch World* (1968), in which she attempts to regain the gift of magic which she lost under the influence of the diabolic Dinzil. As sorceress, and as that part of the human being that functions as spirit to feel, she represents the feminine dimension of a total person, complementing her brothers, who act as body and mind. In this role she manifests a oneness not only with the other two triplets but also with other species, with the animal as well as human world, and with the very countryside. She does not seek to dominate other races nor to master the environment. There is no hostility in her for there is, in a sense, no ego. This very receptivity and responsiveness to the feelings of others unfortunately make her vulnerable to psychic as well as physical attack.

Kaththea suffers captivity for a time but eventually discovers a portal to another world, where she finds her long-missing parents, who have been spellbound all those years without aging. Together with the aid of another prisoner, a powerful wizard, Hilarion, the reunited Tregarths manage their escape and return to the Witch World.

The theme of love becomes more prominent in this final work of the series. Kaththea is painfully aware that Kyllan's relationship with Orsya, the Krogan woman, and Kemoc's with the Lady of the Green Silences, represent a fulfillment that she has been unable to achieve. Since her own attachment to Dinzil proved destructive, she is deeply suspicious of Hilarion, obviously a wizard of great power. Hilarion is, however, a man of total integrity, and Kaththea discovers that between them there can be mutual devotion, with neither ruled nor ruling, but only sharing. The work ends with her realization that with him she is now complete.

The feminist perspective established through the female narrator in this novel is augmented by the theme of androgyny. It becomes clear that the Council of Witches erred in rejecting sexual relationship with men. Jaelithe was ousted by the council for violating their cult of virginity, and Kaththea, her daughter and spiritual heir, resisted their indoctrination, forming her own union with a wizard. In Norton's view neither sex is complete without the other; self-fulfillment involves union with the opposite sex. Furthermore,the relationship between the sexes should be based on equality, not domination. The spiritual superiority of the witches over the physical reliance on steel weapons by men is an underlying assumption in Witch World, but segregation of spirituality is exposed as a false goal. Instead, through androgyny, through acceptance of the Other, weaponry becomes unnecessary. Wholeness through balanced union of male and female, especially on the plane of values, tends to eliminate the need for aggression. Norton is thus the first of the women fantasists to combine the themes of the renunciation of power, the depolarization of values, and the vindication of mortality. Norton's insistence on integration of the Other anticipates Le Guin's ecumenical league of planets.

Androgyny also figures prominently in a subdivision of the Witch World books concerning the Were Riders, a species of shape-shifters. Chronologically two of these works, *The Crystal Gryphon* (1972) and *The Year of the Unicorn* (1965), occur shortly after the first two of the Tregarth series, during the childhood years of Simon and Jaelithe's triplets, and the third, *Jargoon Pard* (1974), occurs about twenty years later and concerns the daughter of the protagonist in *The Year of the Unicorn*. Romance is a major element in these tales, each of which relates the story of a couple engaged in self-discovery and in search of wholeness through discovery of the other.

The Crystal Gryphon is told from an alternating first-person point of view. Half of the chapters are narrated by Kerovan, a young man of ancient lineage mixed with the blood of the Old Ones, and the alternate half by the lady Joisan, his betrothed from childhood through parental agreement. For most of the action the two narrators are involved in separate but related episodes, and they do not actually meet until near the end of the work. This double perspective both enhances the movement of the narrative and deepens the reader's awareness of character development.

Kerovan is one of the most striking examples of Norton's isolated, misfit heroes, for he was marked at birth with cloven hoofs instead of feet, setting him apart from all normal humanity. His search for knowledge about the Old Ones is the focus of his quest for self-knowledge, for clearly spiritual power as well as physical deformity is part of his mysterious heritage. Joisan accepts her engagement to him as her legitimate destiny although it represents a decision made by others. From the start she refuses to believe that her betrothed is a monster, remaining loyal to him through horrendous adversities. When he sends her as token of their eventual marriage a thing of power, a crystal ball containing the figure of a gryphon, she guards it as an object of infinite value.

As Kerovan and Joisan both explore the nature of the Old Ones' power, they learn about themselves and each other as well. Kerovan learns to accept his deformity and his share in the mysterious powers of the Old Ones as differing but positive dimensions of his heritage. Joisan finds her unwavering faith in her unknown betrothed rewarded through his devotion to her, and in her guardianship of the crystal gryphon she also learns much about the nature of power, its proper uses and dangerous abuses. After the double series of dramatic adventures, the meeting and acceptance of the couple is effectively understated in its focus on the theme of identity. At the end of the book Kerovan identifies both himself and Joisan by simply saying her name.

The Year of the Unicorn also focuses on a couple, but the protagonist is the young woman Gillan, who relates the first-person narrative. Gillan is one of the most appealing of Norton's female protagonists. Without at first being aware of it, Gillan is of the blood of the witches of Estcarp. A victim of war, she does not remember her family or ancestry. As a child she was brought to the Abbey Norstead to be raised by the religious sisterhood resident there. She is willful and independent, however, and after ten years in the abbey decides not to remain there for a religious career. She devises a trick whereby she may escape, and her subsequent adventures take her not only into the land of the Were Riders, who are shape-shifters, but also into herself.

Gillan becomes the bride of one of the Were Riders, Herrel the Wronghanded, a misfit among his fellows. Aware of her own difference as a black-haired adept among her fair-haired religious companions, Gillan does not object, but the other Riders resent both her and Herrel and fear her obvious ability to see through their own illusions. Through sorcery they try to gain control of her by separating her wraith from her body.

From this point in the narrative, Gillan is split into two, sometimes more, selves. Her adventures are both diverse and complex but always concentrated on her struggle to find and unify her self. Shape-shifting, illusions, and interdimensional portals serve to confuse and complicate Gillan's quest, and even the careful reader may at times lose track of which of the two or more Gillans is actually present at a given moment. In a final melodramatic scene the apparently literal death of one Gillan in the Other World becomes the metaphorical transition to rebirth of the real Gillan in her own world. Once again Norton is concerned with righting the split between physical and spiritual, preferring the wholeness of mortality to immortality of the separate soul.

It is not surprising that Gillan is one of Norton's most popular female protagonists. Independent, resourceful, tenacious, and courageous, she is a woman of strict integrity and self-discipline as well as of physical and spiritual fortitude. Many Norton fans have written to the author asking for more stories about Gillan.

Although another story about Gillan was not forthcoming, there was to be another story about her offspring. In the third of the Were Rider books, *The Jargoon Pard,* two babies are exchanged at birth, one of them the son of Gillan and Herrel. The other infant is the daughter of the lady Heroise, who is desperate for a male heir. A wise woman attending the two births, which occur at almost exactly the same time, substitutes Gillan's son for the baby girl, who is then given to and brought up by Gillan and Herrel, who name her Aylinn.

After the opening chapter, which explains the exchange of the two infants, the rest of the book is told in the first person by Kethan, the real son of Gillan who is, however, brought up as the heir of Heroise. Kethan discovers his abilities as a shape-changer after he receives the mysteriour gift of a jargoon pard belt from his mother's wise woman. The jargoon is a gem of considerable power, and the fur of the pard is the clue to Kethan's other, latent identity. The double ancestry of the Were Riders, partly human and partly animal, endows them with the potential to live in dual form. Naïve about such transformations, Kethan turns into a pard but is unable to effect a return to human form. His adventures in both forms constitute the main narrative of the book. In an exciting and suspenseful climax, he is finally restored to human form, not through external means but by virtue of his own inner power. The truth about his ancestry as well as that of Aylinn, whom he has encountered along the way as a moon witch, is also finally revealed.

The tight, fast-moving plot of this novel is deepened by Kethan's first-person internalization of the painful conflict resulting from his dual nature. His constant struggle is to harness the bestial nature to the wishes of the man. Although for a prolonged period he must live physically as a pard, hunting and killing his prey for food, he must as a man within the pard's skin respect humans and retain rational thought processes. His success in preserving rational supremacy over his bestial power ultimately makes it possible for him to control his physical shape as well. The device of shape-shifting is a metaphor of divided selfhood.

In one episode Norton offers a disquisition on the various colors of magic, rejecting the dualistic distinction between black and white magic as respectively evil and good. All magic contains elements of both. Red magic is associated with the body; green magic pertains to growing things in nature and to human creations of beautiful things; yellow magic is of the mind, requiring logic and philosophy; indigo is focused on the weather; and brown involves the woods and animal world. Far from being merely arcane, this treatment of magic as a full spectrum is one more way of depolarizing values. In the Were Rider books, then, as in the Witch World series, Norton goes beyond the conventions of sword and sorcery to communicate through her narratives a predominantly feminist vision.

Norton has also written a series of six books for young readers. The common theme in these works is acceptance of the Other. In each case the self-knowledge of the protagonist results not only from the admission of one's own weaknesses but also from the discovery of the Other as worthy of respect. Furthermore, each of these works is focused on a talisman, an object possessing magical powers. Drawing on myth and legend, these novels supplement their fantasy adventures with a moral perspective, for the youthful protagonists all learn about themselves in their experiences with the talisman.

The earliest, *Steel Magic* (1965), is the most juvenile in tone. The narrative draws on familiar Arthurian material, and the three child protagonists undertake their perilous quests in Avalon. The structure is schematic, as each of the three quests for an object of power is introduced separately then completed in the same order. This serial structure both increases the suspense and clarifies the meaning through parallel action.

When Sara wins a picnic basket, she and her older brothers Greg and Eric take it along on their search for a mysterious lost lake where they come upon a ruined castle and enter another world through a gate. There they meet Huon of the Horn, hero of one of Norton's earlier novels, who explains to them the desperate need to find the three missing talismans, Excalibur, Merlin's ring, and Huon's horn. Greg sets forth on the mountain road with only the picnic fork for protection, and eventually finds Excalibur; Eric takes the sea route, taking the spoon, and uncovers the horn; Sara, armed with the knife, rescues the missing ring. The law of fairyland, endowing cold iron with magical power, converts the three ordinary stainless steel table implements into potent weapons. The three quests are imaginatively handled as each child encounters and subdues his or her worst fears in magnified form. Sara, for example, is transformed into a cat for a time, giving her perspective on herself and on her inordinate fear of spiders. As Huon points out, the traveler through the mirrored wall does not return unchanged from the journey. Fantasy's mirrored wall becomes an image of seeing oneself in the Other, thereby gaining understanding of both self and Other.

In *Octagon Magic* (1967) the talisman is an eight-sided doll house, a miniature replica of the mysterious so-called "witch's house" in which it is discovered by eleven-year-old Lorrie. The gentle elderly lady who resides there, Miss Ashmeade, is anything but a witch to Lorrie, a Canadian girl who feels alienated in her present surroundings at home and at school. In Miss Ashmeade's gracious company, with her tales of life in the past, Lorrie finds comfort and escape. When she rides the rocking horse alongside the doll house, both toys become real and transport her into an adventurous past, where she helps runaway slaves. Lorrie is thus able to lose her feelings of alienation by overcoming her own attitude toward others as alien. Her new sense of tolerance and cooperation leaves her feeling less resentful of her schoolmates. In this tale of gaining self-knowledge through magical contact with the Other in a different world, the elderly Miss Ashmeade, with her strong respect for traditional values, may well represent the author.

Fur Magic (1968) draws on Norton's knowledge of Indian lore. Framing the story is the mythic figure of the Changer in the form of a coyote. According to the Plains Indians, the Changer created the Old Ones, animals and birds who lived as rational beings before the coming of man. Young Cory, spending a summer in the West with his Indian foster uncle, is perturbed by fears, afraid of the woods at night, of horses, and even of his uncle. Cory is transformed into a beaver, Yellow Shell, whose adventures occupy most of the book. The boy's experiences in animal form teach him to feel at home in nature and dispel his fear of the unknown. Norton successfully communicates the way humans find their own identity through taking on the nature of the Other, here encompassing both the animal world and the culture of the Plains Indians.

In *Dragon Magic* (1972) the talisman is a jigsaw puzzle consisting of four different dragon pictures. Four city boys, of different ethnic backgrounds, attending the same school but scornful of each other as "kooks," find the puzzle in an old unoccupied house. The first to discover it is Sig Dortmund who pieces together the picture of the silver dragon, whereupon he has a vision in which he relives the Fafnir legend. As Sig Clawhand he accompanies the hero Sigurd on his quest, witnesses

Fafnir's destruction through greed for stolen gold, and recognizes in his own desire to possess the puzzle the same ugly greed.

The three other boys have similar visions on separate visits to the puzzle. The black boy, George Brown, puts together the blue dragon. He then envisions the tale of a monster-dragon called the "sirrush-lau," as he reenacts the life of Sherkarer, a Nubian prince in the biblical era who has been captured in war and sold into slavery. As slave he meets Daniel, whom he helps kill the monster whose existence is a threat to their lives. Gaining his freedom through cooperating with a man of another race and religion, George learns that working together is better than hatred and resentment of the Other. Artie Jones, of Welsh descent, puts together the red dragon, symbol of King Arthur, and finds himself back in early Britain as Artos, riding to battle under the banner of the Pendragon. Through his discovery of Mordred's treachery he learns the danger of choosing the wrong side. In school Artie had been concerned with joining a certain "gang." Finally Kim Stevens, an adopted Chinese boy, is enabled by the gold dragon he assembles to become Mu-Ti, messenger in the service of a great leader, Chuko Liang, or "the slumbering dragon." In that role Kim learns the bitter consequences of misjudging others. He has similarly misjudged his fellow students as unfriendly whereas the fault has been his.

The myths of the past are thus fulfilled in the fantasy quests of the present. For each boy a dream vision becomes a reality. Gaining respect for his own ancestral past and thereby for himself, each boy learns to accept the Other as friend and equal.

Norton's style is more experimental than usual in this book. Although it is straightforward and colloquial in the present scenes, when the action shifts to the past the style changes accordingly. In the adventures of Sig and Fafnir, for example, she uses the heroic style of the saga. In the Mu-Ti story, with an oriental setting, she adopts for the dialogue the ornate, elaborately polite formality of an ancient Chinese court.

In spite of its juvenile protagonist, *Lavender-Green Magic* (1974) is the most mature of the Magic series. A sixth-grade black girl, Holly, is the central figure in this tale involving a background of witchcraft in Massachusetts. Since her father, a soldier, has been reported missing in action, Holly, together with her twin younger siblings, Judy and Crockett, are to move out of the city and stay with their grandparents while their mother goes to work in a nursing home. Sensitive, resentful of the ill fortune that seems to be ruining her life, Holly expects the worst in every new situation. She is embarrassed to learn that her grandparents own a junkyard, although most of the local school children regard it as an exciting repository of treasures; she mistakenly anticipates a prejudiced reaction from the almost all-white school population; and she surrenders to a growing selfishness that has sprung in part from her defensive attitudes.

In the grandparents' cluttered but endlessly fascinating house the children discover the talisman that will produce their magic adventures. It is a dream pillow, filled with herbs to help induce peaceful sleep, and decorated with a strange, mazelike embroidery. When Judy sleeps on the pillow, she dreams that by following the maze in the garden she will come to the house of a mysterious Miss Tamar. Although the maze is overgrown, the children, finding their way by taking only right turns, suddenly enter a house in the past where a friendly young woman, dressed in pilgrim-style clothing, tends her pot at the stove. The kitchen is scented by bunches of herbs hanging from the ceiling. Miss Tamar enchants her vistors and gives them herbs to plant back home, but it is also clear that she is suspected of witchcraft by some of her neighbors who mistrust her herb lore.

The children return home safely from their visit, keeping it a secret. Holly, however, nurses a growing desire to sleep on the magical herb pillow and finally gets hold of it. In her dream she is told to follow the maze, taking left turns all the way. The twins go with her but are frightened at all the wrong signs along the way. The path is slimy and covered with huge toadstools. This time at the center of the maze they find not Tamar but her sister Hagar, who invites them to enter in the name of Hecate. Clearly Hagar is a witch, but what also emerges with growing clarity is Holly's affinity with her. Holly admires Hagar's powers and accepts her herbs, which prove poisonous to the other plants. In an exciting climax that takes place appropriately at Halloween, the three children return to the house at the center of the maze where they encounter both Tamar and Hagar. In their grotesque Halloween costumes the youngsters look like demons to the crowd who have come to kill Tamar as a witch.

The ending is as happy as it is spectacular, with Tamar's good magic reaching forward in time to protect Holly's father. What is more significant than the ingenious plot is the complexity of theme and characterization. The split characterization in the sister witches functions to reveal the split in Holly's own immature nature. Her deep selfishness attracts Hagar, but her better nature is perceived by Tamar. Norton also integrates social issues, in particular prejudice, with Holly's internal conflict. The most sophisticated of the Magic series, this work treats the theme of Otherness through the differing but related issues of racism and witchcraft, with both reflected internally as psychological conflict dividing the adolescent protagonist.

The last of the series, *Red Hart Magic* (1976), also offers a series of visionary dream adventures in the past interspersed with the painful reality of the present. In this case two unhappy children, a boy neglected by his father and a girl neglected by her mother, find themselves thrown together when the two single parents decide to wed. Bitterly resentful of each other and discontented with their lives, they escape when the boy,

Chris, buys a model of an old English inn that has the power to transport them back to the seventeenth century. Through the inn both he and the girl Nan are enabled to display courage and tolerance in their shared challenging adventures, which include saving the life of a hunted priest in Protestant England. Both youngsters find themselves better able to cope with school problems because of their heroic self-images in the past, and both learn to respect members of the opposite sex.

In all of the Magic series, then, a magical talisman serves to integrate and fulfill the individual personality of the protagonist, a transformation that also creatively enhances the relationship of self with society. A necessary step toward selfhood is identification with the Other.

One of Norton's rare single works of fantasy is *Merlin's Mirror* (1975), actually an account of the wizard's life, from his mysterious birth to his final enchantment, set within a science-fiction framework. For the frame Norton uses the theory that in the ancient past of our planet Sky Lords lived on earth in an advanced civilization which was destroyed. Merlin, called at first by his Welsh name Myrrdin, is the child of a human mother and Sky Lord father, destined to restore the lost knowledge and civilization to the human race.

The body of the book is conventional fantasy, including several of the traditional episodes in Merlin's legendary career as wizard. As a youngster he is captured by the men of King Vortigern who seek a fatherless boy to use as blood sacrifice on the crumbling foundation stones of the king's tower. Merlin saves his own life by explaining to the king that the foundation is being continually undermined by the disorderly presence there of two warring dragons, one white and one red. Not only does this diagnosis prove true to observation, but the lad also prophesies concerning the future defeat of the Saxon white dragon by the Welsh red one. Also included are Merlin's arrangement for the birth of Arthur; his raising of the king stone by magic and returning it to England from Ireland for Ambrosius's burial at Stonehenge; and his plan for Arthur's removal of the sacred sword from the stone to prove his right to the kingship.

What is distinctive in this treatment of the Merlin myth is the conflict with his antagonist, Nimue. Like Merlin, Nimue is of the Sky People, but she objects to his determined intervention in the development of the human race. Specifically, she tries to thwart his attempts to bring about the restoration of civilized order through the enlightened rule of King Arthur.

The complex conflict between the wizard and his ultimate enchantress is developed on many levels, assuming various symbolic forms, all reflecting the elemental conflict between male wizard and female goddess. While Merlin has his cave, where he receives guidance and information, Nimue has a tower of stone in the middle of an enchanted lake. Merlin communicates with the magic mirror in the cave whereas Nimue in her tower has a strange crown made of wires which is apparently her communication device. Although the effort virtually exhausts his powers, Merlin uses his wand to destroy the crown. Merlin is at home with earth and stone; Nimue's element is water. Merlin, whose strength waxes with the sun, retires to a brightly lit cave while Nimue, who flourishes in the moonlight, prefers a dark tower for her retreat. Merlin assumes the visage of a male deity, the Horned God, to meet Nimue's huntresses, who wear pendants bearing the moon symbol and who worship her as the Great Goddess.

Nimue is Merlin's opposite, flesh to his spirit. She is not, however, an evil force to be overcome. As opposites they should be united, a fate that Merlin will not allow. In effect Nimue represents Merlin's unconscious, the reality of which he tries to deny. Unable to see her two-sided nature as goddess, he fears her influence and rejects that part of himself that is of her. Their potential for unity is suggested in the myth of the Horned God and the Great Goddess. "The Mother had her rival. In latter years that rival became her mate"(p. 176). Had not Merlin denied his own need for Nimue, perhaps his mission to bring peace to mankind could have been accomplished. On the other hand, perhaps the Arthurian ideal of civilized order is not the best fate for the human race. At any rate, even Arthur stresses the need to understand Nimue. The human race cannot benefit from Merlin's knowledge without acknowledging Nimue.

In this novel, then, Norton returns to the theme of her earlier Witch World works, that of the conflict between the technologically oriented male and the wise, intuitive female. She retains Merlin's wizardry as genuine power inherited from his Sky Lord paternity but has him exhaust himself physically in his vain efforts to help mankind. What Merlin lacks is an understanding of the dark side of himself as well as of humanity. When the wizard is cast into his enchanted sleep, Norton wisely leaves the fate of Nimue a mystery. The reader suspects that when he awakens, she will be waiting. The feminine side may be rejected, but it will not go away.

In her fantasy novels Andre Norton always fulfills and sometimes transcends her declared purpose to tell an entertaining story. In her work she communicates a vision of the world, of the individual, and of society. Her view of the world is essentially sacramental. Her forces of nature are portrayed as animate, sympathetic, willful. Trees, stones, hills, and pools are alive, both in and of themselves and in their subtle awareness of humans. Certain of her imaginative races are close to personifications of nature, like the Green People whose magic is of growing things, and the Mosswives, who seem an intermediate species, part woman, part tree. In her worlds all living species are valued as sacred in their identity, and total acceptance of the Other is the ideal.

Objects may also become sacramental, acquiring enchantment through time by dint of human contact. Norton thus succeeds in casting an enchantment over the real world of the reader.

For Norton the individual, male or female, is of supreme importance. Her respect for the freedom and integrity of the individual is thrown into sharp focus by her preference for the isolated, rejected outsider figure. Almost all of her heroes, women and men, are misfits in their own milieu, whether melodramatically like Kerovan, who is cloven-hoofed, or more mundanely, like Holly, the black girl who feels out of place in an all-white school. Each of these heroes lacks identity within the group but finds it within the self. The quest narrative typically, then, takes the form of a search for wholeness. Frequently the search is literalized as when Gillan is actually split into separate selves, or when the three children of Simon and Jaelithe are depicted as separate components of a single being, i.e., body, mind, and spirit. Wholeness also involves the union of male and female, as is the case of each of the protagonists in both the Witch World and the Were Rider series. Androgyny is an implied mythic goal throughout the novels. Wholeness also involves union of conscious and unconscious, a theme in both the Witch World books and in *Merlin's Mirror*.

Norton's vision of human society also emerges through her works of fantasy. Her most original and distinctive society is that of the matriarchal Witch World, dominated by the Council of Witches. The very fact of their supremacy indicates that psychic power is valued over mere weaponry or other forms of physical force. In these books Norton transforms the meaning of the charged word "witch." After Simon Tregarth's early reference to the biblical injunction against witches as a starting point, the reader learns along with him a new perspective on the word. The witches of Estcarp are wise women, female wizards with great psychic powers, professionally committed to maintaining the balance of nature and society. In keeping with the traditional portrayal of the wizard as a priestly figure, these women forego sexuality in order to devote themselves exclusively to works of the spirit. In that sense they are closer to nuns than to folklore witches, but their theology is of nature and psyche, not of church and deity. The reader learns, however, that loss of virginity does not entail loss of power. For Norton marriage does not violate spirit but rather enhances it.

The Witch World narratives are also charged with renunciation of the power principle. Just as the preferred weapon in resisting force is not steel but psyche, so the goal is peaceful psychic development, not domination, whether political, military, or technological. The witches are not at all mere virgin warriors fulfilling masculine desires for power and glory. Norton is not simply substituting women for men in traditional male roles. It is not that they lack the requisite skills. Gillan and Loyse, for example, counter male force with effective sword play. When the threats of rape and other forms of male domination are dispelled, however, the women do not establish their own pseudo-masculine empires. Their desire is not to dominate the men who sought to dominate them, but instead to assure their own freedom and integrity as individuals and that of others as well.

Norton's novels are thus memorable for their humane and feminist vision as well as for their imaginative fantasy narratives. Not only does she succeed in holding her reader, but her cosmos lingers in the mind, with its unforgettable images of alien species, jewels and talismans resonant with psychic powers, and magical transcendence of time and space. At the center of this original universe, with its startling variety of life forms, is the individual, alone, heroic, supremely important. Whether a schoolboy putting together a puzzle or a sorceress on a distant planet, the individual undertakes a mythic journey toward self-realization. Pervading this imaginative world is a vision of peace, based on the rejection of the desire for power and domination, and of whole-ness, based on the depolarization of opposites, resulting in the unity of physical and spiritual, masculine and feminine.

Susan Cooper

Susan Cooper was born in the Thames valley of Buckinghamshire in western England, a region rich in local legend. Although she moved to the United States in 1963, her fantasy sequence *The Dark Is Rising* is infused with the lore of her native countryside and Celtic myths of the ancient past.[1] The five-volume series is a richly evocative work, interweaving vivid scenes of rural life in contemporary England, Cornwall, and Wales with the haunting past of the Arthurian fifth century. The central theme is the conflict between the forces of the Light and the Dark, a polar opposition more transcendental than the mundane struggle between good and evil. The plot is focused on a series of quests to obtain the magical signs and objects of power needed to save the world from domination by the Dark. Although the sequence has been labeled juvenile fiction, and although the figures engaged in the quests are children, these books are actually mature fantasy. The juvenile tone disappears after the opening volume; the adventures become more dangerous and deadly, involving an adult level of betrayal; and the narrative structure, especially in the final volume, becomes highly sophisticated in its complex architectonics of time and space. The central, unifying figure of the series is Merriman Lyon, introduced as a lovable and eccentric great-uncle, but developed throughout as a profound delineation of the wizard archetype.

The sequence opens with *Over Sea, Under Stone* (1966), which introduces several major characters including the three children of the Drew family, Simon, Jane, and Barney. The trio are effectively drawn as children, with credible details of their petty squabbles and mutual insults, as well as their genuine affection for each other. Barney, the youngest, is a fair-headed lad in love with tales of King Arthur, which he has read and dreams about. When his family vacations in Cornwall, he is quick to note that this western land is the Logres of Arthur. And it is Barney who first realizes that his beloved great-uncle Merry, known to the world as Professor Merriman Lyon, is in reality Merlin (Merry Lion, Merlion, Merlin). Simon, the oldest, is the rational one, and Jane the intuitive.

Initially identified as an old friend of Mrs. Drew's father and well known as an Oxford professor, Merry has no direct relationship to the Drew children. No one knows exactly where he came from, but his deep-set eyes, fiercely curved nose, flowing white hair, and towering stature make him an imposing physical presence. Ancient as stone, he seems at one with sea and sun. It is he who explains the nature of the quest to the three children whose discovery of an old manuscript promises to enliven their vacation in a Cornish fishing village. They assume that the maplike drawing found in the attic must lead to treasure, but Merriman reveals that this manuscript, a 600-year-old copy of a much older original, concerns the whereabouts of the Holy Grail, hidden somewhere in the village. It is their task to decipher the map and find it before the enemy, the forces of the Dark, discover it. In this challenging task he will be their guardian, but not their helper.

The conflict of appearance and reality is strongly emphasized in the roles of the dark figures in the book, who evince an ambivalence and an ambiguity unusual in juvenile fiction. In this respect the first book anticipates the sequels, in which the theme of evil is handled with even more subtlety. The first enemies encountered turn out to be the most friendly people the children have met in the village. Mr. Withers and his sister Polly are presented as aristocratic in appearance, well dressed and formidably polite. They invite the children to spend a day at sea with them on their beautiful white yacht. Jane, for reasons she cannot fathom, does not like them and declines the invitation, but the boys go and thoroughly enjoy their excursion. Some days later, Simon discovers their dark nature when Miss Withers sends a rough youth chasing after him in order to steal the precious map. He sees her face suddenly distorted with fury, as she shouts insults at him. Barney discovers their hidden motives in even more dangerous circumstances. During a street carnival, when he has become separated from the others, he finds himself drawn into a dance by a slim person dressed in the costume of a white cat, who maneuvers him into the folds of a white robe worn by a dancer disguised as an Arab sheikh. Only after they have kidnapped him and taken off in their car does he recognize the Witherses. The symbolic appearance of evil in all-white as well as all-black garb is repeated in later works.

More conventionally wicked, with an identity based on deception from the start, is the ominous figure of Mr. Hastings. Jane meets him when she is seeking the village vicar, not knowing that the real vicar has moved and this dark, forbidding-looking man is simply renting the vicarage. His description befits that of a witch, for his heavy black eyebrows grow together without a break in the middle. A vague but intense uneasiness disturbs Jane as she talks with him and notices his keen interest in her questions about a map of the Cornish coastline. She senses "somthing monstrous" blazing behind his eyes, something not quite human. It later turns out that Merriman has known him by other names in other times, and although he is momentarily subdued by the power of the Grail at the end, he is still alive and the implication is that he will reappear in subsequent volumes in different guises.

The third proponent of the Dark is the most startling because the least expected. The housekeeper for the vacationing family is a beaming, red-cheeked village woman, Mrs. Palk, a buxom image of homely virtues. She bustles about benevolently, offering cups of tea or cocoa, and cheerfully singing hymns while washing the dishes. Only intuitive Jane mistrusts her; everyone else accepts her for the domestic paragon she appears to be. One night she sneaks into Barney's bedroom after he is asleep, obviously looking for the map. Somewhat later, she betrays the children with a blatant and dangerous lie. They have asked her to give their uncle a message about their plans for the day. She falsifies the message, deliberately misleading him as to their whereabouts, as a result of which Barney is kidnapped. Later on, Simon and Jane are told by one of the townspeople that Mrs. Palk will do anything for an extra pound. The reader is totally unprepared for the abrupt discovery that this model housekeeper and nursemaid is actually a villain.

While the children and their uncle seek the Grail using the old manuscript guide, they are continually pursued, intercepted, thwarted, and threatened by representatives of the Dark. The enigmatic instructions on the manuscript itself pose a further problem. Eventually, however, in an exciting climax, the Grail is discovered, but a lead case containing a second valuable manuscript interpreting the inscription on the Grail, is lost to the sea. The sacred relic is for the time being safely deposited in a museum.

The plot of this introductory volume is tightly woven, and the adventures are suspenseful although several last minute rescues by Merry tend to undermine the reader's sense of real danger to the young protagonists. The role of Merry as spiritual guide and guardian is not yet successfully realized, and the proponents of the Dark, not so much defeated as temporarily outmaneuvered in the end, lack moral depth. In itself *Over Sea, Under Stone* is more an adventure story than a true fantasy, in spite of the presence of the Grail as a numinous object, but it serves as effective prologue to what will be a genuine fantasy sequence.

In the second book, *The Dark Is Rising* (1973), Cooper introduces authentic fantasy elements such as magic and the double reality of primary and secondary worlds, coexisting in the present and the past. She also interweaves motifs from Celtic mythology and folklore with her own symbols, adding a dimension of meaning to the work. The protagonist is Will Stanton, youngest of nine children, who learns on the eve of his eleventh birthday that he is in fact the last of the Old Ones, an immortal race of people born to save the world from domination by the Dark. He was born on Midwinter Day, and the events of the book take place between Midwinter Eve and the twelfth day of Christmas. The powers of the Dark are strongest during this period, restrained briefly by the Old Magic on Christmas Eve but waxing until their greatest thrust on Twelfth Night.

In the first section of the book, after a series of frightening episodes preceding his birthday, Will is whisked out of his own time through mysterious doors on a mountain top. In a great firelit hall hanging with tapestries, he meets Merriman and a fragile old lady, who introduce him to the nature of his destiny. His quest is to find the six signs of the Light, made by the Old Ones, and to join them in a circle. He already possesses on his belt the first sign, an iron ornament shaped as a flat circle quartered by crossed lines, given him by a neighboring farmer. The other five signs, all quartered circles, will be made of wood, bronze, water, fire, and stone. In his brief stay in the strange hall Will also learns something of his powers over fire and his ability to travel back in time. When he returns to his home for his birthday, he realizes that the hall exists in the past of five hundred years ago. Part one ends with Will's finding of the second sign, a bronze quartered circle, given to him by the mysterious figure called the Walker.

The second section of the book is focused on Christmas. With meticulous detail Cooper captures the sights and sounds of the family holiday festivity and juxtaposes it with Will's visit to a Christmas celebration in the local manor house a century ago. In the past episode Will undertakes to study the Book of Gramarye, written in the Old Speech. After he has absorbed its precious knowledge, the book will be destroyed. In this section Will also acquires the next two signs, the third one, of wood, from the manor house, and the fourth one, of stone, from the stucco wall of the church. Christmas ends on an ambivalent note, however, as Will goes to sleep both happily contemplating riding his new bicycle and anxiously recalling Merriman's word "danger" in respect to the continuing unnaturally heavy snowfall.

Several terrifying adventures test Will's courage and ingenuity in the third section of the narrative. Nature seems to have gone wild, as devastating snows afflict the whole of England; Will's family is the focus of more immediate violence from the Dark, as his mother is injured and his sister kidnapped. Will nonetheless gains possession of the last two signs, those of fire and water, thus completing the circle. As the almost catastrophic Twelfth Night draws to a close, the snow suddenly gives way to rain and the imperiled townspeople, huddled together in the manor house to avoid freezing, are saved. These events occur in a tense vivid scene in which Will moves back and forth between the manor house of the present and of a century ago. In order to dispel the malign influence of the Dark Will must in the past help to seize the candles of the winter, bluish cylinders burning with a cold white flame, and fit them in a mandala ring of holders that will restore them to their proper use, while in the present the malevolent power of the Walker is subdued by a sedative. This dramatic enactment of the winter solstice in a ritual at once moral and seasonal is one of the most imaginative scenes in the series.

Characterization in this work is also excellent. Will is convincingly drawn as a divided human being, part choir boy and part Old One, a likeable fun-loving lad with the moral fate of the universe on his shoulders. Merriman is much more complexly portrayed than in the preceding work. Subject to moments of anger and irritation, vividly aware of danger, emotionally concerned with personal relationships that at times conflict with his duty to the Light, he is a more appealing Merlin figure. In some ways, however, the most striking character is the Walker. Introduced as an old tramp, he seems from the start a malevolent yet pathetic person. Dirty, uncouth, harsh and whining in speech, he is at once repulsive and pitiable. In one of Will's sojourns back in time we meet the Walker as a young man named Hawkin, who was born in the thirteenth century and raised as a son by Merriman, after his own parents had died. Happy to serve as Merriman's liege man, Hawkin is a bright, cheerful, energetic individual, boyishly proud of his green velvet jacket and altogether delighted that he has been brought forward in time in order to help his beloved lord perform a certain task.

Hawkin does not know that the task endangers his life. In order for Merriman to extricate the precious Book of Gramarye from its hiding place inside the workings of a pendulum clock he must have one hand touching a human shoulder while he reaches for the book with the other. If he fails to grasp the book or if he accidentally touches the swinging pendulum, the human helper will be killed. Although Merriman has chosen Hawkin for this crucial role out of genuine affection and deep trust, he does not realize until too late that it is not fair in human terms to jeopardize the young man's life. He makes the painful discovery that he has put more trust in a man than a mere mortal has strength to take. Of the Light rather than of humanity, Merriman forgets that Hawkin loves as a man, expecting proof of love in return. Shocked and dismayed when he learns the truth, Hawkin betrays his master and aids the Dark.

As a result, bright-eyed young Hawkin in his green velvet jacket becomes the despised Walker, ancient and ragged, doomed to wander, perhaps forever, in his own private hell. His release from dreary immortality takes place in the last book.

The theme of trust betrayed is also exemplified in a minor character, a dairy maid, Maggie Barnes. Apparently an innocent, wholesome person, she is described as "apple-cheeked" and "uncomplicated," with "nothing sinister" about her. In an encounter with Will, however, she turns suddenly vicious and the boy is astonished at her sneering laughter that sounds all the more evil for the "rosy openness" of her face. When she appears in the context of one of Will's travels in time, she is referred to as the "witch-girl." It is she who convinces Hawkin that the lords of the Dark are better, kinder masters than Merriman.

In addition to the high level of characterization and to the ingenious plot with its carefully structured interweaving of two worlds, this book contains rich mythic content. Cooper draws on a variety of Celtic legendary materials to add resonance to the traditional theme of the conflict of Dark and Light, and the enhanced role of magic clearly establishes the work as fantasy.

Greenwitch (1974), the third volume in the series, opens with a news account of the theft of the Grail from the museum to which it had been donated by the three children. The forces of the Dark, only temporarily subdued earlier, are once more abroad. In this work Cooper again utilizes Celtic and English folk customs as well as Celtic and classic mythology to add depth to her lively narrative. Here the Drew children meet Will Stanton, and although it is essentially their story rather than his, the Light needs the services of both. The major characters from the two previous volumes thus come together, sharing the quest to restore the Grail.

Less complex in its symbolism and more straightforward in its narration, *Greenwitch* is nonetheless an exciting book. Somewhat closer in tone to the opening volume, it focuses this time on Jane, the most sensitive and intuitive of the three youngsters. The plot converges on one ritual, the spring rite of the Greenwitch, an image woven of branches and leaves by the women of the small fishing village and flung into the sea to insure good fishing and fruitful harvests. The actual process of making the image may be watched only by women, so that Jane is able to observe but her brothers are not. The image has a hazel framework with a body of hawthorn boughs and blossoms and a head of rowan. Every woman who participates is allowed to make one wish on the image, and Jane, sensing a sadness about the figure to be thrown into the sea, unselfishly wishes only for the Greenwitch herself to be happy. Pathetically grateful to the one human who has treated her as a live being, Greenwitch later appears to Jane in a dream and reveals her secret possession. Deep under the waves she keeps the lead case with the precious manuscript that had fallen into the sea when the Grail was found.

The events in the book lead up to and away from this central episode, beginning with the announced theft of the Grail and ending with the recovery of both the Grail and the manuscript that makes it possible to interpret its inscription. Through the figure of the Greenwitch the concept of Wild Magic is introduced. Neither Light nor Dark, Wild Magic is simply the way of living things in the natural nonhuman world. Greenwitch denies any loyalty to the warring sides but simply asserts her own integrity as a child of the sea. Even though she is constructed by human hands, she is given life by Tethys, Lady of the Sea.

Will and Merriman take an underwater trip to the kingdom of Tethys. Tethys calls Merriman "Hawk," and they appear to be old acquaintances. The description of the sea world is graphic, with an especially effective passage about a giant deadly squid. Tethys herself is not described, for she is simply a presence, "the sea itself." Her world has no light, no joy, but rather is a place of fear and treachery, where fish eat other fish. It is a world of nature, not humans, and its Wild Magic has no concern for good or evil.

The principal exponent of the Dark is a painter, dark-haired and darkly dressed, a clear reminder of Mr. Hastings and the Black Rider. He paints with demented concentration and produces bizarre canvases which turn out to be magical spells. His connection with the Dark is exposed when he steals Barney's drawing for a totem and warns the Drews to keep away from the Greenwitch. It is that poignant leafy image that finally dispels him, however, casting him into outer Time.

Cooper uses the double time device in this book, but to a lesser extent than in its predecessor. In one harrowing episode, when the undisciplined and chaotic power of Wild Magic is loosed in the figure of the Greenwitch before she returns to her mother sea, the fishing village reexperiences the past. A phantom ship appears, and the bloody events of two past time periods are reenacted. Observing from her bedroom window, Jane first sees the onslaught of red-haired, helmeted oarsmen who leap from their boats and rush ashore to savagely attack the townspeople. This barbaric spectacle gives way to the capture of a smuggling ship. One of the ancestors of Captain Tom, whose house the vacationing children are staying in, was a smuggler who betrayed a fellow crew member to the authorities, identifying him as the man who shot and killed a revenuer. In her nightmarish vision Jane sees him as a drowned man piloting a phantom ship while ghostly crowds in the streets cry out the name of the hated traitor, Roger Toms. Distant past and recent past are joined by the present as the painter is forced aboard the phantom ship which flies away over the rooftops, disappearing into the distant skies. The book ends with the recovery of the Grail and the return of the valuable lead case to Jane by the grateful Greenwitch.

The Grey King (1975), next to the last in the series, is set in Wales and juxtaposes the double reality of daily life among Welsh shepherds and the parallel world of High Magic. There are two protagonists, Will who is visiting Wales for a period of convalescence from hepatitis and Bran, a strange albino boy whom he meets on the farm. This pale youngster, with white hair and tawny eyes, identifies himself as "the raven boy," a phrase that Will recognizes from one of the verses he has learned describing his quest. Almost as unusual in appearance is the boy's white dog, Cafall, who has silver eyes, another echo of a phrase from the magical verses. "There fire shall fly from the raven boy,/ And the silver eyes that see the wind,/ And the Light shall have the harp of gold." The meeting of the two boys initiates their shared quest for the golden harp.

Bran occupies a significant role in terms of the whole series. A child of mysterious origins, he was left as a baby with the farmer Owen Davies, abandoned by a mother who seemingly appeared out of nowhere and disappeared again three days later. Ultimately Bran is revealed to be the Pendragon, son of King Arthur brought forward into contemporary times by his mother, Queen Guinevere, primarily out of fear. Although not yet aware of his destiny, Bran has learned from Merriman that he must aid Will in the quest to awaken the six sleepers and thereby discover the golden harp.

Guinevere's appearance in twentieth-century Wales relates the theme of betrayal to an Arthurian motif. Her reason for leaving her own time is her fear that Arthur will not trust her because of her previous betrayal. She is convinced that if you once betray a great trust, then you dare not permit yourself to be trusted again. As she puts it, a second betrayal would be "the end of the world."

The concluding book in the series and by far the most complex of the five is *Silver on the Tree* (1977). Here the cryptic prophecies are fulfilled, the daring quests are completed, and the many narrative strands artfully tied together. Once more Will and Bran are joined by the three Drews, this time at midsummer, and again the setting is Wales although many of the events take place both elsewhere and in different time periods. The adherents of the Dark are active again, not only continuing their conspiracy to obtain the magical things of power but also working to pervert nature and men to their purposes. Deception, bigotry, and cruelty abound, as ugly English boys bully a Pakistani youth because he has dark skin, and vicious minks on the prowl kill chickens for the sake of killing. Here the theme of trust and betrayal receives its most significant treatment, and here also the Celtic mythological background is most effectively woven into the texture of the narrative.

Journeys both back in time and out of time occur in this book. In one such journey we see Will back in the time of the Roman Empire, watching the building of an amphitheater. He slips off his belt with the six magical signs attached to it and buries it in the hollow of a rock in a stone arch in the process of construction. Minutes later we see him back in his own time, talking with an archaeologist at the digging site of Carleon, where he reaches under a rock in a broken arch and retrieves the belt, shaking off the dirt of sixteen centuries. The episode gains meaning from the parallel portrayals of two men at the site. The first is a homesick Roman centurion, working on the structure and complaining about the frigid English weather; the second is an American archaeologist, also homesick, also lamenting the weather, dreaming about his family back in sunny Florida. In a given landscape history repeats itself and human nature remains a constant.

In this final work Jane assumes a significant role again as she did in *Greenwitch*. The parts she plays in the narrative quests involve communication rather than action. Just as in *Greenwitch* her sensitive response to the woven image inaugurated a relationship, so here the mysterious Lady, fragile and delicate yet essential to the success of the Light, chooses to communicate only with Jane because it is "like to like." Her message to the young girl is a cryptic prophecy about a forthcoming quest to the Lost Land. After the visit from the Lady, Jane is terrified by a sudden apparition from the lake, a gruesome monster demanding that she reveal the Lady's words. Although she refuses to betray the message, this surprise threat from the Dark drives Jane into a faint, but she recovers quickly without forgetting the all-important message to deliver to the boys who must undertake the quest.

The adventures of Will and Bran in the Lost Land, where they go for the purpose of finding the crystal sword, occupy about a third of the book and provide the most effectively sustained fantasy episode in the work. The boys travel there on an airy roadway, arched like a rainbow. The land exists far in the past, for its fate was to be drowned in flood waters when a storm broke the dikes holding back the sea. On their arrival, they see what seems at first to be an empty city, but a guide appears named Gwion, who assures them that there is a country and a palace as well. The Dark is also in evidence there, as they encounter frightening phantom riders in an otherwise charming rose garden. The boys undergo other strange adventures, including visiting an empty palace that turns out to be a maze of mirrors, and being pursued by a giant skeleton of a horse, a literal nightmare. They eventually find the tower, where the gifted king, craftsman of the marvelous crystal sword, sits in melancholy brooding, paralyzed by despair. Consumed by doubt and fear, the monarch suspects even his faithful minstrel Gwion of betrayal. But "loving loyalty bright as a flame" shines in the bard's face, and when the deluge begins and the boys are about to return to their own world with the sword, Gwion refuses to leave and stays at the side of the king. "I belong here," he asserts, supporting the shoulder of the failing king and bravely facing the flood.

After Will and Bran return from the Lost Land, another betrayal occurs in the children's own world, this time involving a further example of the apparently innocent Mrs. Palk/Maggie Barnes type. This time it is the kindly wife of the shepherd John Rowlands, an honest man and lifelong friend of Bran. Mrs. Rowlands is portrayed as a gentle, endearing woman, whose warm voice is an appealing feature of her friendly nature. Bran has known her all his life as a good neighbor. The dark side of her nature is not revealed until almost the end, so that the reader is once more, as in the case of the housekeeper, taken by surprise. The scene takes place aboard a train, with Mrs. Rowlands knitting as Bran, Merriman, and the other children are talking. As the train descends into a tunnel, her needles clack ever faster and faster as if saying "into the dark, into the dark." Bran suddenly brandishes his crystal sword and challenges her, much to the anguish of her unsuspecting husband, but Will and Merriman confirm the accusation. Mrs. Rowlands gradually changes her expression, drops her knitting, clings to John momentarily for protection, then chillingly admits her alliance with the Dark. Her warm voice modulates into harsh, sardonic laughter as she taunts the futile endeavors of the Light. In one of the most tense and bizarre moments in the sequence, Merriman gestures to expel the woman from this stream of time and she is caught up in a whirl of light, seized by a white rider who materializes out of the darkness through which the train is moving. Although her voice will later be heard again and her face dimly seen, she does not return, and her stunned husband tries desperately to understand how his beloved wife of many years can actually have been one of the Dark without his knowing it.

At this point both John, the bereft husband, and Bran, the acknowledged Pendragon, face painful alternatives. John finds it intolerable to choose between dismissing his grief at the loss of his wife by remembering her evil and mourning her death by forgetting her complicity with the Dark. He asks the ethereal Lady to make the choice for him. The Lady, unlike Merriman in his relationship with the young Hawkin, makes the decision in strictly human terms. She causes him to forget his wife's betrayal and to endure a time of genuine mourning for her death.

In a somewhat analogous situation, Bran must choose between loss on the human level and loss on the suprahuman level of the Light. Specifically, he must choose between joining his immortal father King

Arthur, freed now from time since the threat of the Dark has been averted and the task for the Pendragon fulfilled, and remaining with his adoptive father to share his rural existence. For Bran the "loving bonds" established in this life in his growing years on a farm in Wales are more important to him than his role as Pendragon. He therefore will forget his participation in the transcendental work of the Light and instead continue to live and age as other mortals do. Both of these choices clearly stress the value of human love over the ideals of the Light although both are made possible only through the victory of the Light.

Silver on the Tree then ends with a magical ritual at the midsummer tree, the tree of life. The Pendragon cuts the silver blossom from the mistletoe with the crystal sword, thereby driving the powers of the Dark out of time. Hereafter the future of the world is in human hands.

Cooper thus skillfully parallels the metaphysical conflict of Light and Dark with its reflected mundane struggle between trust and betrayal. The reader encounters the Dark in its unequivocal manifestations. In its symbolic purity the Dark wears garments of white as well as of black. As Will notes, "[T]he Dark can only reach people of extremes—blinded by their own shining idea, or locked up in the darkness of their own heads" (p. 142). The evil in humans is not merely less obvious, it is often totally disguised by virtuous appearances. The reader, inclined to trust the friendly neighbor, the affectionate housekeeper, and the wholesome farm hand, is quite taken aback when their duplicity is revealed. For this reason, as well as for others, it is a mistake to relegate the Cooper series to the juvenile level. Dante knew that the monster Fraud had the face of an honest man, but such an awareness is quite an adult phenomenon.

Throughout *The Dark is Rising* series Cooper's language ranks her with the best stylists in contemporary fantasy fiction. Her descriptions of daily life are precisely detailed and meticulously concrete. Her dialogue is effective and convincing, always closely related to character and to context. The brief exchanges among the excited children in the Stanton family on Christmas Eve, the awesome high style of Merriman and the Lady, the whimpering, whining tone of the Walker, Barney's childish little explosions of delight all have the ring of authenticity about them. But Cooper's greatest achievement in style is her descriptive power in the fantasy episodes. Shimmering scenes of wonder, like the boy's flight to the Lost Lands, the underwater kingdom of Tethys, the mystical transformation of the mistletoe blossom into a white bird, and the eerie majesty of the great candlelit halls of the past, as well as the scenes of sheer terror, like the pursuit by the ghastly, white-boned horse skeleton, the attack by the slimy, iridescent sea monster, the appalling, abrupt expulsion from time of several Dark figures, and Barney's drug-induced vision in the Grail, testify to her stylistic excellence. Her

language is rhythmic as well as precise and heightened by image and
metaphor, creating a poetic effect. One reviewer described her style as
rich and as eloquent as a Beethoven symphony.

The resemblance to a symphony is apt, as Cooper, in her Newbury
Prize acceptance speech, compared the narrative structure of her series
to that of a symphony in four movements, with *Greenwitch* functioning
as a rondo. More impressive to the reader than the overall structure,
however, is the stylistic handling of themes as symphonic motifs. The
alternating pattern of joy and fear, for example, is handled like a musical
theme. Will's fear materializes in *The Dark Is Rising:* "The thing that
came was utterly silent. It was huge, a column of black mist like a
tornado, whirling at enormous speed upright between the land and the
sky. At either end it seemed broad and solid, but the centre wavered,
grew slender and then thicker again; it wove to and fro as it came, in a
kind of macabre dance. It was a hole in the world, this whirling black
spectre; a piece of the eternal emptiness of the Dark made visible" (p.
185). In contrast, there is the joy of decorating the Christmas tree with
old familiar decorations with "the golden-haired figure for the top of the
tree; the strings of jewel-coloured lights. Then there were the fragile
glass Christmas-tree balls, lovingly preserved for years. Half-spheres
whorled like red and gold-green seashells, slender glass spears, spider-
webs of silvery glass threads and beads; on the dark limbs of the tree
they hung and gently turned, shimmering" (p. 68). The analogy to music
thus applies to the language as well as to the sequential structure of the
series.

The sequence also embodies a philosophical vision of reality and a
sound conceptual grasp of moral perspective. Cooper is in this way
superior to those fantasists who are content to create a magical and
physical landscape for their secondary worlds but fail to give them a
moral or metaphysical foundation. Cooper's human world is controlled
by people but subject to the Old Magic of the earth and the Wild Magic of
living things. Greater than either of these powerful magics, however,
are the loving bonds between human beings, for they are the strongest
force of all. Beyond the world is the universe, which is bound by the law
of High Magic. On the suprahuman level coexist the polar opposites,
Light and Dark. These Platonic forces exist as realities on a plane above
human nature but they are able to influence human beings. The Dark
seeks to dominate the world and the Light to stop that effort at
domination. At the center of the Dark is a great black pit, bottomless as
the universe. At the center of the Light is a cold, white flame. Both are
beyond human attributes.

Cooper's attitude toward time is a significant part of her vision.
Although time travel is a common device in fantasy and science fiction,
in her case the device is employed as a dimension of meaning, and not

merely for its technical virtuosity. Cooper sees a unified pattern of experience in differing periods of time, as when the Roman centurion of sixteen centuries ago was echoed by a contemporary archeologist in his complaints about weather and loneliness. The past events in a given location hover, so to speak, both in their original form and in subsequent versions. Near the climax of the battle between Light and Dark in the final volume, for example, the participants suddenly see the battle of Mount Badon going on concurrently.

The trips in time begin in *The Dark is Rising* with Will's movement through the great carved doors on the snowy mountain top. Those same doors reappear near Will's home at the end of the volume, when Merriman passes out of time through them. During the course of the narrative Will visits the local manor house a century ago, and in one of the last episodes moves back and forth in time in that same place. In *Greenwitch* the past returns to the present, as Jane watches from her bedroom window two separate incidents from history taking place in sequence in the village streets below. Similarly, in *The Grey King* Will observes the past without actually traveling there. In this way he learns about Bran's destiny as he envisions King Arthur and Bran's mother, Guinevere, first in our time and then retiring to a stone abbey in their own time.

Silver on the Tree incorporates several time journeys, beginning in the opening chapter when Will, sitting on the riverside, suddenly perceives a double landscape. Through his brothers, who have become phantom forms, he sees several small, dark-haired people dressed in tunics, gathering bundles of spears, arrows, and sticks, and apparently running away from something. Somewhat later follows the brief episode at the Carleon digging site, and finally the long series of adventures in the Lost Land. Barney too travels back in time but only to be turned over to the irate Welsh leader Glyndwr as a possible spy for the English. In all of these journeys in time, with their visions of people and events in other eras, the sense of place is very important. The object of time travel is a past moment in the same location. A given event is not just a random happening but develops a sacramental meaning conferred in terms of both its place and its time. Time and place are for Cooper dimensions of reality.

Along with their high style and their profound moral and metaphysical vision, Cooper's books are distinguished by their use of mythology and folklore. This organic incorporation of mythic materials also confirms the sense of significant time and place and exemplifies the vision of unified time in a well-ordered universe bound by the law of High Magic. Details of Celtic lore confer meaning on particular items in nature. The holly berry, for example, is a good luck talisman, and flowing water provides protection from evil magic.

Trees have special prominence in Celtic lore. It is no mere coincidence that the Greenwitch is made of hazel, hawthorn, and rowan. The hazel was a sacred tree among the Celts; the spirit of the hawthorn was believed to take revenge on anyone who cut it down; and rowan wood was regarded as a charm against witchcraft. In the Lost Land, when Will and Bran are pursued by the equine skeleton, they are saved by blossoms falling from a hawthorn tree, which cause the bones to fall apart and lie in a dismantled heap. Will also applies his learning in tree lore when he must gather twigs from seven different trees in order to enter the glass tower: elder, the tree of fire; willow, the enchanter's tree; along with birch, hazel, apple, holly, and oak, all having their own distinctive properties. Individual characteristics of trees figure into the ancient poem of Taliessin, which details the performance of trees in aiding Gwydion in his battle aginst the Dark. The elder led, the elm stood firm, the holly and hawthorn fought heroically, and the birch, although brave, took too long to prepare itself for action. In this poem and in Celtic folk song and custom, trees are depicted as inhabited by spirits. A time-honored custom in Cornwall is to greet the apple tree with wassailing on Twelfth Night.

Another popular motif in Celtic myth is hunting, which is featured in several episodes in Cooper's works. In *The Dark is Rising* Will is led by Merriman to witness the funeral of the wren. An ancient rite in Britain involves the hunting and slaying of the wren on St. Stephen's Day (December 26). According to one of the related legends, the wren is a shape assumed by a fairy maiden who taunted hunters. In Will's eyes the wren suddenly is transformed into the person of the delicate Old Lady. In *The Grey King* the phantom hounds recall the ancient Welsh belief that the souls of the dead fly through the air by night in the form of hounds, spurred on by a supernatural huntsman. The "wild huntsman" of souls appears in several early Welsh tales. Herne the Hunter, familiar to most readers from Shakespeare's *The Merry Wives of Windsor*, appears in *The Dark is Rising*, where he puts on the stag's-head mask given to Will by his brother as an exotic Christmas present, and again in *Silver on the Tree*. Since the consummation of the last quest involves cutting the mistletoe, Herne the Hunter is present at the oak tree, of which he represents the tutelary spirit. Will notices that Herne, like Bran, has tawny eyes. Herne assumes the role of the wild huntsman as he drives the Black and White Riders out of time, after the blossom has been transformed into a white bird. The wild huntsman is also referred to in an ancient Welsh poem relating the story of the mythical prince Gwyddneu, ruler of a lost country now covered by the waters of Cardigan Bay. This legend is the source of Cooper's Lost Land adventure.

The seasonal rituals underlying the cyclical view of time in the series also reflect Celtic tradition. The series as a whole begins and ends in summer, thus coming full circle. Within each individual work, one seasonal holiday is stressed. *The Dark is Rising* takes place during the twelve days of Christmas, a time associated with the rising powers of the Dark. Will's midwinter birthday coincides with the winter solstice, the shortest day of the year. In *Greenwitch* the figure woven of branches and blossoms is the focus of a spring ritual designed to insure good harvests on land and from the sea. In *The Grey King* Halloween is the crucial date, both as the first day of winter according to the ancient reckoning of the calendar, and the traditional day of the dead, as it evolved in the Christian mythos. Finally, in *Silver on the Tree* the focus is on midsummer's eve, preceding the longest day of the year, an important festival for the Celts and carried over into the Christian calendar as the feast of St. John.

Finally, along with other motifs and themes from Celtic myth and legend, Cooper borrows materials concerning King Arthur. The setting is frequently Arthurian. Not only are several of the narratives set in Cornwall, or Logres, but one scene offers a reenactment of the battle of Mount Badon. The summit of the mountain Cader Idris, known as Arthur's seat, appears in *The Grey King*. The tradition maintains that whoever dares to spend a night alone on that seat will on the following morning be either poetically inspired or mad. King Arthur actually appears in person in several scenes but speaks only once. He appears frequently as a silent, blue-robed figure, and in the final work of the series he speaks to his son Bran. The major Arthurian characters in the series are Bran as the Pendragon, with his dog Cafall, and Merriman Lyon as Merlin, who is the unifying, central figure throughout. The image of the king is peripheral to the central themes of magic and the conflict between Light and Dark.

The Dark is Rising series is a distinctive fantasy of high literary quality. Susan Cooper is a superb stylist, one of the two or three best under consideration in this study. Her work is also superior in its complex narrative structures which reflect a view of the relationships between time and space. Time travel is not a mere device, but manifests a philosophical vision of time as continuous and organic rather than linear and repetitive. Finally, the series is outstanding for its integral use of Celtic myth and legend, not merely to provide highlights in the plot but to deepen the meaning of the events by remythologizing the contemporary world.

Although Susan Cooper is not writing consciously as a feminist, her vision of life is spiritually allied to the feminine as defined in contemporary psychological and anthropological theory. Her Celtic background, with its emphasis on the seasonal cycle and its sacramental view of nature, is the product of a matriarchal society. And although the protagonists of the series are boys, the roles they play in the conflict between Light and Dark are not the traditional roles of heroic action, with its usual emphasis on strong arms and stronger weapons, but rather those of inner strength and sensitivity. Will and Bran, in particular, assume their destiny through moral courage, intuitive understanding, and deep love. And the spiritual center of the work is not King Arthur, the warrior and ruler, but Merlin, the archetypal wizard, guide, and guardian. Furthermore, through the characters of Bran and John, Cooper asserts the theme of the vindication of mortality. When Bran is asked to decide on his future destiny, he chooses the loving bonds of mortal human life over the abstract appeal of immortality. The rejection of immortality is reflected on the level of human forgetfulness, as both John and the children forget their participation in the transcendental conflict and resume their mundane life.

Finally, Cooper's vision of Light and Dark, although morally polarized, recognizes that both of these absolutes are in their essence inhuman. The Dark, as she points out, is appealing to people who are blinded by the Light. In this recognition of the danger inherent in absolutes, even within her ultimate dualism she rejects the total polarization of values on the strictly worldly level.

4.

URSULA K. LE GUIN

LE GUIN'S WIDELY ACCLAIMED EARTHSEA TRILOGY is a major achievement in contemporary fantasy.[1] Earthsea is an intricately detailed and fully realized secondary world, with its own geography, history, and cultural heritage. Central to this world is magic, the essence of which is language. The most knowledgeable inhabitants of this world are the wizards who devote their lives to mastering names, and the protagonist is a wizard who becomes an archmage: Ged. *A Wizard of Earthsea* (1968), *The Tombs of Atuan* (1971), and *The Farthest Shore* (1972) deal with the major events in Ged's youth, maturity, and old age, thereby tracing his lifelong journey to self-knowledge. Le Guin regards fantasy as the medium best suited to a description of that journey because "only the symbolic language of the deeper psyche" will fit the events of that voyage "without trivializing them."[2]

Drawing on cultural anthropology, philosophical Taoism, and the archetypes of Jungian psychology, Le Guin explores in depth the several themes discussed in the opening chapter. In *A Wizard of Earthsea* the emphasis is on the renunciation of power; in *The Tombs of Atuan,* on the depolarization of values; and in *The Farthest Shore,* on the vindication of mortality. Throughout the trilogy, stress is on the Taoist goal of noninterference with the balance of nature, maintaining ecology in the

"Ursula K. Le Guin," © copyright 1984, is reprinted in revised form with the permission of Twayne Publishers, a division of G. K. Hall & Co., Boston.

natural world and nonaggression in the political, while favoring a wise passivity on the individual level. The themes are immanent, however, not imposed from without and as such are inseparable from plot, setting, and character. In fact, aesthetically these works are among her best in their total integration of plot, character, and theme, as well as in their lapidary style.

As the title indicates, the setting throughout is a sea strewn with hundreds of islands. A few of the islands are portrayed in their disparate cultures in some detail, whereas many others are named but not actually introduced into the narrative. (A map is provided for the reader.) The world of Earthsea is relatively primitive. There are no references to machines, and even the large merchant ships are powered by oars and sails. It is also a world in which magic is operative, and every island or town has its local mage to take care of problems concerning weather, medicine, war, and minor repairs. The protagonist is a mage, first introduced as a young boy named Duny and called the Sparrowhawk by his friends, who matures to become ultimately both a dragon-lord and an archmage whose real name is Ged. In terms of this central character the overall plot of the trilogy recounts Ged's journey to self-realization, but the congruent patterns of narrative include on the social level, a movement from disorder to order; on the religious level, from transcendence to immanence; and on the metaphysical, from imbalance to balance in the natural and moral realms.

The secondary world of Earthsea was introduced to readers somewhat before the appearance of these three books. "The Rule of Names" and "The Word of Unbinding," seed stories of the later novels, appeared in *Fantastic* in 1964. "The Rule of Names" has direct bearing on *The Wizard of Earthsea,* while "The Word of Unbinding" foreshadows *The Farthest Shore.* The central character in the earlier story is also a wizard, an apparently inept one named Mr. Underhill who, however, turns out to be a dragon in disguise. He is actually the dragon Yevaud, whom Ged will eventually bind to the island of Pendor. The theme of the story is the vital importance of true names as opposed to mere use names. Knowing the true name of a person, be he wizard or dragon, confers power over him. To share one's true name with someone is thus to show absolute trust. A light touch characterizes this humorous short piece which precedes the rather more somber account in the novel of Ged's quest for selfhood.

A Wizard of Earthsea is largely focused on Ged's struggle to find and name the mysterious shadow that relentlessly pursues him. As Le Guin explained in her essay "The Child and the Shadow," the archetypal shadow in the Jungian sense—"the dark brother" of the conscious mind—is both a dangerous threat and a valuable guide on life's journey. "It is inferior, primitive, awkward, animallike, childlike; powerful, vital, spontaneous. It's not weak and decent . . . it's dark and hairy and unseemly; but without it, the person is nothing.''[3] Realized in this novel as a separate entity, the shadow is both cause and object of the hero's quest.

The hero is introduced as a young boy nicknamed the Sparrowhawk. Motherless and neglected by his father, the lad is a mere goatherd, but he shows a remarkable talent for deeds of magic. When he succeeds in routing a barbaric invasion by his skill in fog-weaving, the news of his gifted abilities spreads through the islands. On his thirteenth birthday, he is visited by the mage Ogion, who confers on him his true name—Ged—and takes him away from his native village to become his apprentice in wizardry at Re Albi in his home, called the Falcon's nest.

Life with Ogion is a meditative retreat for the impatient boy eager to perform great deeds of magic, but he learns much natural lore. It is also during his brief apprenticeship with the wise old man, and before Ged goes off to the College for Wizards, that the shadow appears for the first time. He sees it as he pores over a forbidden book of runes: "[S]omething was crouching beside the closed door, a shapeless clot of shadow darker than the darkness'' (p. 22). His subsequent journey to the island of Roke to attend the college is on board a boat prophetically nam- ed *Shadow*.

On the island of Roke, an old Scottish word meaning mist or fog, Ged completes his training in wizardry and also his rites of passage to adulthood. Always proud as well as impatient, Ged lets the taunts of his fellow students prompt him to undertake a greater display of power than is either wise or safe. Chafing under the boasts of a rival student, Jasper, Ged foolishly summons from the dead the spirit of a legendary woman, Elfarran. In an awesome scene, he recites with more skill than wisdom the Spell of Summoning, and succeeds in invoking a fearful shadow- beast. The dreadful apparition turns with fury against its summoner. The young man's friends are unable to save him from its wild attack. On- ly the superior magic of the archmage Nemmerle can dispel the ominous shapeless thing, but the old man is utterly exhausted by the effort and dies shortly thereafter.

Profoundly humbled by this devastating experience, Ged accepts a professional post as mage in the modest fishing town of Low Torning, which has been under threat of a dragon attack. In this village Ged makes friends with a fisherman, Pechvarry, and his son, Ioth. They are the lonely wizard's only companions apart from the little wild animal, the otak, whom he has adopted. When the boy becomes mortally ill, Ged tries unsuccessfully to save him, almost losing his own life as he pursues the lad's dying spirit close to the dry lands of death. In doing so Ged has violated the balance in the world, once more challenging the natural separation of living and dead, as he had when he summoned the spirit.

This time Ged's life is saved by the loving intervention of the pet otak. In its instinctive wisdom the little beast licks his companion, thus summoning through his touch the lost spirit.

Although this attempt to save a child's life is a personal failure, Ged achieves a major success for the town. He seeks out the threatening dragon who has occupied the abandoned island of Pendor for four generations. He confronts it with knowledge of its name, Yevaud (the same dragon who appeared in the story "The Rule of Names"). Not only does Ged resist the dragon's tempting offer to him to reveal the shadow's name in exchange for betrayal of the town, but he actually negotiates with the wily dragon, binding him with an oath never to leave his own island of Pendor. Yevaud will never threaten the archipelago again.

In spite of this success, Ged is continually plagued by dreams about the nameless shadow. Without knowing its name, he is helpless against it. He cannot even return to Roke by boat because the Roke wind is set against him. On the advice of a mysterious person he meets on board the vessel, he sails instead for the Court of Terrenon. This person is revealed later to be a "gebbeth," a body that "has been drained of true substance and is something like a shell or a vapor in the form of a man, an unreal flesh clothing the shadow which is real" (p. 107). He is eventually driven by the pursuing gebbeth into the castle of Terrenon, where he encounters Serret, whom he had known earlier as the sorcerous daughter of the Lord of Re Albi but who is now the wife of Lord Benderesk. In this castle he faces one more severe temptation. The Stone of Terrenon carries the strong Old Power, which can reveal the name of the shadow to Ged but which also threatens to possess his soul. Ged rejects the offer of this power that would ultimately enslave him and escapes the castle by transforming himself into a hawk. In this form he returns to his master, Ogion, who restores his body, renews his spirit, and shapes him a new staff of yew. Thus renewed he sets off to hunt the shadow that had been hunting him. The decision is a spiritual turning point in his journey to selfhood.

Among his adventures as he now heads eastward in pursuit is an encounter with an elderly man and woman on a remote island. Marooned there since early childhood, the two people have little to communicate, but the woman gives the wizard a mysterious half-ring. This talisman will be the focus of his quest in the next volume of the trilogy. Also on this journey Ged meets his old friend from Roke, Vetch, who is now a mage on the island of Ismay, and Vetch decides to accompany Ged in his boat, the *Lookfar*.

The quest culminates at an ultimate point in the east, where the sea turns to sand and no wind stirs. "There were no directions here, no north or south or east or west, only towards and away" (p. 178). There

Ged finally confronts the shadow and learns its name. Identifying it raises this unconscious horror over the threshold of consciousness even as the sea has given way to land.

> Aloud and clearly, breaking that old silence, Ged spoke the shadow's name and in the same moment the shadow spoke without lips or tongue, saying the same word: "Ged." And the two voices were one voice. (p.179)

The hunt is over; the quest is completed. All that remains is for Ged to accept and integrate the shadow that is a part of himself after all:

> Ged reached out his hands, dropping his staff, and took hold of his shadow, of the black self that reached out to him. Light and darkness met, and joined, and were one. (p. 179)

This climactic episode, which occurs near the end of the book, is a major event on Ged's journey to self-knowledge and to adulthood. The newly integrated shadow will continue to be his guide on the journey toward light.

Throughout *A Wizard of Earthsea* the narrative structure of the quest is thematically enriched by Le Guin's skillful interweaving of symbols and motifs. In addition to the shadow as central symbol she incorporates birds, dragons, and stones for their symbolic suggestiveness. Birds are representative of the soul in folklore and legend all over the world. Separation of the soul from the body at death has been traditionally likened to the flight of a bird from a cage,[4] and becoming a winged being has been a metaphor for the process of spiritualization. Ged as wizard is a spiritual figure, identified from the start with the sparrowhawk, a bird consecrated to the sun by the ancient Egyptians, Greeks, and Romans, who attributed to it all of the powers associated with the sun. The mountain home of the mage Ogion is called the Falcon's Nest. The elderly mage Nemmerle keeps a pet raven, which disappears at the death of his master. When Ged wants to escape from the Castle of Terrenon, he transforms himself into a hawk in order to fly back to Re Albi to be restored by Ogion. On the other hand, the enchantress Serret transforms herself into a gull, only to be destroyed by pursuing winged black creatures, a negative and destructive form of spiritual power.

Le Guin also uses dragons and stones in both traditional and original ways to enhance her narrative. Her dragons are ancient and guileful beings, who speak the magically endowed Old Speech. No one dares look into the green eyes of a dragon, and his laughter is seen rather than heard as yellow smoke that issues from his nostrils. The dragon of

Pendor is an impressive giant, "lean as a hound" and "huge as a hill" (p. 89), with grey-black scales "catching the daylight like broken stone" (p. 89). Like dragons, certain stones are invested with the Old Powers. The Stone of Terrenon tests Ged even as the dragon of Pendor had done. And like the dragon, which Ged binds to the island of Pendor forevermore, the Stone of Terrenon is bound to its present location. We learn that it is so with the Old Powers, "being bound each to an isle, a certain place, cave or stone or welling spring" (p. 123).[5]

The style of *A Wizard of Earthsea* is suitable to its subject of mythic magery. Artful yet simple, the language is largely Anglo-Saxon in diction, strongly alliterative, and suggestively resonant of an austere heroic age. The alliteration is pervasive, recalling the oral tradition of the heroic poem *Beowulf*.[6] ("The beasts began to bleat and browse . . ." [p. 3]; "You witless woodenhead! . . . you spineless slave-sons!" [p.32]; "the soft singing of spells . . ." [p. 129]). And, like *Beowulf*, *Wizard* is also marked with gnomic formulas. ("To light a candle is to cast a shadow." [p. 44]; "Infinite are the arguments of mages." [p. 161]; "Only in silence the word." [p. 181]). Above all, language is not merely a matter of style but is itself a subject of *A Wizard of Earthsea*. In the world of Earthsea, the word is creative. All spoken languages derive from Old Speech, which is now understood only by dragons and wizards. But the true names of everything are those of the Old Speech, which is the heart of a wizard's education. "Who knows a man's name, holds that man's life in his keeping" (p. 69). This "rule of names" applies not only to men but to all created things. That is why magic is "the true naming of a thing" (p. 46). It is also the magic of Segoy, creator of Earthsea, "the language Segoy spoke who made the islands of the world" (p. 47). For Earthsea, the beginning was the Word.

The theme of names is also central to the second volume in the trilogy, *The Tombs of Atuan,* which in many ways parallels the *A Wizard of Earthsea*. Like its predecessor, *The Tombs* is about coming-of-age, but is focused on a girl rather than a boy. As Le Guin put it, "The subject of *The Tombs of Atuan* is, if I had to put it in one word, sex. . . . More exactly, you could call it a feminine coming-of-age. Birth, rebirth, destruction, freedom are the themes."[7] In this treatment of female coming-of-age, not only the rule of names but also several other themes recur but from a contrasting point of view to that of the male-centered *Wizard*.

The island of Atuan had been introduced fleetingly but significantly into the narrative of *A Wizard*. We learned in the opening chapter of the earlier book about the Kargish empire, of which Atuan is one of four islands. We learned also that the Kargs are a fierce, even savage people, white-skinned and yellow-haired, given to raiding and violence. They apparently worship twin masculine deities, for they rush into battle crying the names of the White Godbrothers Wuluah and Atwah. It is an attacking band of Kargs that Ged dispels with his magically produced fog. Near the end of *A Wizard* Ged finds the broken ring of Erreth-Akbe which will eventually lead him on his quest to find the other half in the tombs of Atuan.

Although the presence of Ged unifies the three works, the young wizard does not actually appear until the middle of *The Tombs of Atuan*. The first half of this book is exclusively concerned with introducing the female protagonist, Tenar, and with developing the exact nature of the feminine religion that is observed in the symbolic setting of the ancient tombs of Atuan. This religion is dedicated to the worship of the Nameless Ones, dark and destructive forces that exist far underground, "the ancient and holy Powers of the Earth before the Light" (p. 107). Ged's sudden appearance in these mysterious tombs thus has a very different meaning for him than it has for Tenar.

A series of complex symbolic polarities surrounds the very birth of the girl-child Tenar. It is believed by those who follow the religion of the Nameless Ones that its High Priestess is repeatedly reborn in the body of a girl baby born close to the time of the former priestess's death. It is Tenar's awesome but grim destiny to be thus chosen as the incarnation of the recently deceased priestess. She is introduced to the reader as a lively, healthy child of three with black hair and white skin (in obvious contrast to Ged's dark skin.) The polarities of dark and light are intensified when, in spite of her mother's frantic attempts to rescue her from her destined role, she is duly initiated at the age of six. Clad in a black robe in a ceremonial enactment of the conflict between the forces of light and darkness, she enters the dark Place of the Tombs and surrenders her old identity as Tenar. Now in the service of the Nameless Ones she adopts the new name of Arha, which means the Eaten One. Her individual identity is thus sacrificed to her assigned role as priestess of the ancient underworld powers. Her supposed rebirth as a priestess represents her death as an individual.

For the next eight years, until the age of fourteen when she makes her crossing into womanhood and becomes formally acknowledged as the highest priestess of the Tombs, she remains in this remote and sterile location, surrounded by women and engulfed in ritual.[8] During this period of training her life consists almost entirely of ceremonial details and traditional womanly skills such as weaving and spinning. Whereas Ged attended a college for wizards and gained much knowledge about the nature of the world, Tenar learns only about rituals and the unexplorable world of the dark tombs where no light ever appears. Furthermore, while Ged erred in the direction of too much consciousness, Tenar's problem is that of almost total unconsciousness. The solar-oriented Sparrowhawk was guilty of pride and ambition, while the lunar priestess remains entombed and enslaved to an endless round of ritual.

> Nothing happened. Once the ceremonies of her consecration were over, the days went on as they had always gone. There was wool to be spun, black cloth to be woven, meal to be ground, rites to be performed; the Nine Chants must be sung nightly, the doorways blessed, the Stones fed with goat's blood twice a year, the dances of the dark of the moon danced before the Empty Throne. And so the whole year had passed. . . . (p. 24)

Arha's life is thus virtually limited to an unconscious level, as she moves through her daily round of prescribed and habitual religious duties. Unlike the young Sparrowhawk, who chose unwisely and acted rashly, Arha has no opportunity for either personal choice or voluntary actions. Her development as a conscious individual is totally stultified. She is indeed "eaten."

Her relationships with other people are also extremely limited in both number and depth. The matriarchal community is, of course, limited by definition to females and eunuchs. Arha's closest friend is the gentle eunuch, Manan, who provides an element of almost maternal love in his care of her. His affection is not so much returned as taken for granted by Arha, who enjoys teasing her rather pathetic "potato-faced" guardian. Her closest friend of her own age is Penthe, a cheerful, sensuous girl, completely unsuited to her life in training as a priestess. "I'd rather marry a pigherd and live in a ditch. I'd rather anything than stay buried alive here all my born days with a mess of women in a perishing old desert where nobody ever comes" (p. 40). Her frank admission of doubts about the Nameless Ones puzzles Arha, who is not sufficiently free from the control of her dark masters to sense the sheer vitality implicit in that sunny skepticism. Arha's other close associate is Kossil, the grim, older woman who has hardened in her years of service to the Nameless Ones so that she no longer feels warmth toward anyone. Her harsh life is an image of futility. As Ged later explains, "I think they [the Nameless Ones] drove your priestess Kossil mad a long time ago; I think she has prowled these caverns as she prowls the labyrinth of her own self, and now she cannot see the daylight anymore" (p. 107).

Arha's first conscious act in her role as head priestess occurs at age fifteen, when she orders the death by starvation of three male prisoners who have defiled the tombs. For any male to enter the secret underground precincts is of course a symbolic rape, and the ritual sacrifice of the male intruder is standard practice for this matriarchal cult. This destructive action has its negative effect on Arha, however, and she faints, falling into an illness that lasts for several days. During her illness she has several dreams, one of which is particularly rich in its imagery of the feminine archetype. "She dreamed that she had to carry a full bowl of water, a deep brass bowl, through the dark, to someone who was thirsty. She could never get to this person" (p. 38). Since nourishment is the primary function of the great-mother archetype, this dream clearly reflects the tension in Arha between the positive and negative manifestations of the mother image. The dream is also prophetic, for she will have a literal opportunity to provide or to deny nourishment, to sustain life or to destroy it.

Part of Arha's training in the hands of the older women is an inculcation of hatred for the wizards of the Inner Lands, regarded as masters of deception and trickery. The wizards admittedly work magic, but Kossil tries to denigrate their achievements as products of deception. Conscious action, based on knowledge of the words of power, seems to her a matter of subtle trickery, quite unlike the more profound spiritual power of the Nameless Ones. Her vehement rejection of the superior rational powers of wizards is also linked with her rejection of the masculine world, and its corresponding worship of the Godking in neighboring lands.

This quiet, empty world of feminine mystery is interrupted by the unexpected appearance of the wizard Ged, whose werelight Arha detects in the undertomb near the entrance to the labyrinth. Ged, who has violated the sanctity of the tombs in his effort to recover the missing half of the Ring of Erreth-Akbe, is trapped underground and finds himself completely at the mercy of the young priestess. Her dream of the cauldron is realized, as she must now choose whether to leave the intruder to die of thirst or to help him survive by bringing him food and water.

Her first impulse, dictated by the Terrible Mother element in her own unconscious, is destructive.[9] "She would not give him any water. She would give him death, death, death, death, death" (p. 74). But this negative impulse is suppressed by an even greater one—curiosity. Her prisoner may be blasphemous, but he is also interesting, and she decides to bring him the food and water necessary for his survival if only to permit her to learn more about him. Her eagerness to learn about life proves to be on the side of life itself.

Before her encounter with Ged, the tombs represented for Arha an undifferentiated unconsciousness, deep, demanding, and dumb. With his sudden challenging appearance, she must for the first time act. She must now find within herself the counterpart of the rationality that the wizard represents for her. Her unreasoning devotion to the terrifying nameless gods has kept her existence almost entirely on the level of intuition. Psychologically, as well as literally, she has been living out her years underground. But it is also in the underground—at once womb and tomb—that the transformation begins.

In her talks with Ged, as she brings him "water and bread and life" (p. 84), she begins to discover herself. She is astonished to find that the wizard knows her real name, and it is through him that her first sense of self-knowledge comes. She has been, as her name indicates, "eaten," with her individuality totally consumed in the dark, meaningless round of her ritualized existence. But Ged leads her to rediscover the individual Tenar. "You must be Arha, or you must be Tenar. You cannot be both" (p. 113).

She also learns that he is the possessor of the broken fragment of a sacred ring. When Ged explains to her that he has come to this holy place to investigate the hitherto undisturbed treasure room in order to search for the missing half, she reveals to him that as priestess, she has in her possession a sacred semicircle on a silver chain around her neck. In a climactic moment of illumination for both of them, Ged places in Tenar's hand the other half of the fabled ring that once belonged to the legendary hero, Erreth-Akbe, and she places it next to her half on the silver chain. The new totality of the rings is matched by her new awareness of totality in herself. The ring newly made whole is obviously a symbol of totality, and it represents for her the birth of the ego, much as the integration of the shadow-beast had meant this for Ged. On the social level the ring, marked with a bond-rune, signifies peace and unity for Earthsea.

Now that Ged has in effect restored her true name, Tenar casts aside the role of Arha, instinctive votary of the destructive gods of darkness. She is now able to choose freedom. No longer enslaved to unconscious obedience, Tenar is free enough inwardly to decide in favor of undertaking a dangerous escape. "You have set us both free," Ged exalts, as the two set out on the dark and labyrinthine path that leads to daylight (p. 115). As John Layard has pointed out, "The labyrinth always has to do with death and rebirth, is almost always connected with a cave, and is always presided over by a woman, though it may be walked through by men. The labyrinthine way represents part of the individuation process."[10] Like Kossil, Tenar "prowls the labyrinth of her own self" (p. 107).

But freedom does not come all at once. There will be moments when Tenar temporarily regresses, succumbing to the pull of the consecrated Eaten One. The first such moment occurs at the entrance to the tombs when Ged's staff and voice force the rocks blocking their escape to break open for them. Under the starry sky just paling toward dawn, Tenar falls to the ground and refuses to follow Ged, who suddenly appears to her like a black-faced demon. He persuades her to come with him by reminding her of the ring, and as the two move away from the ominous opening to the tombs, an earthquake shakes both the huge Tombstones and the Hall of the Throne: "[a] huge crack opened among the Tombstones. . . . The stones that still stood upright toppled into it and were swallowed" (p. 123). Tenar then realizes that Ged's work held back the earthquake long enough for them to escape; that his magery subdued the anger of the dark powers. Ged's mentor, Ogion, the reader recalls, was famed as the mage who held back an earthquake.

Tenar suffers one more relapse. One more time the Nameless Ones reach out to recapture their votary. As she looks at Ged, finding him momentarily abstracted, deep in his own thoughts, she suddenly feels an unreasoning fear, and reaches for a knife. "The little blade was sharp enough to cut a finger to the bone, or to cut the arteries of a throat. She would serve her Masters still, though they had betrayed her and forsaken her. They would guide and drive her hand in the last act of darkness. They would accept the sacrifice" (p. 140). But as she turns on him with the knife poised, his expression clears and he addresses her softly, trustingly, seemingly not even noticing the weapon. Her rage dissipates, and she is again ready to join him in their journey back to civilization.

Tenar's story ends with their arrival in the port of Havnor. Hand in hand with the wizard, she enters the white streets of the city. Only sixteen years of age, she is alone and somewhat afraid but free to grow. She is ready to face her future. Tenar does not reappear later in the trilogy—a disappointment to some readers—for her coming-of-age story is completed here. We hear of her only once more, when Ged refers to her in *The Farthest Shore* as "The White Lady of Gont" (p. 8). *The Tombs of Atuan* thus parallels *A Wizard of Earthsea,* with its focus on the female adolescent's rites of passage rather the male's. Whereas the wizard must cope primarily with the problem of an inflated ego, the priestess must deal with the threatening power of the unconscious. Ged's shadow was separated from him and needed to be reintegrated, but Tenar's shadow is not merely within her but overflows her whole psychic being, so that her feelings, like her body, have been entombed. In Havnor, with the completed silver ring about her wrist, she is liberated from the darkness.

This story of feminine coming-of-age has its parallels in myth as in modern life. Le Guin uses two myths as implicit structural motifs, that of Theseus and the Minotaur and that of Demeter and Persephone. With her close knowledge of the maze of paths in the tombs, Tenar is like Ariadne leading Theseus out of the labyrinth. She is also like Demeter, whose devotion to the underworld powers is a blight but whose reappearance in the world heralds a new spring. But these experiences are universal and immediate as well as mythic. The enslavement to the Nameless Ones, to the dark forces of the unconscious, is in fact reflected in the lives of all adolescent females who bear the burden of past tradition and feel compelled to accept a traditionally imposed identity. As one critic put it, the contemporary young woman must break away from "the accumulated demands and expectations of mothers and grandmothers and great grandmothers."[11] Like Tenar, she must consciously choose her own identity and not simply accept herself as a reincarnation of a past role.

The Tombs, along with the worship of the Nameless Ones, represent a collective religious shadow for the islands of Earthsea. Another form of collective shadow appears in the final volume of the trilogy, *The Farthest Shore*, where the vitality of Earthsea is endangered by the loss of distinction between life and death.

The Farthest Shore is about death, which is also a coming-of-age—as Le Guin has pointed out, "in the largest sense,"—for the final stage in this process is the acceptance of one's own mortality.[12] It also implies the moral and social integration of the fact of death. In this volume Ged has become an aged wizard, grey-haired and contemplative, but he is accompanied by a young man, Arren, who awaits fulfillment of his noble destiny as king of all Earthsea. The paths of the old man and the young—wizard and prince—meet at the rowan tree, the center of the island of Roke and, by extension, the center of the world.[13] There they agree to undertake together their quest to free Earthsea from the mysterious evil that has upset the equilibrium between life and death.

The world of Earthsea has been afflicted with a devastating spiritual plague of joylessness, together with a failure of magic, blurring of distinctions, and loss of meaning. "There is a hole in the world and the sea is running out of it. The light is running out" (p. 154). The evil seems to be associated with a widespread rejection of mortality, and there are ominous whispers and mutterings about the opportunity to live forever. Ged sees in this apparently unmeasured desire for life on the part of human beings a threat to the balance of nature. As he sees it, death is "the price we pay for life," and he sets out with Arren on the journey westward in an effort to restore the balance of nature by reestablishing mortality.

As they move westward, the direction of the setting sun and the opposite of the eastward quest recounted in the opening volume, Ged and Arren reflect on the differences between age and youth and between magery and kingship. As Ged explains to his young companion, "When I was young, I had to choose between the life of being and the life of doing. And I leapt at the latter like a trout to a fly. But each deed you do, each act, binds you to itself and to its consequences, and makes you act again and yet again. Then very seldom do you come upon a space, a time like this, between act and act, when you may stop and simply be. Or wonder who, after all, you are" (pp. 34-35). Arren is impatient for action, but Ged compares himself to the ancient dragons, who are both the oldest and the wisest of all beings, who have stopped acting in favor of simple being. "They do not do; they are" (p. 37).

Although Ged may in theory ally himself with existence as opposed to action, in fact he is at once both active and contemplative, both involved and detached. He acts many times in the course of their adventurous journey westward. He acts decisively, he acts courageously, and he acts imaginatively. He dons a disguise in order to go about asking questions undetected; he risks ambush in a lonely room on a dark night in a dangerous part of a drug-ridden town; he daringly rescues his young companion who is captured by brutal slave-traders. Such exploits are scarcely those of a person who has entirely given up on activity.

Arren also plays an active part in these adventures. A young man with a regal heritage, he is destined for heroism as well as kingship. The name Arren means "sword," and he carries on the quest an enchanted sword that cannot be drawn for revenge or aggression, but can only be used in the service of life. Arren is also born to fulfill the prophecy made by the last king who reigned 800 years ago. "He shall inherit my throne who has crossed the dark land living and come to the far shores of the day" (p. 17). Arren agrees to accompany Ged on the quest as they stand beneath the rowan tree, and we learn later that the prince's real name is Lebannen, which means "rowan tree."

In the pride of his youth and ancestry, Arren is confidently eager to help Ged find the source of the mysterious evil. He learns, however, that he is subject to temptation and that he is capable of failure. In the episode that takes place in Hort Town, where many inhabitants are victims of the drug Hazia, Arren fails in his duty as guard. While Ged attempts to enter in spirit the drug-induced dreamworld of the former sorcerer Hare, Arren stands guard. As the lad watches the two men, he finds that he cannot resist following the lord of shadows who beckons him with a tiny flame, no larger than a pearl, offering eternal life. Because of this lapse of attention, Ged is knocked unconscious and Arren himself hauled off by slave-traders. Later, when Ged has regained consciousness and also managed to find Arren and free him from his captors, the young man is chagrined with the sense of his own failure.

In a subsequent episode, Arren experiences an even greater spiritual failure. They are at sea. Ged has been wounded, their companion Sopli has drowned, and Arren surrenders to a feeling of despair about his own survival. He tends Ged's wound listlessly, and instead of trying to sail their boat to a port, he simply lets it drift aimlessly through the open sea. Having lost faith in magery, he looked at Ged "with the clear eyes of despair and saw nothing" (p. 108). From this dark night of the soul,

Arren is rescued, together with the scarcely conscious mage, by the Raft People, a community who spend their entire lives on rafts, floating on the open sea. Their stay with the Raft People is a dreamlike experience, a time of rebirth. It is also a time for Arren to recognize his own shadow, his fear of death. He admits that he neglected Ged out of fear of death. A boy of seventeen, he has not yet been able to accept the fact of mortality. His own weakness thus reflects the very evil that is the object of his quest. But he has now learned that "to refuse death is to refuse life" (p. 121).

When Ged recovers, the companions continue their westward quest. The climactic events occur when they complete their journey in the "dry land" of the dead. At the very edge of that grim, grey landscape they meet their enemy, the source of the evil that has brought Earthsea into a state of despair. There, before the stone wall that separates the living and the dead, they meet the former sorcerer, Cob, who has surrendered his humanity to his overpowering urge to cling to fleshly existence. It is Cob's magic that has opened the door between life and death, turning the living world into a world of living death, where the sun is dimmed and life is joyless. Cob's body is killed in a self-sacrificial attack by a dragon, but Cob's spirit climbs over the wall into the land of shadows, where Ged and Arren must follow. It is a dismal journey through that land where stars shine but do not twinkle, where shadows meet but do not speak, and where there is only dust to drink. But the old man and the boy persist until they come to the fatal door that Cob's misguided magic has opened between that world and theirs. Ged then uses all the magic he can muster, asserting a superhuman strength in the weakness of his age, to close that door. Shaky yet strong, he sways a little, then stands erect. He commands in a clear voice: "Be thou made whole! . . . And with his staff he drew in lines of fire across the gate of rocks a figure: the Rune Agnen, the Rune of Ending, which closes roads and is drawn on coffin lids. And there was then no gap or void place among the boulders. The door was shut" (p. 184).

In their long and difficult journey back to the world of the living, Ged and Arren need each other. The aging wizard is able to act as guide, but his physical strength is unequal to the challenge. The young prince, however, musters an endurance even beyond hope, carrying his mentor safely over the edge of darkness and back to the light. Although Arren lifts Ged to safety over the wall, both are at that point totally stranded on a deserted beach far west of the nearest human habitation. Left to themselves, they would perish. But there on the beach they encounter a superbly ancient and wise dragon, Kalessin, who addresses them in the Old Speech and offers to fly them back to civilization.

As the companions mount the dragon, Arren suddenly sees the wizard's staff lying on the beach, half-buried in the sand, and reaches down to get it. The wizard stops him, however, explaining that he has spent all of his powers in the dry land of the dead. The staff can no longer help him: "I am no mage now" (p. 193).[14] But the loss is also a gain. Although Ged as mage has lost the ability to perform feats with his staff, he has gained a higher form of wisdom. The staff served as a kind of medium between the wizard and the things of the earth, between spirit and matter. Now Ged is closer to the air-born dragons. In his eyes there is now "something like that laughter in the eyes of Kalessin . . . " (p. 196). This is not to say that he has lost all contact with human responsibility. He is yet to undertake the important duty of establishing Arren on his rightful throne. But in his more transcendental nature, he influences human behavior without actually being part of it. Ged's spiritual guidance has made possible the fulfillment of the prophecy: "He shall inherit my throne who has crossed the dark land living and come to the far shores of the day." His physical presence is also necessary to inaugurate the reign of the new king.

Ged acknowledges the new king by kneeling in homage and wishing him a long and successful reign. He then takes his departure from the scene of human activity. He flies off in an easterly direction on the neck of the great dragon, Kalessin. As does the *Odyssey*, this last volume of the Earthsea books offers alternative endings. In one version, Ged attends the crowning of Arren in Havnor, after which he sails off in his boat, *Lookfar*, never to be seen again. In another, Ged does not come to the coronation, although the young king has sought him. Hearing rumors that Ged has gone alone and afoot into the forests of the mountain, the new king does not search further for the wizard but acknowledges that "he rules a greater kingdom than I do" (p. 197).

Ged's final, mysterious flight into the unknown on the back of a winged dragon is an apotheosis appropriate to a mythic hero. Throughout the Earthsea trilogy Ged as protagonist has exemplified the paradigmatic career of the mythic hero. From the first book, in which he demonstrates the divine signs of talent characteristic of the childhood of mythic heroes, Ged has moved through the other traditional stages, including trial and quest, periods of meditation and withdrawal, symbolic death and journey to the underworld, and, finally, rebirth and apotheosis. Interwoven with Ged's complete career are the partial careers of Tenar and Arren, both richly indebted to mythic motifs. Tenar is the priestess of the underworld, devoured by forces of darkness until her rescue through the light of wizardry. Arren is the young prince destined to fulfill an ancient prophecy and restore peace and unity to his fragmented kingdom.

Along with the mythic roots of character and narrative, Le Guin also endows the landscape of her imaginary world with mythic features rich in suggestiveness. The name Earthsea in itself suggests a reconciliation of opposites, a balance of conscious and unconscious. The sea is associated not only with the unconscious but also with death, so that the sea journey to an island is at once expressive of a new level of self-consciousness and of resurrection. Ged's integration with the shadow thus occurs at the point where land and sea meet and are one. An important part of this mythic cosmology is the world tree at the center. Like the tree Yggdrasill in Norse mythology, the Immanent Grove is the center of Earthsea.

The center of it is still, and all moves about it, but the Grove itself often seems to the confused viewer to be moving. "And they consider—the novices, the townsfolk, the farmers—that the Grove moves about in a mystifying manner. But in this they are mistaken, for the Grove does not move. Its roots are the roots of being. It is all the rest that moves" (p. 9).

Integrated with the mythic patterns that infuse setting as well as plot and character in the trilogy are patterns of imagery. The central image is that of the spider weaving a web. We learn early in the first book that Ogion watches the spider weaving, and in the last book Ged describes the spider as a patterner. The web images both creation and destruction. The world of Earthsea is a web, with the Master Patterner at its center in the Immanent Grove. But the web is at once light and dark, a black center filled with silver threads catching the sunlight. Evil in this world is the web woven by men. The name of the magician who opens the door between life and death is Cob, an archaic word for spider (as in cobweb). Although the spider image is both central and recurring, the most pervasive imagery is that of light and darkness. There is scarcely a chapter in the trilogy without a pattern of light and dark images, in continual movements of conflict and reconciliation, ranging from Tenar's white skin and Ged's dark to the bright yellow star over the dark waters of the South Reach.

Both myth and image are successfully integrated with theme in these artfully written books. Like the patterned web, all is part of the whole. No symbols are imposed and no episodes introduced that are not integral to the world of Earthsea and the story of its master wizard who maintains the balance, restores a king, and finds himself. Earthsea is a convincingly authenticated world, drawn with a sure hand for fine detail. A mature narrative about growing up, a moral tale without a moral, a realistic depiction of a fantasy world, the trilogy is also a paradoxical work, but the paradox is at the heart of its inherent Taoist view of life. One of the many gnomic sayings in the work, "To light a candle is to cast a shadow," is a metaphoric summation of this view.

5.

EVANGELINE WALTON

MANY CONTEMPORARY FANTASY WRITERS have drawn on the materials of the *Mabinogion,* a collection of traditional Welsh tales from myth, history, and folklore. Although there are several translations available, these stories are frustrating reading, for they are fragmentary and essentially incoherent. They lack both characterization and narrative credibility. Evangeline Walton has undertaken a retelling of the *Mabinogion,* not merely translating it, but creating an expanded and structured modern version. She has made additions and deletions for the sake of dramatic effect, narrative structure, and heightened style, but she has never altered any of the original material. Deepening character, adding dialogue, and providing local color, she has achieved a powerful restatement of these provocative but chaotic works.[1]

Walton's initial publication in the series was the book originally entitled *The Virgin and the Swine* (1936) which was not a success and quickly went out of print. Lin Carter republished it in 1970 as part of his new adult fantasy series for Ballantine, giving it the more appealing title, *The Island of the Mighty.* The prompt success of this work encouraged the author to bring out her thirty-year-old manuscript dealing with the second branch, called *The Children of Llyr* (1971). The two remaining volumes, *The Song of Rhiannon* (1972) and *Prince of Annwn* (1974) completed the other two branches. In these four works Walton effectively orders the disjointed narrative of the *Mabinogion,* conferring on its strangeness a certain degree of plausibility and supplying both psychological and sociological motivation without destroying the sense of wonder. She delineates the mythic worlds with imaginative details. In short, she turns the mythic raw materials into literary fantasy.

The retelling of the first branch, *Prince of Annwn,* is a good example of how Walton fleshes out the sparse account in the original tale. In the brief opening scene of the *Mabinogion,* Pwyll, the prince of Dyved, encounters Arawn, king of Annwn, the underworld, while both are out hunting. Somewhat recklessly, Pwyll permits his dogs to take over the stag that has been brought down by the other hunter, a serious breach of courtesy. Since the other hunter as king is of higher rank, he asks Pwyll to pay the necessary face-price for the insult. Pwyll's designated price is to kill Arawn's rival king. The two rulers then exchange places and identities for a year and a day, at the end of which Pwyll defeats the rival, and both return to their own courts. All of this is told economically in about four pages. There is no characterization, almost no use of descriptive detail, and no sense of contrasting worlds. Pwyll's year in Annwn, for example, is summarized matter of factly: Pwyll spent that year hunting and singing and carousing, in fellowship, and in pleasant talk with his companions. In Walton's expanded version, the initial hunt itself occupies seven pages, in which the contrasting atmospheres of the two worlds are carefully developed, and several subsequent chapters are devoted to Pwyll's experiences in Annwn. Walton thus transmutes the bare, jumbled, but intriguing elements of the myth into effective literature.

Walton draws on her extensive background knowledge of the Celtic world. She writes from the inside, infusing the third-person narrative with the Celtic outlook on the world. For example, for the Celts the world we know was only one of many. The otherworld closest to ours was Annwn, the abyss, place of the dead and primal womb of creation. Here most human beings returned at death; here also nameless beings struggled upward until ready for birth on earth. A few people, however, were able after death to go to a higher, brighter place. The Celts also believed that there were certain points of entry directly from our world into another, so that the living might go there through a grove, a pool, or a burial mound. Walton gives us two of those otherworlds, Annwn, which Pwyll reaches through the forest, and the Bright World, which he enters after traveling through a mystical burial ground.[2]

Arawn's kingdom, quite unlike the popular notion of a dark and dismal place of the dead, is a moonlit land of Middle Light. Neither bright sunlight nor dark night exist there, but instead there is a continual twilight. When Pwyll first meets Arawn, the king appears to him grey, but when actually in Annwn he discovers that his own skin, although transformed into the likeness of Arawn, is not grey at all. At first Pwyll had anticipated a nightmarish appearance of the inhabitants of the dead world, whom he logically expected to be decaying corpses. In contrast he finds everything there much brighter than on earth. Just as the grey man is no longer grey, so all things in his kingdom are of vivid, heightened hues. His palace shines with walls of pale gold, and the roof sings, consisting of a mass of living birds. The faces of all the people are beautiful, with eyes brighter than those of mortals. The food and drink are exquisite, the sensuous atmosphere is overpowering, no artificial light is needed to supplement the shining walls, and a glow of rose and gold hovers in the air. The realm of death is more alive than Pwyll has ever known life to be.

Later in the narrative Pwyll also visits the Bright World in order to win his bride. In order to arrive there he first enters the mound of Gorsedd Arberth, descending through the tomb of King Heyevydd, whose skeleton, holding a gleaming sword in his hand, stands in a golden chariot. In the Bright World Heyevydd is still alive, living in a palace even more stunning than Arawn's, walled entirely with crystal. This sunlit world is even more brilliantly beautiful than Annwn. The startling sight of a hawk sitting next to a singing bird on a branch reveals to the young prince that its beauties are deeper than mere appearance. This is a land where nothing can ever hurt, where all is peace and harmony. Unfortunately, as Pwyll learns later, it is vulnerable to corruption from other worlds.

Walton's worlds are linked in an evolutionary chain, symbolized in the first book by the varying degrees of brightness. The movement upward through worlds is based on the doctrine of rebirth, exemplified in the case of the skeleton buried in this world who is presented as a living king in a higher and brighter world. In the other books in her series, Walton further develops this vision of several worlds, each, as she puts it, the shell of another. Central to this vision is the image of the cauldron as the vessel of rebirth, a metaphorical womb. Celtic art depicts warriors killed in battle being thrown into the cauldron for rebirth.

Walton succeeds in making Pwyll a convincing and appealing character. Daring, proud, impetuous, filled with zest for life yet with a warrior's ready willingness to sacrifice it, he is a young man sent on a quest who grows inwardly as a result of his experiences. Walton internalizes his character by printing his thoughts in italicized passages, making the reader aware of his doubts, his fears and denials of fear, his attempts to cheer himself up. In his first quest, to help Arawn by defeating his enemy, King Havgan, his characterization is developed through two allegorical episodes. Both of these episodes occur after he leaves Arawn, having assumed the latter's shape and appearance, and in both he is tested and strengthened. In both he is alone except for Arawn's horse, the Grey, whom he comes to love almost as much as his own adored mount in Dyved, Kein Galed.

His first test comes about while he is galloping through "grey sightlessness and grey soundlessness" toward the abyss of Annwn, when he suddenly hears an ominous sound. Quickly deciding either to make friends with it or to kill it, he advances eagerly to discover what sort of creature it is. The reader has been warned through eerie evocative imagery that it is a dreadful foe. Even Pwyll, trained warrior that he is, is not prepared for the monstrosity it turns out to be, black, foul, and enormous, with two human heads dangling from its forepaws. Shrewdly, Pwyll tries to throw his two spears through its two eyes, but only one meets its mark. Although Pwyll is viciously wounded by the claws of the thing, he is able to subdue it with the unexpected aid of the two heads, who come to his rescue when they are dropped in the struggle. First blinded, then killed, the vile creature melts into the ground, its huge corpse destroying the area about it. Pwyll is magically healed of the severe wounds inflicted by the monster and learns from Arawn that the foe was actually Fear. In this test, Pwyll is inspired by the loyalty of his grey horse and by the assistance of the two skulls, whom he honors by giving a respectful burial.

The second test, also allegorical, occurs in the twilight world of Annwn, beginning when the swirling mists seem to shape themselves into serpents, but the truly dangerous serpent is within, torturing Pwyll with doubts of Arawn's integrity. He suspects that the grey man has misled him, simply because, as the serpent diabolically suggests, the immortals like to toy with men out of sheer boredom. But Pwyll is strong enough inwardly to set his heel on the serpent's head, to use Walton's interesting but anachronistically Christian image for the psychological test of her Celtic hero. The next monster facing Pwyll is a giant bird, sitting atop the lintel of a three-columned gateway. There are three vertical niches in the central pillar, the two top ones occupied by skulls, the lowest one empty. Each side pillar has one niche with a newly severed head in it. The loquacious skulls explain that the monstrous bird ate their flesh away because they died in despair, unable therefore to come to the cauldron of rebirth. Pwyll tries hard to resist despairing thoughts, assuring himself that even if he is killed on this journey his life has been good. He longs once more to ride his Kein Galed, and soon such images of hope are joined by those of beauty, as lovely singing birds suddenly appear, their beauty condemning the monster as a blasphemy of the very idea of a bird. Thus armed with hope and sensitive to the beauty that justifies all existence, Pwyll sees the pillars suddenly collapse, burying the monstrous bird along with the structure. As he later learns, this monster was named Despair.

From these tests Pwyll learns to recognize his own susceptibility to both fear and despair. He also learns pity for others, as he regrets having dragged his men and hounds away from their breakfast simply to serve his own sporting urge to go hunting. Proud of himself physically, especially of his sexual and martial prowess, he learns a touch of humility in dealing with these essentially spiritual foes, more threatening than any ordinary man or beast. Strengthened by these encounters, Pwyll is prepared to deal with further tests in Arawn's kingdom. First , he is able to resist the temptation to make love to Arawn's wife. Out of courtesy and loyalty to Arawn he represses his sexual desire for a whole year and a day. Second, he faces an even greater challenge to his self-control when he meets the godlike Havgan, Arawn's enemy. When the handsome, young, seemingly gentle Havgan begs to be beheaded quickly rather than left wounded and suffering, Pwyll finds it difficult to grant his wish, even though Arawn had warned him against this peril. (The severed head would survive, to do more evil.) He does refuse, however, thus saving both Annwn and his own world from the threatened deprivations of Havgan's black-bearded followers who obviously would ultimately destroy any land they occupied.

Not all of Pwyll's experiences are tests. One positive encounter occurs in a mysterious green wood, where he sees a beautiful woman making wooden images of birds come to life. This woman is the goddess Rhiannon, also an outstanding and complex character in this first work of the series. Pwyll is astonished and delighted when he drinks from the golden cup beside her blue well and learns that she plans to come to his world and be his wife. She will take on human mortality in order to wed him. As both goddess and woman she is both immortal and mortal, both the mother of all and the wife of one. She later tells Pwyll that she has been wife to the past kings of Dyved as well.

Rhiannon is in fact more than goddess or woman, for she also symbolizes the matriarchal principle in the Celtic world. Walton is one of several women fantasy writers to create a matriarchal society. But whereas Norton conceived an original version of a matriarchy based on magical powers and training, Walton and several other writers have imaginatively revived the matriarchal societies of the ancient world, particularly the Celtic. (See chapter 11 on Marion Zimmer Bradley and the *Mists of Avalon*.) In the Walton books a major theme is the conflict between the old religion based on worship of the goddess and the new patriarchal religion, moving in from the east, with its devotion to a male god. This shift in religion brings about changes in social structure as well as in relationships between men and women and between people and their environment, since the mother goddess represents the earth as well as woman.

For the Old Tribes, devoted to the goddess, the womb is sacred. The earth is the womb of the mother, assuring fecundity in nature. Procreation is associated exclusively with the female, the male role in conception not having been discovered yet. Women are sexually free, with none of the restraints of marital bondage. Descent is matrilinear, with the kingship passing to the son of the former king's sister. The Old Tribes also believe in reincarnation, which takes place through the metaphorical womb of the cauldron of rebirth. The danger inherent in male control of female symbols is demonstrated in the third book, when the cauldron functions to produce not genuine rebirth but monstrosity. Related to the concept of rebirth is that of the spirit residing in the head, which can survive the death of the rest of the body. Talking heads proved helpful to Pwyll, and in the third volume the spiritual survival of a leader's head transforms the history of a nation.

In contrast, the New Tribes prefer man-gods. They introduce the radical new idea that men play a role in procreation, thereby initiating revolutionary new concepts such as marriage, legitimacy, and inheritance through the male. For them, the heads cut off in battle are but trophies, mere signs of their own physical prowess as warriors, and they even revere as trophies the cut-off breasts of women captives. They deliberately pervert the worship of the goddess in several ways, including the blasphemous rite of requiring the new king to mate with a white mare, after which he kills her and drinks her blood. Rhiannon as exemplar of the mother goddess deplores this barbarian custom as a mockery of her sacred meaning. Although Pwyll is ostensibly a member of the "enlightened" New Tribes, aware of paternity, he also honors the goddess and refuses to participate in the ritual of the white mare. The conflict between the two views is an intensely personal one for the young ruler.

Arawn's foe Havgan is also a representative of the new religion. His followers ravish and despoil the earth, which they do not honor as the mother of all life. Their attitude toward death is also totally different. Not accepting the idea of death as gateway to rebirth on a higher level, they regard death as final and even suggest the possibility of eternal torment for some after physical death, with no opportunity for spiritual evolution. Clearly an anticipation of Christian ideas, this new religion from the east worships a male god who will subject his enemies to everlasting burning after death. Havgan is portrayed as a sun-god, pale and beautiful yet evil. In lands where the sun parches the earth and destroys growth, where people and crops burn when exposed to its intense rays, the sun is not wholly beneficent but can often be a threat to survival. Pwyll, who has difficulty accepting the evil nature of this radiant young god, notes that his strength wanes after noon when the sun begins to decline.

In the first half of the book, then, Pwyll completes his quest in Annwn, surviving the physical and spiritual tests and returning home to Dyved a better prince for the experience. In the second half, Pwyll's quest is for a bride. The dreamlike event in the green wood, where he encountered the radiantly beautiful woman with the birds, has shown him an image of his wife-to-be but a seemingly unattainable one. Although Pwyll does not realize it, his own forebearance in sleeping chastely with Arawn's wife has prepared him for attaining the woman he desires. One night the queen of Annwn revealed that she was the goddess. Unknown to the sleeping Pwyll, she rose from bed to be greeted as Mother by the birds who constituted the roof. She then complimented the young prince as if he were her child, "born of Me as all the sons of women are born of Me." She explained that although Rhiannon shaped the birds, she as Mother of all gave birth to Rhiannon, as she does to all that lives, even Havgan who threatens to ravage the land that is her womb. Her assurance is that of rebirth, "All that die are born again of Me. Light and darkness, both have their times, their places; both are Me" (p. 74). Time and Death are but her children, Death the son who brings home her Sheaves to escape the weariness of age and become young again. Immortality is thus rejected as a false notion belonging to the godly religion. For the worshippers of the goddess the cycle of rebirth is accepted as part of the natural order. Rhiannon's statement encapsulates two major feminist themes, the vindication of mortality and the depolarization of values. Just as death is the way to birth, so light and darkness coexist.

The goddess next appears in the episode that takes place on the mysterious Mound of Gorsedd Arberth, where it is said the man who dares to sleep beholds either great dangers or great wonders. Pwyll wishes to sleep there, together with his faithful companions, eager for either eventuality. As they all sleep, the High Druid, who objects to the young prince's ideas, tries to kill him with his golden sickle, but on that windless night a sudden strong wind knocks the sickle out of his hand to the ground. The goddess is protecting the prince. What Pwyll experiences is both danger and wonder. The wonder is in the form of a beautiful young woman riding a horse. Attracted to her, Pwyll tries to catch up with her, but although her mount seems to be ambling along at a slow, steady pace, he cannot catch up with her no matter how hard he spurs his own horse. In his passion to overtake her, he almost kills Kein Galed by pushing him too hard in this impossible race. When he finally realizes what he has been doing, he fights against his own pride, determination, and will, and begins to take pity on his horse. He decides to do what the men of the New Tribes would never tolerate, i.e., ask the woman to stop. He does, and she stops, replying sharply that courtesy has accomplished what physical force would never be able to do. This is clearly another victory for the goddess. Pity has won out over the will to power, courtesy over force, feminine perseverance over masculine drive. The goddess is thus an embodiment of the renunciation of power and aggression.

Further wonders follow. The woman identifies herself as Rhiannon, and her birds circling about the suffering horse completely heal him. Rhiannon is both goddess and the queens of old, in her present manifestation the daughter of the king whose bones lie under the magic Mound. By analogy every woman is a manifestation of the goddess, an exemplar of her nature as mother and mistress, a being whose force consists of the denial of force in favor of birth and healing.

Pwyll undergoes one more test in the hall of Heyevydd. Although his journey there is undertaken with courage and fortitude, while he is there he drinks a bit too much of the heady wine of that world, leading him to make a rash decision. Rhiannon had been pledged by her father to marry Gwawl, but she had preferred Pwyll. When Gwawl asks a boon of the young prince, Pwyll, who had been learning pity, now misuses it and agrees to grant anything requested by this apparently unhappy young man who has been deprived of his intended bride. The mistake is disastrous, for Gwawl naturally requests his bride back. Rhiannon is angered at her befuddled bridegroom but orders him to return after another year and a day, at which time she will put a plan into effect that will accomplish their marriage and eliminate Gwawl as suitor. The irony of the situation lies in part in the identity of Gwawl. Pwyll gradually becomes aware, through his wine-befogged wits, that this man is Havgan, the summer-white, blue-eyed foe of the other world. Pwyll has failed this test, but the goddess is not so easily defeated in her plans to take on mortal form and marry him.

When the preliminary night on the Mound is repeated a year and a day later, the High Druid tries once more to kill Pwyll but is again defeated by the intervention of the goddess. When he raises his golden sickle, lightning suddenly strikes him, while the fragrance of the goddess fills the air. He retires bitterly, his beard scorched but his resolve undiminished. Pwyll goes to the hall of Heyevydd, equipped with a small leather bag as Rhiannon had instructed. He asks the king to fill the bag with scraps of food, but the bag seemingly holds an endless amount so that not all of the food in the hall will fill it. The only way to fill it is for Gwawl to step in it with both feet. When he does so, the bag shoots up like a great widening pit about him, and its mouth closes over him so that none in the hall can open it. Pwyll then summons his men, who surge in, bind Gwawl's followers, and proceed to kick the bag soundly. In this world that has never known violence, the deed is an outrage. When Gwawl leaves the hall, his cold blue eyes are filled with hatred for the young prince who has twice defeated him. His threat of revenge will follow the bridal pair. The book thus ends on a negative tone. Not only will Gwawl strike again, but also the High Druid has prophesied that Pwyll will never bear a son. The marriage of Pwyll and Rhiannon has introduced violence into the Bright World, and the shadow of that deed will haunt their lives. The reader at this point is eager to go on to the other branches, having entered the Celtic world and met two such appealing mythic figures.

The Children of Llyr, based on the second branch, deals with many of the same themes but is quite different in tone, setting, and event. The conflict is between Ireland and Britain, here called the Isle of the Mighty. Worship of the goddess is still thematically important, but here the only major female figure, Branwen, is entirely the victim of male domination. The principal characters in the novel are the five children of the British sea-god, Llyr, only one of whom survives at the end of the book: the giant Bran, his sister Branwen, his brother Manwyddan, and their twin half-brothers Nissyen and Evnissyen. Many remarkable events are recounted, but they lack the colorful glow of the otherworld scenes in the preceding book, and they all end in appalling tragedy. This is a powerful but grim novel.

The tragic sequence of events begins with Bran's agreement to marry his sister Branwen to the Irish leader, Mathnolwch. Bran has an ulterior motive in that he wanted his own son Cardoc to inherit his place as leader, and his sister's presence in Britain would put her son first in line, according to the matrilinear succession. In spite of a traditional rivalry between the two kingdoms, the royal festivities seem at first to be both elegant and amiable, with a special pavilion built for Bran, who cannot be held by any ordinary house. The fatal flaw in the plans is the failure to invite Evnissyen, the villain of the story. Although Nissyen is a friendly and peace-loving man, with a gift for turning strife to harmony, his twin is just the opposite. Spiteful, revengeful, an inveterate troublemaker, he deliberately sets about to ruin the marriage and stir up hostilities between the tribes. He first brutally mutilates the Irish king's horses. Bran recompenses him with sound horses and several other valuable gifts, but in spite of his generous efforts, Matholwch's relatives demand that he punish Branwen for the insult he has suffered at her brother's hands. Matholwch, who is a weak and cowardly man, agrees, although Branwen has been a good wife, and he sends her to work in the kitchen under very demeaning circumstances. He forbids that any word of her mistreatment be sent to Bran.

Branwen's ingenuity in getting a message to Bran is another example of Walton's artful expansion of the original. The *Mabinogion* tells us in a few lines that the unhappy woman taught a starling to speak so that it could carry a message for her. Walton devotes an entire chapter to the episode, describing how Branwen, while kneading dough at the trough, spent three years in secretly teaching the bird how to speak. When the bird fulfills its mission at the end of the three years, Bran immediately sets out for Ireland to revenge the wrong done his sister. Too big to fit in any boat, he walks through the sea.

During her time in Ireland Branwen has born Matholwch a son, Gwern, who becomes a pawn in the ensuing political battle. When the forces of Bran march on the Irish leader's land, Matholwch quickly agrees to let Gwern inherit the throne in order to appease Bran. He also builds a house big enough to hold Bran, in a further attempt at peace-making. For a time it appears as if the gathered warriors of Ireland and the Island of the Mighty will be able to achieve peace, forgetting their mutual insults and even their disagreements over the succession, but they do not reckon on the unregenerate evil of Evnissyen. As the men sit together in the great hall, many of them praising the charming young son of the royal couple, Gwern, their harmonious gathering is abruptly shattered by a violent action. Evnissyen, apparently greeting the child, seizes him and thrusts him head down into the roaring fire. Bran manages to stop Branwen from following her son into the fire, but he cannot abate the fury of the fighting that follows.

This brutal episode is told so bluntly in the *Mabinogion* that the reader does not feel the force of it. Walton's description, however, makes it electrifying. The ensuing battle is also vivified through Walton's descriptive detail. The actual fighting lasts a long time because the Irish are able to revive their dead by dipping them into the magic cauldron of rebirth, ironically a gift from Bran. The creatures who emerge from the cauldron, however, are not reborn warriors, but monstrosities, parts and fragments of bodies, soulless perversions of the human form, fighting with relentless ferocity. At the end of this melee of horrors, most of the Irish warriors are finally dead, along with all but seven of the men from the Island of the Mighty. Bran is killed although his head remains alive to console his surviving men. Branwen lives long enough to help the wounded but dies of a broken heart when the fighting is over. Nissyen, too, is killed, but just before his death he shows a moment of tenderness toward his evil twin who has been seriously wounded.

Evnissyen is one of the most memorable characters, another example of Walton's use of psychological motivation. In the *Mabinogion* he is simply totally evil, with no individual personality apart from that given fact. Walton depicts him as evil, but as a man with a warped personality, a man who is convinced that no one likes him. He is jealous of his popular twin and sensitive to efforts of others to be kind to him, for he realizes that they should not have to try. When he finally discovers that Nissyen likes him for his own sake, in that fleeting moment of kindness just before the twin's death, he decides to perform a good deed for the first time. This pathetic yet despicable man whose whole life has been a torment to himself and to others finally helps someone but through destructive means. He is tossed into the cauldron by a couple of brawny Irishmen, who expect him to emerge as a monstrous fighter on their side, but once inside the cauldron Evnissyen musters superhuman strength in order to kick apart the sides of the vessel, thereby breaking it. This psychotic, self-pitying twin, who has always taken out his frustration on others with unspeakable cruelty, undergoes a change of heart and endures the torture of the flames in order to save a remnant of his countrymen. As his only surviving brother Manawyddan remarks, "He saved us by destruction, that is his one gift" (p. 170).

The explosion of the cauldron is an apocalyptic episode, turning the green countryside into a wasteland of ashes. The poison fumes freed by the bursting cauldron hang over the land like a death cloud, while birds fall from the air, cattle drop dead in the fields, and people die in their houses. Although the scene was written in the 1930s, it has an uncanny resemblance to an account of a nuclear explosion and aftermath. This episode along with the grisly account of the cauldron of rebirth are both masterful examples of Gothic horror writing.

The impact of horror and tragedy is somewhat alleviated by the elements of renewal and survival. The mere fact of Bran's head living on to comfort and entertain his seven surviving men for eighty-seven days (the *Mabinogion* says less convincingly eighty-seven years) lessens the sense of loss. Among the seven who return from Ireland are Pryderi, supposedly Pwyll's son, and Manawyddan, son of Llyr, who will be major characters in the third branch of the story. The aura of doom is also somewhat modified by the sense of wonder in the strictly fantasy elements of the story. Bran's size, like Gulliver's among the Lilliputians, is both marvelous and comic. The speaking starling, painstakingly trained by Branwen, is a touching tale of wonder. Branwen's years in the kitchen were spent standing in a waist-high pit where the cooking was done, with the huge spit placed on her shoulders, making her bow beneath its weight, sweating in the flames. According to historical records, this inhumane custom was actually practiced in medieval Ireland.

Of the four novels retelling the four branches, this is the most tragic, but even here the sense of rebirth and renewal is maintained. It is not like *Hamlet* or *King Lear*, where all of the major characters are dead at the ending, but more like the Oedipus trilogy where there is both survival and transformation. Pryderi and Manawyddan are alive, Bran's head survives at least for a time, and the pathetically beautiful episode of the trained starling offers hope for the human imagination to triumph over injustice and cruelty.

The third branch, *The Song of Rhiannon,* begins with the sad return home of Pryderi and Manawyddan. It also begins with Walton's use of an expository device in order to clarify what the *Mabinogion* cites but fails to explain. Does the birth of Pryderi to Rhiannon mean that the prediction of the Druids, i.e., that Pwyll would never have a son, has proved false? The reader learns the truth gradually, first from the lips of an old woman in a shepherd's hut that the two men visit on their way back to Britain, then from Manawyddan's own memory of the occasion. It seems that Pwyll came to realize after his sojourn in the underworld of

Annwn that he would not be able to sire another child. Desperately wanting an heir, he arranged for his close friend Manawyddan to spend one night with Rhiannon in order for her to conceive. Meeting always in the dark, Rhiannon would never know which night it was. A gentle and loyal man, Manawyddan loved Rhiannon that night, so that the conception took place in accord with the Ancient Harmonies, but since then he never uttered a word about it. Now, recalling all this, he feels totally alone and alienated, with no kin to turn to. Close friends with his unsuspecting son, however, he agrees to go with Pryderi to Dyved, where the prince will return to his own wife, Kivga, and where, as Pryderi also suggests, Rhiannon will be happy to accept Manawyddan as her mate.

Back in Dyved, the two couples become inseparable friends, living happily by themselves. Pryderi, conscious of his duties as prince and young enough to want to prove himself by daring deeds, tells his people that he intends to sit on the Mound of Gorsedd Arberth as his father had done, awaiting what marvels might occur there. When he does so, in the company of his wife and friends, a different kind of magic strikes. A mist arises, hovers, then dissipates, leaving the entire countryside stricken into a wasteland, with no living creature left except for themselves.

The storm that brings such desolation is also traumatic for the four survivors. Traversing their land for two years, they find nothing human and are forced to survive on honey and wild game. Eventually traveling out into other lands, they are able to make a living through handicrafts, but each time they stir up the envy and enmity of other craftsmen because of their own superior work. Driven out of several localities, they return to Dyved to live by hunting. Their drifting lives and deep despair are at once psychological and physical.

Once when the men are chasing a wild boar, they see both boar and hounds disappear into a hillside, and Pryderi goes in after them. Manawyddan realizes too late that it is a trap, that they have been led to the same fearful mound where the disastrous otherworldly storm had come from. He does not follow Pryderi but waits many hours, then returns to tell the women the ill news. Rhiannon races out, condemning Manawyddan for cowardice. The older man and younger woman are left alone. When neither the prince nor his mother returns, they decide to struggle to stay alive. Manawyddan vows never to violate Kigva, and in spite of their woes they feel that their friendship will help them through. Without their dogs, hunting is impossible, but Manawyddan plants some wheat, while Kigva takes care of the cooking and household chores.

Their lonely struggle is lightened by the appearance of a "bogey" in the household. The mischievous doings of this prankster add considerable humor to the novel. A grotesque little creature out of Celtic folklore, with whiskers growing upward rather than downward and out of his ears and eyebrows as well as his chin, he is helpful but occasionally malicious. The little trickster dislikes Kivga, who is unable to even see him, but he enjoys chatting with Manawyddan, who is a magician, someone with whom he feels a certain grudging kinship. Cynically superior to humans, whom he calls the Clumsy Folk, the bogey is tamed by Manawyddan, who knows the appropriate curse to threaten him with: He will raise a wind to blow the bogey into the upper air over the eastern sea for the span of twice seven generations. He is therefore gratefully happy for a bowl of milk left for him overnight. In one of his talkative moods he tells Manawyddan about the farmer and his wife who had been living in the same cottage when the land was abruptly desolated. They were both instantly turned into dragonflies.

When Manawyddan finally succeeds in growing wheat, he is again visited by misfortune. One morning when he goes to the fields he finds that the sheaves have all been eaten. When this mysterious consumption of the wheat happens several times, he decides to wait in the fields overnight to ascertain the cause. The culprit is revealed as a group of mice, tiny but nibbling away with ferocious energy at the precious crop. They run away when he makes his presence known, but he captures one plump, apparently pregnant mouse who cannot run so fast as the others. Desperate for revenge, Manawyddan decides to hang the captive mouse as if it were a convicted criminal, constructing a tiny gallows for the purpose in the stricken wheat field. Before the sentence can be carried out, several visitors appear who try to talk him out of it. They turn out to be the same visitor in a series of disguises, namely the Grey Man of another world, a friend of Gwawl's who has planned all this as revenge on Rhiannon. Manawyddan agrees to release the mouse, who is actually the Grey Man's wife transformed, in return for the release from enchantment of Pryderi. At this point the Ancient Harmonies are restored, and the land of Dyved returns to normal life again.

This version of the third branch of the *Mabinogion* is less unified than its predecessors. Although the narrative for the most part is focused on the two survivors, father and son, it is also somewhat strained by virtue of its essentially transitional nature. Part of its purpose is to provide an expository link, explaining such matters as Pryderi's paternity. In one scene the appearance of Branwen's starling provides a link with the preceding volume. The nature of Gwawl's revenge connects the work with the first branch. The result of all this is more exposition and less dramatic happening.

On the other hand, some of the events, although not central to the main plot, add a touch of humor which is largely lacking in the other branches. That delightful trickster, the bogey, provides comic relief from the scenes of desolation that precede and follow his appearance. In another episode, which takes place while Pryderi is visting the court of

High King Caswallon, a feat of magic breaks the tension. A ragged stranger visits that court at the same time, a gifted harpist and a talented magician who performs a remarkable trick. Based on the famed Indian rope trick, it involves unrolling a spool of thread, sending it high into the air until its end is beyond human sight, then sending up it first a hare, then a dog, then a boy, and finally a girl. Several more breathtaking flourishes to the trick stun the audience, but only the king himself realizes that the magician is none other than Manawyddan.

Although less unified than its predecessors, *The Song of Rhiannon* is gentler in tone and more humane in its emphasis on love and loyalty. Although it does not have the tragic inevitability of *The Children of Llyr*, it movingly depicts the poignant sadness of the survivor, Manawyddan. And although it does not have the theme of an individual quest to the Other World, it certainly is much concerned with the forces of otherworlds at work in Dyved. As the novel ends, the Grey Man restores the land of Dyved after its seven years' blight, and for a moment it seems that Manawyddan has achieved peace. But in the Bright World to which the Grey Man returns, there are further plans to test this brave man's soul.

Walton's version of the fourth branch of the *Mabinogion* is not only the oldest but also the longest in the series (368 pages) and in many ways the most complex. The central figures are the ancient necromancer Math and the seven children of his sister, the goddess Don, especially his nephew Gwydion, his heir and also a magician, and his niece Arianrhod, a sorceress. The narrative is divided into three books, "The Pigs of Pryderi," "Lleu," and "The Loves of Blodeuwedd," separate but continuous stories dominated by Math and Gwydion. The mood is varied, tragic in respect to the doomed children of Arianrhod and comic in several episodes concerned with magic and trickery. Above all, however, the tone resonates with the sense of wonder. Both creative magic and destructive sorcery flourish in the world of this book, where the presence of Faery is ever palpable.

Math is an impressive Wise Old Man. He is the avatar whose duty is to guide his people upward on their destined path of evolution. As an archetypal wizard, he is close to being essential spirit. He rarely moves, most of the time lying on a couch, with his feet in the lap of a virgin. He listens to the "myriad vibrating sounds of the universe" and enjoys ineffable serenity no matter what calamities come to pass. And calamities do occur quite frequently. He has little need of food or sleep and is able to see into the thoughts of other people at a long distance. His subtle awareness moves through the air on the wind. When his nephews feel a sudden cold chill, they recognize his penetration of their thoughts. As Walton beautifully describes his spirituality:

Math did not need sleep to bridge the gulfs between the worlds. He could rest without sleep, so perfect was the freedom he had attained even in this body from the troubles and blindness and earthy heats of flesh, that the spirits of common men flee from, wearied by one day's sojourn, back to the purer, lighter worlds that lie on the other side of memory; realms that all of us visit nightly—though, waking, our brains are too gross to retain their loveliness. (p. 249)

Math's task is to enlighten although in the case of Gwydion he resorts to punishment as a means toward enlightenment.

The first tale is focused on Gwydion and his brother Gilvaethwy. Gwydion here is an archdeceiver, first tricking Pryderi, ruler of Dyved, out of several pigs, gifts from Annwn, then tricking his uncle by arranging for his brother to seduce Math's virgin footholder. The first deception has far-ranging political consequences, for Pryderi starts a war over the loss of his pigs. Feeling guilty that men are dying because of his action, Gwydion agrees to settle the dispute in single combat with his opponent. When the heroes fight, brains win over brawn, and Pryderi the warrior is victim of Gwydion the wizard. Although the reader may prefer magic to martial prowess, the young wizard does not gain much sympathy at this point. His other misdeed brings about Math's decision to punish his nephew. First rewarding the young woman footholder who valiantly tried to fight off her seducer, Math then transforms both of his nephews into beasts in order to start their evolutionary journey anew at a lower level, equivalent to the bestial behavior they have manifested. After living for two years each as deer, hogs, and wolves, they are returned to human form, duly enlightened by the experience. Gwydion becomes gentler and wiser, more concerned with the inward nature of things than with overt trickery. Already an amalgam of Merlin and Hermes, a shape-shifter and the poet who introduces writing, he becomes a more balanced and unselfish human being as well.

The subsequent books, "Lleu" and "The Loves of Blodeuwedd," are focused on Gwydion's sorceress sister, Arianrhod, thus returning to the theme of the feminine. Guardian of a magic well, living in the Castle of the Silver Wheel, Arianrhod is a strong, power-hungry woman, not above lying, scheming, and treachery to attain her goals. Although she is not a virgin, she applies for the post of footholder for Math, who exposes her deception through his own magic. In his surefire virginity test for his scheming niece, she abruptly bears a child, then, as she races out of the room, drops another small object on the floor, which Gwydion immediately picks up, wrapping it carefully in silk cloth. Not only is her flight from the test a confession of guilt but, more importantly, a rejection of motherhood, a sacrilege that will ultimately destroy her. In the world of goddess worship the ultimate crime is the denial of motherly nature.

The small object dropped by Arianrhod after the abrupt birth of her baby actually turns out to be a second infant, not yet ready to be born. Gwydion, who wrapped it in silk, deposits it in a chest by his bedside until it is ready for birth. When it is born out of the chest as out of a womb, he adopts it and loves it as his own son, but when he takes it to Arianrhod she curses the boy three times, i.e., with namelessness, with never being able to bear arms, and with never touching a woman. Each of the three curses Gwydion tries to circumvent with magic. With the aid of Math, he even creates a woman out of flowers for the young man, Lleu, when he reaches maturity. Gwydion thus functions as surrogate mother in several ways, placing the unborn infant in the womblike chest, "bearing" it and caring for it in childhood, then creating rather than bearing a mate for him in adulthood.

Although he has symbolically borne Lleu, Gwydion proves unable even through his magic to preserve his life. The wizard tries by determining that Lleu can be killed only by a virtually impossible combination of several bizarre factors. The innocent young man makes the mistake of telling his wife, Blodeuwedd, what these circumstances are. She reveals them to a lover who wants Lleu out of the way. As he explains, a charmed sword must be fashioned, worked on only during the time of weekly druidical sacrifices. Then the sword must be thrown at Lleu as he stands in his bath at the edge of the forest, with one foot on the edge of the cauldron and the other on the back of a goat. After the fatal sword has been fashioned accordingly, Lleu naïvely agrees to demonstrate the theoretical death scene for his villainous wife. When he is killed, Lleu's soul enters an eagle and flies off. The bereaved Gwydion seeks him in that form.

Blodeuwedd is a chilling portrayal of mingled innocence and evil. Because of her artificial nature she exists on a low level of being, with no sense of either guilt or responsibility. Falling in love is for her a step up the ladder of evolution simply through aroused desire and will. The results are morally negative, as her selfishness becomes a matter of deliberate choice. In keeping with her not-quite-human nature, her death will not permit rebirth. Instead, her ultimate destiny is transformation into an owl, a bird that wakes only at night and is despised by other birds.

With Lleu dead, Arianrhod arranges the death of her other son, completely revoking her motherly role. Before her own melodramatic death, she suffers from both guilt and loneliness. Thwarted in both love and ambition, with all the love she had never permitted herself to feel "curdled within her, soured and perverted," this embittered woman is haunted by images of her dead sons and her brother who she feels has used her as a tool. Becoming slowly mad with a passion for revenge, she resolves to unleash the profoundest curse possible in order to deny the soul of Lleu refuge, to bar him from the ocean, the heavens, the fields, and the womb of woman. Her purpose is so malign and unnatural that her fellow guardians of the well leave her in fear and horror. As she releases the primal powers of destruction with her spells, her castle is flooded, and she drowns. Walton makes the sorceress a sympathetic character by portraying her weeping by the seaside for the love she never felt. Like Evnissyen in the earlier book, she is not merely a wicked person but also a suffering, lonely individual hungry for love. Her fatal flaw in the Celtic scheme of things is her failure as a mother. To hurt rather than nurture one's own children is a fundamental violation of the Ancient Harmonies, and Arianrhod must pay.

The children of the goddess Don thus suffer tragic fates as did the children of the god Llyr. In this work, however, the tragic intensity is modified by the emphasis on transformation. Death is presented not as the end but as a turning. Aging Math remarks that he feels near to making the change. The change may come about in a different form of life, as in the case of Lleu's transformation into an eagle. In Walton's mythic vision death is a transition to rebirth.

The theme of rebirth is intricately interwoven with the theme of multiple, layered worlds. The many otherworlds are all of Faery, but there is movement from one to another. The first layer above our own is but one step away from the moment of birth and death. When we are born into this world we bring with us a memory of that Other, as Wordsworth's poem puts it, "trailing clouds of glory." The gods in this context are depicted as men who have worked their way upwards to freedom from earthly flesh. The task of a leader such as Math is to aid the evolutionary process for others through guidance and education. The conflicts that develop during this process result from the transient dualism of earthly life. Here there is war between men and women, humans and animals, adults and children, but eventually all consciousness will unite with the One and dualities will give way to unity. In this world we cannot value light without darkness, but in other worlds there is neither dark nor light. Walton is clearly opposed to the polarization of values.

In this beautifully written book, even the most bizarre episodes do not seem quaint or primitive in the telling, but rather become totally credible in their eloquent presentation. Largely through the evocative power of her style, Walton creates a world in which these strange things happen. A man stands on the edge of a forest with one foot on the rim of a cauldron and the other on the back of a goat. When a man is killed, his soul enters an eagle. An embryo is kept for nine months in a chest, then born as a healthy infant. These are indeed marvels but so suitable to Walton's fantasy world that they seem almost mundane in context.

Some readers may object to an occasional authorial intrusion, as when Walton deprecates science in comparison with magic:

> For the secret of magic is that it is a science that requires marvelous control and concentration of mind, just as the intricate metal machinery with which men of today work their miracles requires marvelous planning and shaping and fitting. And that is why magic is now denied and discredited by many who, lacking the mental vigor to carry out or envision the process, dismiss it as children's tales and phantasy; and clumsily substitute telephones and radios for the all-penetrating thought of Math. (p. 146)

Through such passages, however, Walton achieves an intimacy with the vision implicit in the original material. One feels in reading her work that she is herself a reborn Celt, sensitive to the meaning of that world not from the distant perspective of the twentieth century but from within, long ago.

Walton thus goes much beyond translation to recreate the four branches of the *Mabinogion*. Her work avoids the discontinuities and abruptness of the original, with such disconcerting features as characters who appear and disappear for no apparent reason, as well as the frustration of complex events summarized in a single sentence. Without altering the original material, she has added to it for the sake of both authenticity and literary effectiveness. Most of her additions are from Celtic lore so that they suit the world of the narrative. Two such examples are the talking skulls and the bogey. The episode of the skulls in *The Prince of Annwn* is based on the artifacts of Bouche Rhône in France, where ancient Celts actually placed skulls in specially provided niches. Similarly the bogey, whose pranks provide comic moments in *The Song of Rhiannon*, is a well-known figure in the folklore of the Celtic peoples. Walton's omissions are also based on a desire for authenticity. She omits all Christian references on the assumption, accepted by most scholars, that they would have been added much later by monks copying the original material. One example is the forging of the spear with which to kill Lleu. In the text that has come down to us the spear must be worked on only during mass on Sunday, but Walton has it that it could be forged only during druidical ceremonies, certainly much more appropriate to the context.

Walton's profound and intimate understanding of the Celtic world enables her to write perceptively of its social and cultural assumptions. In particular, the thematic motif of rebirth to a higher spiritual level comes through not as a distant doctrine but as immediate and personal belief. In a recent interview Walton asserted her own belief in the doctrine. "Spiritual evolution through reincarnation seems to me to be the only religious concept that makes sense. . . . The whole theory sounds like a ferocious amount of work, requiring infinite patience, but for that very reason it makes more sense to me than any other theory of the afterlife I've ever heard."[3] The concept of reincarnation also adds depth to her characterization. An outstanding example is the goddess Rhiannon, who functions both in her role as deity and in her reborn manifestation as wife and mother.

Walton also writes with a deep and sympathetic understanding of the matriarchal society of the Old Tribes, who honor all women through the goddess. Belief in the goddess as mother also has ecological implications, for to wound the earth is to wound the mother whose womb it represents. In contrast to the mother principle she sees technology as masculine, admitting to a fear of the machine age which threatens the earth once held sacred. In her four novels we see the movement away from the matriarchal to the patriarchal pattern of society, a movement which has continued until our own time. Her view of this development is ironic: "[W]hen men took over they invented nothing really new until our own machine age appeared, an almost exclusively masculine creation. Pollution has dimmed that last glory a little" (*PA*, p. 178). Correspondingly her treatment of masculine "heroism" is highly ironic. Not only are the great heroes killed, e.g., Bran and Pryderi, but their people suffer great losses. When Pryderi is slain by Gwydion, the hero principle is defeated by the wizard's craft. As C. W. Sullivan perceptively points out, however, it is only Pryderi as representative of the Heroic Age who is defeated, for his people, the New Tribes, have established the patrilineal succession. Even Gwydion has accepted the belief in fatherhood and seeks a son to succeed him.

Although Walton may not be writing consciously as a feminist, her positive portrayal of a matriarchal society is in effect a feminist achievement. In addition, her strong characterization of two major female characters and her sensitive depiction of the goddess as an ever present force are feminist dimensions of her recreated Celtic world. The major female roles are Rhiannon and Arianrhod, who might also be seen as positive and negative embodiments of motherhood. Rhiannon is more fully developed in her varied roles as coy mistress, proud bride, gentle mother, and spiritual guide. At the heart of her role, however, she is the Great Mother, the creator and renewer of all life. Arianrhod is more of a

Terrible Mother, a sorceress who turns her own remarkable powers against life, against even her own natural sons. But she has strength and a terrible will. Underlying both roles is the myth of the goddess, who may seem to lose out to male domination but who clearly transcends any temporal defeats. As Rhiannon points out to the sleeping hero who is on one level her lover and on another her son: "The Mother is mighty; She has many bodies. . . . She may yet heal Her wounds and make earth bloom again—yes, raise up you men along with it, even if She has to bear your whole race again" (*PA*, p. 174).

6

KATHERINE KURTZ

BORN DURING A FLORIDA HURRICANE, Katherine Kurtz has led a whirl-wind life ever since.[1] A onetime medical student, an expert hypnotist, currently a senior technician with the Los Angeles Police Academy, and an active member of both the Swordsmen and Sorcerers Guild of America and the Society for Creative Anachronism, Kurtz is by no means a retiring, reclusive writer. As an avid medievalist she is also knowledgeable about heraldry, manuscript illumination, church liturgy and architecture. It is not surprising that when she turned her hand to fantasy fiction she chose a medieval setting. Her two fantasy trilogies, *The Chronicles of Deryni* and *The Legends of Camber of Culdi*, are distinctive achievements in the genre, representing what might be called the subgenre of "historical fantasy." These works are set in a world that closely corresponds to a given place and moment in our own history, in terms of religious and cultural background. The setting is Gwynned in Wales, the period of time from about 900 to the early 1100s. *The Chronicles,* although written first, contain several references to historical events of two centuries earlier, the period in which *The Legends* take place. The second trilogy is thus what Tolkien would call a "prequel." All of the works feature historically accurate detail in such physical matters as food, armor, horses, falconry, ships, and costume, and all deal with the spiritual milieu of the tenth and eleventh centuries. They are also unequivocally fantasy fiction, with a large measure of magic informing their exciting episodes.

In addition to being historical fantasy, the trilogies of Kurtz also represent the category of feminist history. What the author achieves within her fantasy framework is a reconstruction of an actual historical period with a focus on feminist themes. She is particularly concerned with the witch mania of the Middle Ages, which becomes a subtextual analogue to the oppression of the Deryni, a race of sorcerers noted for their occult powers. In a subtler psychological way her Deryni also represent the hidden, repressed, feminine side of the human mind, intuitive and mysterious rather than clear and rational. The failure of church and state officials to accept even the beneficent powers of the gifted Deryni, such as their skills in the arts of healing, reflects the deep-seated prejudice against the feminine inherent in doctrinal Christianity. One of the most neglected of all the women fantasy writers, Katherine Kurtz is one of the most important and one of the most political because of the feminist revisioning of medieval history implicit in her sympathetic portrayal of the outlawed race of Deryni.

The first volume, *Deryni Rising* (1970), sets the stage for future action. In the country of Gwynned a profound antagonism has existed for centuries between the human population and the Deryni, a race of sorcerers. A popular and successful human king occupies the throne, but his life is in danger from a vicious Deryni sorceress, Charissa, whose father was killed in a duel years ago by the king's closest advisor, Morgan, himself a half-Deryni. When Charissa manages to kill the king by means of magic, the latent tensions surface, posing further threats to the heir to the throne, a boy of thirteen. Morgan is wrongly accused of complicity in the strange death of the king, and among the accusers is the king's widow, the prince's mother. Morgan's cousin Duncan, a priest of the rank of monsignor and spiritual advisor to the throne, is also in danger. His own half-Deryni ancestry has been kept secret, but revelation is threatened through his inevitable involvement in the intrigue surrounding the murder and the ensuing coronation of the new king. Morgan and Duncan achieve their purpose, to establish young Kelson on the throne, but only after a series of harrowing adventures. The pace of the plot is unusually fast. Most readers are surprised when they realize at the end that, after the first chapter, all of the events have taken place in a twenty-four-hour period.

The medieval setting is precisely delineated. Scenes in the marketplace, the hunt, church, and court are authentically described. Especially vivid are colorful passages devoted to costume and heraldry, reflecting two of the author's personal interests. The king's hunting outfit is described meticulously, from the silk beneath the chain mail to the outer wool cloak and hunting leather, topped with a white-plumed scarlet hunting cap. Heraldry is also elaborately visual and sophisticated. A detail concerning the heraldic gryphon, *sergeant rampant,* becomes a significant clue in the later working-out of the ritual formula by which Kelson takes on the inherited powers of the kingship. Street scenes capture the international flavor of the medieval bazaar, with its exotic oriental features such as sedan chairs and an occasional Turkish emir. Such scenes would be very effective on film. Above all, however, the medieval church is overwhelmingly present as a force. Frequent reference to both doctrine and ritual make the church a vivid, immediate reality. Many passages from Latin liturgy are included, the hierarchy of the bishopric is expounded, and the dominant role of the church in daily life is clearly demonstrated.

One of the most intriguing features is Deryni magic. Ranging from healing to hypnosis through telepathy, telekinesis, teleportation, and shape-shifting, their magical powers, whether used for good or ill, are condemned by the church as witchcraft. Fundamental to Deryni magic is the power of telepathy, or mind-seeing. A Deryni is able to see the truth in another person's mind regardless of what that person says or does to the contrary. This ability proves useful in detecting hypocrisy or betrayal. Closely related to mind-seeing is the technique of hypnosis, which is much more developed than the art as we know it. Through it the Deryni are able to enforce a receptive state by a simple gentle touch on the forehead exactly between the eyes. Even more awesome is the power of instantaneous teleportation. This action is called the portal transfer and can take place only between specified portals. From these precise locations the Deryni can transport themselves great distances in an instant.

Among the most artful kinds of magic are shape-shifting and warding. Their shape-shifting ability permits the Deryni to take on the physical identity of another person for an indefinite period of time. Disguise thus becomes a major weapon in their hands. Warding is even more intriguing by virtue of its strangeness and its complexity. A mysterious, ritualistic procedure, it involves black and white cubes which lock into place when the proper words are spoken over them and the proper touch sparks them into a glowing light. The resulting ward provides a magical safety barrier. Morgan employs the warding technique in order to ensure the safety of the prince during the night before his coronation, when his life is most in danger.

But the most far-reaching magical skill is the art of healing by touch. This skill is limited to a few of the Deryni, among them Morgan, who performs it twice, once on himself and once on a wounded follower. Kurtz explains the fact that only a few Deryni are capable of healing as a result of heredity. The author, as a former medical student, supplies a carefully worked out genetic code to explain the relatively rare inheritance of this feature through x and y chromosomes. One of the minor characters, Rhys, is a sympathetic portrayal of a gifted healer.

Magic informs the dramatic climax of *Deryni Rising*. Kelson is challenged by Charissa to a duel arcane, i.e., a duel involving an exchange of magical spells rather than swordplay. Charissa recites the opening spell which must be quickly countermanded by Kelson's spell. These expert duelists invoke ever more complex and demanding spells until it seems that Kelson will be overcome by Charissa's invocation of a dense black vapor that materializes into a creature with scaly hide, claws, and vicious teeth. Kelson fights back with a prompt invocation of bright light that destroys the monster, letting it writhe and thrash about in pain for a time, before melting away into nothingness. In a final tense encounter, so strong in its emanations that the noon sun drops in the sky, Kelson defeats the sorceress, who fades away even as her shadowy creation had done.

The major Deryni characters are deftly drawn. Morgan and Duncan are particularly likeable and engaging. Morgan is a soldier, an aristocrat, debonair, dashing, and endowed with an ingratiating sense of humor. His cousin Duncan, the priest, is thoughtful and introspective, a man with a profound inner conflict. Their relationship is one of relaxed friendship and total loyalty. The young human prince, whose coming-of-age story this first novel is, comes through less successfully at first but gains through the narrative. His best moment occurs in a council meeting when he deliberately delays the discussion until the stroke of 3:00, at which time he turns fourteen and legally becomes king. From this moment on he is no longer the diffident boy, caught up in political maneuvers beyond his control, but a forceful young man determined to assert his authority. Most of the minor characters are convincing with the exception of Charissa, the Shadowed One and the Lady of the Mists, who seems more an abstraction than an individual.

Closely related to the emphasis on magic is the central thematic role of the Catholic Church, introduced in this novel and continued through both trilogies. In Kurtz's rewriting of medieval history with a focus on feminist themes, she perceptively introduces the idea of the two magics, the orthodox magic of Catholic ritual and the heretical magic of sorcerers, in this case, the Deryni. The church has unequivocally condemned all occult arts, thereby in effect condemning all Deryni. As a member of the priesthood Duncan tries to resolve his own inner conflict between his role as church emissary and his Deryni nature through the belief that he uses his God-given gifts, such as his healing ability, only to do good, but his indulgence in magical practices is never condoned by his church. Yet the church fails to recognize the transformational magic in its mass. The parallel to the position of the medieval church on the subject of witchcraft is obvious. There were no "good" witches.

An unusual device—unique, I believe, in fantasy—is Kurtz's use of scriptural passages as chapter headings. With very few exceptions, every chapter in the six volumes is introduced by a scriptural passage, all of them thematically related, mostly from the Old Testament with a scattering of Apocryphal references. In keeping with the double magic of priest and sorcerer, the visionary presence of Saint Camber hovers in the background of the events in the Deryni books, appearing fleetingly at the coronation to place the crown on Kelson's head. Camber the Deryni had two centuries earlier helped to restore humans to the rule of Gwynned and was subsequently canonized by the church as the Defender of Man. His story, the subject of the second trilogy, is prepared for in the first, directly and indirectly.

The second volume in the *Chronicles, Deryni Checkmate* (1972), is more maturely written, with a finer integration of theme and character and with more natural dialogue. Although the plot is technically centered on the problems in the new reign of the youthful King Kelson, the real focus is on Morgan and Duncan as victims of prejudice. An intensifying conflict develops between the bishops and the Deryni, particularly Morgan who is the highest placed Deryni official in the country. Believing all Deryni categorically evil because all magic is evil, the bishops place Morgan's duchy under the interdict of the church, thereby leaving the population spiritually stranded, without benefit of baptism, marriage, or any of the other sacraments.

Many innocent victims suffer in this country seething with a hatred of differentness, the core of all prejudice. The tragic romance of Morgan's sister, Bronwen, and Duncan's brother, Kevin, is a moving account of such victims. As the young lovers happily prepare for their wedding, a young man who wanted Bronwen for himself seeks the aid of a local old woman with a reputation of witchcraft, especially for love charms and potions. This pathetic yet evil creature concocts a love potion made of poison because she wants to destroy Bronwen whom she knows to be a Deryni. The fatal potion, left on Bronwen's dresser, kills both her and Kevin. The human witch has been permitted to practice her dangerous craft even while innocent Deryni, adept at healing, have been arrested as witches.

Probably the most original and haunting character portrayal here is the fanatic Warin, who focuses in himself the conflict of religion and sorcery. Warin's remarkable charisma convinces people that he is a messiah. He is of nondescript appearance except for his eyes, which have the expression of a mystic or a seer. With those eyes, Warin "could bore into a man's soul, they said; could heal in the manner of the ancient prophets and holy men" (*DC*, p. 163). And this man believes himself appointed by God to destroy all Deryni. Although Kurtz never lets the reader into his mind, through two scenes we are led to accept his remarkable powers. In one he demonstrates his ability to heal, and in another, Morgan's closest friend sees a halo glowing around Warin's head. Possessing some of the qualities of a saint, he is also a religious fanatic who feels himself called in a divine mission to destroy those who are different. In this portrayal Kurtz captures the paradox of religious fanaticism. Warin is ambivalent, sincere and endowed with extraordinary powers, yet at the same time a biased, cruel man with a fiery desire to destroy the Other.

High Deryni is the last and longest volume in the trilogy, and the most intense in its handling of the theme of prejudice. The point of view particularly stressed here is the conflict within the church in respect to its official attitude toward the Deryni race. A few of the bishops refuse to accept the prevailing legal code that represses Deryni activity. As a race the Deryni are prohibited from holding public office and from owning land. Similar repressions were of course practiced in the Middle Ages against both Jews and women. Those few bishops who respect Duncan and who question the ideological premise of denying justice to a person simply because he happens to be born to the wrong parents prefer to find the significant differences between people a matter of moral behavior. For them differences are spiritual rather than physical.

The Deryni antagonist in this novel happens to be a brutal tyrant, Wencit. Like the Hitlers and Genghis Khans of this world he is evil in his actions, not in his ancestry. Wencit can and does use magic, but his preference is for the kind of torture and tyranny that do not require those skills. He deals in and exploits fear, terror, and hatred—all human traits. His atrocities on the battlefield and his corrupt reign are unsparingly related by Kurtz, giving this volume a heavy dose of physical realism along with fantasy.

An element of romance is also introduced into the otherwise rather grim events of this concluding work with its emphasis on warfare. Morgan falls in love with the Lady Richenda, wife of Bran Coris, a nobleman who betrays Kelson and joins Wencit's side in the ensuing conflict. Since hers was an arranged marriage, she had not loved her husband, but she has borne him a son. Ironically, Morgan is about to go into battle with the express purpose of killing Bran. With delicate restraint, they communicate their deep feelings for each other but without touch or hope, as Morgan goes off to war to kill or be killed by the traitorous husband.

The climactic final episode is again a duel arcane, with Wencit and three supporters (including Bran) on one side, and Kelson with three Deryni on the other. As the duel is about to begin, however, one of Wencit's supporters confesses to being in a shape-shift disguise in order to achieve vengeance on Wencit. He has poisoned the drink that he offered his fellows, who are now doomed to a painful death. Although this sudden reversal seems contrived, the genuinely moving ambiguity of the ending compensates for the artifice of the climax.

As his enemies lie dying, Kelson is called upon to demonstrate his courage and his judgment as never before. The dying men beg a prompt death at his hands, for the lingering poison in their veins will bring them prolonged suffering before they die. By showing mercy, Kelson will become a murderer. On the other hand, by not taking their lives promptly, he will become as cruel as they had been. No matter what he does will be wrong. He bitterly wishes that the duel could have taken place to let him achieve either death or mastery in an honorable way. Now there can be no honor, only pain. The scene contrasts with his victory over the sorceress. Then, having defeated her in fair struggle, he was able to go forth proud to welcome the greetings of the crowd. Here, too, the crowds are waiting, ready to cheer his victory. But this time it is a mature, suffering king who goes forth to acknowledge his people. Either way he will bear the burden of guilt. Kelson is now of age, having learned the bittersweet nature of triumph in this world, the inevitable intermingling of joy and pain, of guilt and pride, of victory and defeat, and of right and wrong.

The trilogy *The Legends of Camber* concerns events that take place about two centuries before the reign of Kelson. These works reveal Kurtz's careful plotting, as they explain the scattered references in the Deryni volumes to the apparition of Saint Camber and also the frequent mention of historical rulers. But for a solution to the ultimate mystery of Camber's appearance centuries after his death, the reader must wait until the final scene of the third volume—probably one of the best-kept secrets in the history of literature. It was Camber, a Deryni, who broke the hold of a dynasty of Deryni rulers and restored the human line to the throne through the Haldane family, thus preparing the way for Kelson Haldane one day to assume the kingship. For that achievement the legendary Camber was at first canonized as the Defender of Man, then later repudiated as a demonic and heretical Deryni. The trilogy tells the whole story.

In *The Legends* Kurtz's rewriting of medieval history from the viewpoint of feminist issues is even more incisive than in *The Chronicles*. She continues the theme of the conflict between humans and Deryni with its emphasis on prejudice against differentness. She also continues the conflict between the two magics, the orthodox magic of the Catholic Church and the unorthodox magic of the Deryni sorcerers. The new focus is on Camber himself as participant in both sides of these conflicts. A Deryni supporting human rule, he is also a sorcerer with unorthodox powers cast in the role of a priest of the orthodox church. Furthermore, after his death he is at first acclaimed as a saint, then later condemned as a heretic. In this ambivalence he resembles Joan of Arc, at once saint and witch. In his own person, then, Camber exemplifies the paradox of the feminine in medieval society.

Camber of Culdi (1976) is largely concerned with efforts to restore human rule in protest against the current Deryni ruler, Imre, a tyrant. Not a warrior like Wencit, Imre is a sly politician, capable of deep treachery, as well as a sensualist, guilty of committing incest with his sister, Ariella. He is more of a Nero than an Attila. Camber is touched directly by Imre's irrational violence because his own son has been stabbed in the back by the ruler while in a friendly embrace. The human heir to the throne, a descendant of human rulers from the past, has been a monk for several years, and is now known as Brother Benedict. Camber, with the aid of his other son, a priest, tries to persuade Benedict to step forth and claim the throne for the sake of saving his people from further senseless tyranny. The monk, whose worldly name is Cinhil, is torn by a profound conflict. He has lived according to his monastic vows for a decade, and having so totally renounced the world he finds the prospect of returning to it as a political leader wildly inappropriate and distasteful. Most difficult of all for this monk to accept is the necessity of marriage in order to provide for a successor. Camber persists, however, supported by his son, daughter, and her future husband Rhys, the Healer. Cinhil ultimately yields, whereupon he is subjected both to rigorous training and to ritual magic to prepare him for his new duties. He learns the art of concentration and receives the hereditary Eye of Rom, jewel of kingship. He also agrees to marry Megan, a ward of Camber's, and when they later have a son, the human succession seems assured. Cinhil is trained and ready to assume power, but Imre will not surrender the throne. When the tyrant orders the murder of Cinhil's infant son at the baptismal fount, Cinhil goes to war to depose him. Imre is killed in battle, but his sister Ariella escapes.

When Megan later bears twin sons, the succession again seems safe, but all is not well. One son is born with a club foot which Cinhil interprets as a divine sanction against him for breaking his monastic vows. Cinhil suffers more and more from his divided nature, his spiritual conscience struggling with his political office. Inevitably his relationship with Megan becomes strained as he longs for a return to monastic solitude. He also blames Camber for making him abandon his sacred vows in favor of secular authority.

The inward turmoil of the new king is the focus of *Saint Camber* (1978). Ironically, the newly restored human king begins to manifest prejudice against the Deryni whom he considers a threat to his beloved church. Early one morning on a battlefield, before the fighting starts, Cinhil comes upon what he fears to be some arcane Deryni ritual taking place in a tent. He peers in to investigate the mysterious goings-on to find the magic a familiar one, the celebration of the mass. He is overcome with emotion as he swallows the communion bread and stammers the liturgy. The resurgence of devout feelings leaves him in a virtual trance for several minutes. The scene effectively points up the similarity between the two magics, one acceptable and the other banned as unorthodox.

Although Camber is out of favor with the king, it is a time when Cinhil most needs his advice. In a fierce battle against the forces of Ariella, one of Cinhil's closest friends is slain, Bishop Alister Cullen. When Camber discovers the bishop's body in an obscure corner of the battle area, he ponders the situation and makes a startling decision. He decides to use his shape-shifting ability to take on the identity of Bishop Cullen himself, leaving what will appear to be his own body as dead. Although it will be a sacrifice of his own identity, in the guise of Cullen he will be able to advise Cinhil. Informing only his immediate family of his decision, he undertakes the transformation, an awesome process.

On one level this unorthodox spirituality is allied to the kinds of heresy attributed to supposed witches in the Middle Ages. On another, the sacrifice of one's own identity in order to perform a personally or socially useful function is an experience familiar to women through the ages. The woman who must sacrifice her femininity in order to maintain a "masculine" executive position and the woman who, like Ibsen's Nora, must pretend to be helplessly "feminine" while performing paid work usually limited to men are but two examples.

The immediate consequences of Camber's transformation are ironic. Once he is believed dead, stories of his supposed miracles begin to spread, and soon a popular movement is under way to have him canonized. The so-called miracles, of course, are instances of Deryni magic, in theory outlawed as heretical. The church hierarchy becomes firmly convinced of his claim to sainthood, however, although his family tries in vain to prevent the plan. From here on Kurtz is concerned to present the painstaking investigation of the claim to sanctity. Her researches into medieval ecclesiastical practices have enabled her to make this episode both convincing and absorbing reading. Concurrent with the objective search for evidence and opinion is the growing torment within Camber. Now that Cinhil's inner state is stabilized, Camber becomes more unstable. What will God think of his strange role? Can God forgive such a monstrous deception? "[W]hat would a just God have to say, in the final reckoning, to a man who was allowing His Church to be led astray and call holy one who knew himself not to be as he appeared, whose entire present existence was based upon a grand deception?" (SC, p. 415)

Camber the Heretic (1981), the final and longest work in the series, begins with the death of Cinhil. Camber in the guise of Cullen is present at the dying king's bedside, where he has a vision of the departure of Cinhil's spirit from his body and his entrance through a gate into the other world, with heavenly escort. Kurtz, unlike the other women writers discussed in this book, accepts the idea of immortality. Although Cinhil's twin sons survive to succeed him, as minors they are subject to the influence of a group of extremely intolerant men, confirmed in their antipathy to the Deryni. With determination they systematically try to strip the Deryni of all property and power, laying waste all the gains in tolerance that had been achieved through the efforts of Camber. Even worse is the wave of violence that ensues, with murders and executions a daily occurrence. Most of the victims are Deryni, and it is no longer safe to admit to being Deryni. Slaughter of the Deryni is justified on the grounds that they are not human. One is reminded of the medieval scholastic debate, sometimes jocular but often serious, over the question of whether women were human.

Camber's death concludes this work which is redolent with the theme of mortality. But just as his life has been extraordinary, so is his death. It is at this point that the reader first learns to understand references to Camber's apparitions in the earlier trilogy. Without giving away details of this remarkable finale, let it suffice to say that the visionary nature of his presence in the world two centuries later is indeed accounted for. Quite apart from the institutionalized formalities of the church, Camber is a saint, and his ghostly visitations at the coronation of Kelson and to Morgan and Duncan in times of crisis manifest his saintly function to guide the living from the world beyond. The dual trilogies are thus of a piece, one story, intricate in the relationships of its parts. Camber is a defender of men, restoring human rule under Cinhil, then protecting the boy-king Kelson, but he is also a defender of the Deryni, devoted to bringing about peace and mutual tolerance between the races.

Kurtz's double trilogy is a many-leveled achievement. Simply as fantasy, it has much to offer its readers. Richly imaginative in its handling of magic and of a convincing secondary world, with deft, memorable characterization, and a highly suspenseful plot, it is a satisfyingly structured fantasy quest. On reflection, however, it offers much more. As historical fantasy it is richly detailed concerning medieval life, especially the medieval church. Furthermore, it goes beyond historicity to a creative revisioning of the period it so concretely represents. In many of its thematic concerns, it offers a rewriting of history with a focus on women's issues. The usual metaphorical quest for meaning and identity at the heart of fantasy here reaches beyond the individual quester to women as a group, in particular those women who suffered from accusations of witchcraft. Deryni sorcery, a gift and yet a curse, reflects the repressed feminine side of human nature.

The most prominent theme in these books, one which is not limited to the feminine, is the problem of prejudice. Because of their unique kind of "difference" the Deryni serve as a far-reaching model of historical victims of prejudice. The prejudice that results from perceived differences of race or religion is intensified in the case of the Deryni because their difference is not readily visible. Although their psychic skills are racial in that they are biologically inherited, they are not immediately detectable. This inherited difference is also potentially either a boon to society or a threat, depending on how it is used. This ambivalence makes it even more feared. Since some of their skills are magical, they become readily associated with antireligious practices like witchcraft. Even Cinhil, who should know better, expects as he peeks into the tent on the morning of the battle to find some weird magic rite being performed, and is surprised to find that it is actually a celebration of the mass. The prejudice against this psychically gifted people also takes a social form, as when the members of the council deny the Deryni the right to own property or to hold office. In its extreme form this prejudice against the Deryni difference takes the form of genocide. In the last volume of the Camber series there are mass murders and executions, both of Deryni and suspected Deryni sympathizers.

By making the fundamental "difference" that marks the Deryni for discrimination, ostracism, and mistreatment simply a "skill," Kurtz captures the inherent absurdity in all prejudice. She also is concerned with the less obvious type of prejudice against an aspect of the human mind. In Western history, with its prevailing emphasis on logic and reason, the intuitive and the fanciful have been victims of prejudice. Whereas in some societies dreams are taken very seriously by people in positions of leadership, in ours dreams are scorned or relegated to psychiatric case histories. The society that represses and discriminates against the Deryni is prejudiced against those aspects of the mind that the Deryni represent, i.e., the intuitive, the visionary, the fanciful, the creatively magical.

Another important theme is power, its use and abuse. The Deryni themselves illustrate the subject in the varying ways they use their own occult powers. The destructive use of Deryni skill is exhibited in several characters, including the murderous Charissa and the tyrannical Imre, but the hunger for power and the exploitation of others is practiced more pervasively by humans, exemplified in both religious and political leaders. Throughout these works the desire for power as such is offered as a negative goal. The power implicit in skill should be limited to helping others.

Closely related to this attitude toward power is the notion of using one's gifts wisely. The principle example is Cinhil who at the age of forty is asked to give up his chosen calling in order to fulfill his duty as the only living heir to the throne. Camber's dilemma is the opposite in that he must take on the identity of a clerical man in order to better fulfill his own determination to advise the reluctant king. For many, of course, any use of their talents might endanger their lives. Camber's decision to make proper use of his own talents leads him to sacrifice his identity for the sake of his king and country.

The oppression of unorthodoxy is another theme that runs through the story. The older, more conservative bishops who represent the orthodox position of the church are eager to pronounce an anathema against the Deryni. Only a few of the younger bishops recognize the genuine spirituality inherent in the Deryni unorthodox magic. Just as Jews and witches in the Middle Ages were blamed for all sorts of natural disasters, Kurtz has the priests blaming Deryni black magic for the outbreak of the plague. The vacillation in public opinion and in church officialdom between conferring sainthood on Camber and denouncing him as a heretic illustrates the thin line between orthodox and unorthodox spirituality.

Kurtz's description of the desecration of a chapel honoring Saint Camber vividly evokes the actual ransacking and destruction of monasteries during the Reformation period. So quickly and so totally does orthodoxy descend to unorthodoxy in time. "Nor did they spare the Lady Chapel, with its cool, jewel-like panels of blue glass let into the walls, and its rich hangings; . . . The statue of the Deryni saint was pulled from its base and beheaded, . . . Even the mosaicked hemisphere on which the statue had stood was attacked with club and mace . . . A torch was set to the once-exquisite wooden screen which had taken years to carve, and the fire cracked and blackened what the soldiers had spared and which would not burn" (*CH*, p. 371). The passage reflects the author's love of medieval church architecture and ornamentation as well.

Paralleling the theme of orthodoxy is that of the two magics. Bishop Cullen once refers to the mass as "this greatest magic" (*SC*, p. 95). With total respect Kurtz presents the rituals of Catholicism such as the mass as rich in transformation symbolism central to the concept of magic. In these works the two magics, the transcendental, liturgical magic of the church and the individual psychic magic of the Deryni reflect and confirm each other. They are complementary rather than conflicting. The magical Portal Transfer, for example, gains credibility by analogy to the parallel religious image of a dead man's soul sliding away from his body. Death is another kind of portal transfer. Kurtz avoids didacticism, but such parallels embody a lesson of respect for another's magic.

Kurtz's two trilogies are a unique achievement in fantasy. Like the other women writers under consideration she stresses the depolarization of values and the renunciation of power, but unlike them she incorporates the theme of immortality. The feminism in her work is not, however, a matter a theme but of approach. In the framework of historical fantasy she revisions an historical period, the Middle Ages. On the social level the repression of the Deryni by church and state is equivalent to the repression of women and Jews in that period. Psychologically the repression is of those qualities traditionally regarded as feminine, such as intuition.

Kurtz's style matures dramatically in the course of the trilogies. Although the first Deryni volumes suffer occasionally from banal language, the later books are beautifully written. The language becomes richer, more metaphorical, more rhythmic, and effectively modulated by biblical overtones. When, for example, Camber holds a dying friend in his arms: "[H]e felt the ethereal, detached sensation as the silver cord began to unravel and the ties of earth-binding were loosed" (*CH*, p. 478). Many of her finest touches of poetic language occur in descriptions of the moment of death: " . . . and then a nothingness which was pervaded by a blinding, incredibly beautiful light of all the colors of time" (*CH*, p. 296). But her descriptive powers are not limited to spiritual moments, for her physically detailed depiction of the horrors of war and execution is often both moving and shocking. Although almost totally neglected by scholars, *The Chronicles* and *The Legends* are rewarding reading.

MARY STEWART

MARY STEWART'S UNIQUE ACHIEVEMENT IN FANTASY is the humanization of Merlin. Her trilogy (*The Crystal Cave, The Hollow Hills,* and *The Last Enchantment*) offers a first-person narrative of the life of Merlin from his mysterious conception in a cave to his final enchanted sleep in the same cave, all reported from the vantage point of old age and with the benefit of visionary experience.[1] Not an archetypal wizard, neither suprahuman nor extrahuman, this Merlin grows and develops through time, has doubts and fears, feels pain and fatigue, even gets seasick. Although sympathetically human, however, Stewart's Merlin is by no means an ordinary man. He is a prophet and seer as well as a gifted poet, musician, and brilliant engineer. Though not a magician in the usual sense, he possesses second sight. He interprets this gift of "the Sight" as the voice of the god within him, giving him messages of importance, first to himself, and later to King Arthur. Although Stewart retains all of the legendary events traditionally associated with the mythic wizard, she naturalizes and rationalizes them, leaving only his inner power as seer to set him apart from other men.

In a prologue to *The Crystal Cave* Merlin narrates his visionary dream of his own conception in the cave. He envisions a cave in a Welsh hillside, with his mother Niniane lying with an unidentified young prince. Then he envisions himself in the same cave, old and grey-haired, with a young girl also named Niniane. Although he does not understand the dream for a long time, it clearly depicts his beginning and end in a circular pattern.

According to the legend of Merlin as recounted by the twelfth-century Robert de Boron, the conception of Merlin was the result of a diabolic plot. Demonic spirits conspired to bring about the birth of an anti-Christ, a man who would, like Christ, combine human and supernatural ancestry, but in this case from fallen angels in order to fulfill the devil's purposes in human form. The devil chosen would appear to the woman as an incubus, make her pregnant, and disappear directly afterward. This plan seemed at first to work, but the young woman, who was a devout Christian, foiled it by confessing to her priest and taking the newborn infant to him for prompt baptism. The infant Merlin thus inherited supernatural powers from his diabolic father but was saved for Christianity by his virtuous mother.

Stewart's version demythologizes this legend. Although Merlin's mother, daughter of a king, is secret about her love affair, preferring to hint at sorcery and the otherworldly paternity of her child, it is clear that his father, although not at first identified, is human. The first few chapters realistically concentrate on Merlin's childhood as a bastard. A lonely and solitary child, he perceives himself as an outsider. His only friend is an uncle, who promptly rejects him when the boy recognizes, as if by magic, a poisoned apricot. One day, on his solitary wanderings, he comes upon a cave with an inner chamber floored, roofed, and lined with crystals. The cave is occupied by Galapas, who has been expecting the boy and who becomes his teacher. Merlin discovers that he can see the future in the bronze mirror on the wall of the cave. He learns much from the hermit, including how to make and play a harp. The lonely boy's happiness with Galapas ends abruptly when through a tragic accident his Saxon servant brings about the death of Merlin's grandfather. When the servant is then killed, Merlin sets fire to the room where his body lies in order to give him the ritual burning his Saxon beliefs call for. Even at this young age Merlin, the outsider, feels empathy with the racial and religious Other.

Merlin is forced to flee to Brittany. Stewart's next bold variation on the original legend concerns the revelation of his paternity. In Brittany he is captured by two soldiers, Uther and Ambrosius. Impressed with the gifted lad, Ambrosius takes him to his own headquarters where he treats him in princely fashion, even letting him sleep in his own room. Merlin soon discovers what Ambrosius had recognized from the start, that the soldier who welcomed him so richly is actually his father. Ambrosius was the prince in the cave. Although there is no basis in legend for this relationship, Stewart is borrowing from Geoffrey of Monmouth, the historian who gave us our first information about Merlin. Geoffrey brazenly conflated two stories about a boy prophet, one called Myrrdin and one Ambrosius, explaining simply that they were one and the same.

It was an early historian, Nennius, who told the tale of the young prophet Ambrosius and King Vortigern's castle. According to this legend, Vortigern, then king of Britain, had been trying in vain to build a strong tower. What the stone masons built during the day collapsed overnight. Consulting his wizards for advice, the king was told to find a boy with no father, slay him, and sprinkle his blood over the foundations to make them firm. His messengers searched the kingdom for a fatherless boy, whom they eventually found being taunted by a disgruntled playmate for having no father. Taken to the king, Merlin shamed the wizards by telling them why the foundations repeatedly crumbled. There was a pool under the foundations, continually undermining them, wherein two dragons, one red, one white, quarreled. The king ordered the pool drained, after which the dragons woke and fought fiercely until the red one killed the white. Merlin then interpreted the fight as signifying the defeat of Vortigern by Ambrosius, whose banner was the red dragon.

Stewart follows the legend closely up to the arrival of Merlin at Vortigern's castle. There Merlin's behavior is not that of the all-knowing wizard but of an inspired seer in the grip of forces beyond his control. As he shows the king the dragon-shaped rock in the pool, he suddenly goes into a trance, uttering wild prophecies about boars and dragons and eventually a bear, "artos." Much of this is simply reported afterwards to Merlin, who loses consciousness during his "delirium." The superstitious king is duly impressed by the performance, however, and sends Merlin some robes befitting the man who will now become the king's magician. Merlin scorns the white robes of office, much preferring his own black robe with the dragon brooch, a gift from Ambrosius. In this totally rational depiction of Merlin he is not at all the mythic wizard. Although he repeatedly professes to have no magical powers at all, yet the voice of a god speaks through him. He is more a medium than a wizard. The god is with him, for after the pool is drained and found empty, he is saved from Vortigern's anger by the sudden appearance of the red dragon star streaking across the sky.

The next legendary achievement of Merlin that Stewart deals with is his supposed moving of the giant stones from Ireland to England. This time Stewart is somewhat more mysterious than usual in her attempt to explain all of Merlin's mythic feats in naturalistic terms. Merlin first devises what he calls "engines" to bring the kingstone from Killare, Ireland, to put on Ambrosius's grave at Amesbury. Then he must raise the remaining stones into upright positions to complete the Giants' Dance. Although he is never explicit he attributes the feat to music and mathematics, for he had once heard a blind harpist sing about the magic of the ancient peoples who had first raised the stones. When Ambrosius is buried under the kingstone in the giant circle of stones, Merlin lovingly arranges the grave so that it will forever be decked by the light of dawn. This detail is in keeping with the actual careful orientation of Stonehenge to the sunrise.

The final mythic exploit of Merlin to be narrated in this work is his arrangement for the conception of Arthur by Uther Pendragon and Igraine, wife of Gorlois. Uther asks Merlin's help in gaining Igraine's love, suggesting that magic would be useful, but Merlin again disavows any magical powers. When Uther mentions the kingstone as an example of magic, Merlin simply cites his superior mathematics. In the medieval story, of course, Uther came to Igraine in the magically conceived likeness of her husband Gorlois. Stewart also uses disguise as the means, but describes it in realistic terms, with much reliance on details of costuming to convince the guards that the visitor is really the master returning home. Merlin sees the plan as part of a mighty destiny with the king and Igraine as but tool and vessel, and himself but "a spirit, a word, a thing of air and darkness," with the will of a god like a wind blowing through him. The plan works in spite of the confusion following news of Gorlois's death on the battlefield. Uther is outraged, for he realizes that by waiting one day he could have married Igraine and conceived the child legitimately. Merlin's prophetic insight assures him, however, that the child of destiny had to be conceived that night. The voice of the god is not to be ignored.

Stewart's Merlin is thus a seer, a wizard but not a magician. He possesses a gift of insight and understanding that transcends normal vision and perception. In his reliance on intuition he is at odds with the military minds about him. A man of remarkable imagination he neither seeks nor accepts power. His qualities are precisely those that King Arthur will lack.

The Crystal Cave ends with the conception of Arthur, and *The Hollow Hills* covers the years from his conception to the moment when he draws the famous sword from the stone thus proving himself rightful king of Britain. During Igraine's pregnancy Merlin is subject to doubts and fears, but when the boy is born on Christmas Eve, he quickly persuades Uther to let him entrust Arthur's upbringing to Sir Ector, an old friend with an infant son of his own, Cai. In this volume Stewart also introduces several other figures in the Arthurian mythos including Morgause, Morgan, and Lot. Merlin's activities are focused on the destined sword, which he dreams about, then travels far to discover. In this greatly elaborated account of the sword Stewart also incorporates the legends surrounding Merlin's period of living in the woods as a hermit.[2]

In this work the pervasive thematic importance of the dream stresses the intuitive nature of Merlin's role. As prophet and seer he has complete faith in what his dreams communicate to him. Several concern the sword destined for Arthur. In one dream this finely burnished sword is described in the imagery of jewels, ice, and stars sliding down from the sky into a waiting standing stone. Merlin knows that the sword of his dreams must one day belong to the boy whose birth he so carefully engineered and he undertakes a search for it. Free to travel while the infant Arthur is well cared for, he sets out for Rome and Constantinople, where he sees a picture of the ancient King Macsen holding that very sword. He learns, however, that it was long ago lost in Less Britain.

Continuing his travels with renewed hope, Merlin has several more significant dreams. On one occasion a half-waking dream about the small gods of remote places becomes reality as he finds that he has been captured by diminutive men who speak the Old Tongue, dwellers of the Hollow Hills, descendants of tribesmen who fled the Romans long ago. Through them he learns of another prophecy concerning the sword. Laid down by a dead king and waiting to be lifted by a living one, it is hidden in a floating stone awaiting release by fire. With dreams as his guide, Merlin continues his quest for the sword which he eventually finds in an abandoned green chapel. His quest is spiritual and fulfilled through the promptings of his unconscious, quite unlike the conventional medieval quest of the warrior knight.

It is in *Hollow Hills* that the boy Arthur first meets Merlin, who undertakes to teach him, not magic, but more practical matters like maps of earth and sky. It is here that the relationship between them develops, with the future king both a rational administrator and a fearless and skilled warrior, with his mentor providing the feeling side, the meditative and the intuitive powers that Arthur lacks. Arthur's coming-of-age at fourteen finds him fighting fiercely on the battlefield, riding a white stallion and flashing the kingly sword given him by Uther. The boy who turned man in battle also acts the man the night after when he is lured to bed by a beautiful woman. What he does not realize is that the lovely seductress, Morgause, is actually his sister, a "sideslip" of Uther's, one of his many children born out of wedlock. Merlin discovers the act too late but orders the "witch" to leave.

The central episode of the Arthurian myth, the ritual removal of the sword from the stone, occurs in this work but is deemphasized since it is Merlin's story, not the king's. Merlin's deep magic of the perceptive imagination, of the inspired insight, is the spiritual source of meaning in Arthur's reign.

The ominous themes of mortality, massacre, and destruction open the concluding volume, *The Last Enchantment*. Igraine is mortally ill. A Herod-like massacre is planned in a desperate attempt to kill the offspring of the incestuous union of Arthur and Morgause. Saxons are killing Britons, and followers of the new god of the Christians are destroying the old religious shrines. It is a dark time for Britain, rent by disorder, violence, and factionalism.

It is also in this final novel that the fabled Camelot comes into being, constructed on a site chosen by Merlin, who takes charge of the operation. An ingenious engineer, he is credited with magical powers which he again refutes, asserting rather the "magic" of human cooperation. When Arthur chooses Guinevere for his queen, Merlin recalls a shadow cast over the king by a white owl, the Celtic word for which is "guenhwyfar," and feels a sense of doom about the impending marriage. The influence of Christianity at the new court is intimated in the brooch sent to Arthur by his dying mother, a brooch with "Maria" inscribed on it. Although Arthur remains receptive to all religions, the image of Mary seemingly inspires his victories in battle.

At the royal wedding Morgause is obsessed by her single-minded desire to destroy her enemy, Merlin. She succeeds in slipping poison into his drink and more into the flask he takes with him when he leaves the court. The two doses do not quite kill the aging enchanter, but they drive him mad, making him wander off to live as a wild hermit for several months. When he is found, his only companion is a piglet whose broken leg he has splintered. When restored to health and reason, Merlin will not betray his knowledge of Morgause's attempt on his life because he wants her to bear the four sons who will one day become Arthur's champions. Stewart thus explains the legend about Merlin's period of madness while living as a wild man in the forest.

Because of his madness Merlin has moments of doubt about the god's presence, but his faith is restored when he has a vision of the impending battle of Mt. Badon, where Arthur and his men race to the scene and score a decisive victory. Without Merlin's prophetic warning, all would have been lost. In this case, as in others in this work, Merlin functions as a dimension of Arthur. Merlin represents the insight and imagination that the great leader and warrior completely lacks.

Merlin, however, begins to suffer from a falling sickness, a further result of his prolonged bout with Morgause's subtle poison. His visionary powers continue undiminished but do not save him from naïveté in worldly matters. When he takes on a boy as his apprentice, he never suspects, as Arthur later points out to him, that the boy is actually a girl in disguise. The apprentice is Nimue, a former devotee of the goddess who has left her training at the shrine in order to learn the magical arts from Merlin. The old enchanter ominously recalls Morgause's prediction—and curse—that he would die deceived by a woman.

The final section of this concluding volume is written with an air of mystery surrounding the events. Stewart attempts to solve the problem of Merlin's "last enchantment" by having him buried alive, by mistake, in the crystal cave, from which he escapes and then to which he voluntarily returns. The initial burial takes place after Merlin has spent a happy year with Nimue, during which they travel widely and he teaches her about the cave of vision and the hidden treasures buried beneath the temple. Merlin reports to the reader how he awakens in a large cavern, obviously buried as dead, but with food, water, and candlelight available to him for survival. Eventually Merlin is rescued by a faithful servant who takes him back to Camelot. After a brief stay in Camelot, where he takes a fond farewell from Nimue, he returns to the cave where he is visited regularly by Arthur.

One of Stewart's aims throughout the trilogy is to naturalize the elements of magic in the traditional legendary material. Merlin's paternity is not that of a demon or incubus, but instead his father is Ambrosius. When as a boy he is captured by Vortigern who plans to kill him, he convinces the king that there are dragons under the pool by making the most of an optical illusion, dragon-shaped rocks. Merlin's period of madness is caused by Morgause's poison, and his final enchanted sleep is voluntary burial supplied with means of survival.

Naturalizing the magic by no means eliminates it. Merlin's inspired plan for moving the giant stones from Ireland to England perhaps best illustrates Stewart's sense of the meaning of magic. When Merlin designs the engines that will lift and transport the stones, the "magic" he uses is a mixture of men, music, and mathematics. This magic is of the human mind and imagination, which are capable of creative transformation. In this way Merlin functions as the spiritual dimension of Arthur.

Stewart's Arthur is a conventionally heroic figure, an energetic leader and warrior, but essentially the instrument of Merlin, whose ideals of peace and justice the king tries to implement. Ironically the incestuous union of Arthur and Morgause, which Merlin could not have prevented, he repeatedly blames himself for. But the old enchanter as the spiritual voice of the young king simply was not there when Arthur the knight became Arthur the lover.

Although Merlin as narrator does not understand women, several strong females enhance the trilogy. The most fully realized women are Igraine, Morgause, Nimue, and Niniane, all characters taken from the Arthurian legends but handled quite differently. In addition, several minor characters, original to Stewart, emerge as strong examples of vigorous, self-willed females. Merlin tends to speak only contemptuously of women who are either stupid or narrowly domestic, but he encounters many women whom he must admire for their intelligence, ambition, and determination. There is no condescension in his attitude toward these women, formidable as either friends or enemies.

The most important female role is that of Igraine. Unlike the traditional portrayal of her as a tool of Merlin's and Uther's plotting,

Stewart's Igraine arranges the sexual meeting that will produce Arthur because of her own strong desire for Uther. Her pride as queen, however, is never subordinated to her lust. When she first informs Merlin of her love for Uther, she is lying in her bed, but "it is as if she were a queen giving audience" (*CC,* p. 467). Clearly she is "no man's toy," boasting "I am the daughter of a king and I come from a line of kings" (*CC,* p. 468). Throughout their conversation Merlin feels that he can speak with her as if she were a man. Their arrangement is made as a cool calculation, with Igraine never for an instant appearing in any way weak or passive. Introduced in *The Crystal Cave,* she appears again in both subsequent volumes. In *The Hollow Hills* the reader sees her totally concentrated on planning her son's future. More political than maternal in her motivation, she agrees to turn him over to Merlin for training. In *The Last Enchantment* she is terminally ill but still actively involved in political strategies. Queenly and proud to the last, Igraine dies, not pathetically but richly robed and dignified.

Morgause and Nimue are also drawn as forceful women. In her villainous role Morgause is more political than sensual, luring Arthur to bed not out of lust but as a means to achieve power at court. As Merlin attempts to foil her plotting, he becomes her avowed enemy. Cold and vicious under her "rose-gold beauty," she views Merlin with malice and hatred, eventually poisoning him. The dose is not fatal but causes a madness that leaves him wandering lost for months. Morgause's will is as strong as his, although her sorcery is no match for his prophetic inner voice.

Nimue, also ambitious and iron-willed, is not a villainess although she does cast the final spell on the old wizard. Instead, she appears as genuinely devoted to him as his apprentice in enchantment and also as loyal to Arthur long after Merlin's disappearance. When Merlin returns briefly from his false entombment, he kisses her once with passion, and once with love before he returns to his cave to sleep.

Other female roles are slighter but strong in unconventional ways. Arthur's queen, Guinevere, is weak but sympathetic. As Harold J. Herman notes in an article about Stewart's women, hers is the first example of a genuinely sympathetic Guinevere.[3] Merlin's mother, Niniane, appears only briefly but she is fiercely independent and courageous. Stewart also adds several minor female roles not found in the original materials, such as Keri, a prostitute who attempts to seduce Merlin, and Moravik, Merlin's governess. As Herman also observes, the only weak female roles are those few who are mere stereotypes of domesticity and duly scorned as such by the narrator.

Stewart has solidly researched the period of fifth-century Britain as realistic backdrop for her retelling of the legend. Unlike T.H. White, who chose to deal with the chivalric Arthur of Malory and the Round

Table, Stewart has chosen the Arthur who was *Dux Bellorum,* fifth-century warrior. The reader is given a graphic tapestry of life in these appropriately called Dark Ages. The text abounds in vivid visual images of the time: deep forests where tribes of outcasts live, primitive farms with wooden plows, dangers lurking along any pathway where brutal men with knives and cudgels await the unwary traveler, the smell of a burning hut where Saxon raiders have been, remains of Roman fortresses now matted with brambles, and in striking contrast, the halls of the rulers, with fine paneled doors of oak, embroidered and bejeweled hangings, inlaid tables with exquisite chess pieces, and goblets of silver.

Stewart's religious background is also historically sound. At this time there were three religions in competition for the worship of the Britons, i.e., the ancient local religions of the goddess and the new rival religions of the male gods Mithras and Christ. Merlin also refers frequently to classical deities. On the hill before his cave stands a figure of the Irish god Myrrdin, for whom the wizard is named. Religious rituals with druidical sacrifices still function in an underground fashion.

The conflict between Mithraism and Christianity becomes significant in the Arthurian destiny. Mithraism had been most successful and widespread during the early years of the Roman Empire. It was particularly appealing to soldiers as it required feats of courage and strength for initiation. Through soldiers it followed the frontiers of the empire all the way to Britain. Mithraism was essentially a mystery religion involving secret rites simulating death and rebirth. Its central mythos was the slaying of the Cosmic Bull, representations of which survive in cave sanctuaries where such ceremonies were performed. Merlin as a boy has a vision of a ritual bull-slaying. Mithras is accepted by both Uther and Ambrosius, whose installation as king is celebrated in a secret underground ritual, with no women permitted to attend. For Merlin, however, all of the gods of light are one. Arthur, receptive and tolerant toward all religions, eventually accepts Christianity, bearing the banner of Mary victoriously into battle.

Stylistically these works are strong in descriptive passages but occasionally weak in dialogue. Whether the descriptions are of real life in fifth-century Britain or of dreams about mystical swords, they are couched in vivid, concrete prose. In dialogue, however, some of the attempts to modernize fail to come off convincingly. More importantly, the dialogue does not sufficiently distinguish the varied conversational styles of the individual characters.

The descriptive brilliance unfortunately does not always enhance the narrative movement. The reader is likely to find some episodes hard to recall because they are so heavily clothed in conceptual and visual detail. The sense of dramatic event is thus undermined. A more fundamental problem is the strain of the first-person narration. Such scenes as

Arthur's first victory in battle followed by his seduction by Morgause are filtered through Merlin's perception of them. The episode of Guinevere's kidnapping is communicated partly through her own later, obviously lying, report and partly through the unconvincing device of Merlin's dream about the event. Even Merlin's own most dramatic experiences, such as his rescue from the cave, come about slowly and lyrically, bathing the reader in sensations of dark and light, silence and sound. The reader can remember the smell of the air in the cave better than the act of rescue.

As often happens, the novel's greatest strength is the reverse side of its greatest weakness. Since Merlin is an introspective narrator, the narrative inevitably lacks drama. What comes through in a powerful way is the supple, sensitive, meditative mind of the enchanter set against the dark background of fifth-century Britain. The sense of place and atmosphere is strong because of Merlin's responsive depiction of them. A first-person narrative is a challenge to the writer, not merely because it limits the direct account of events to those witnessed by the narrator, but also because of the danger of a monotonous perspective on those events. Merlin's intricately detailed exposition does at times become tedious, and even annoying when he indulges in frequent self-pity and self-blame when things do not go right.

In one sense, however, Merlin is himself a dramatic figure. He embodies a dialectic at work in the Arthurian mythos in two different ways. First, Merlin functions as a medium, a link between two worlds. Just as the hollow hills provide a physical point of entry from this world to the otherworld, Merlin as their human counterpart provides "the meeting point for the interlocking worlds of men, gods, beasts, and twilight spirits" (*HH* p. 493). The idea is inherent in the nature of the mythic magician who is himself half-human, half-divine. Second, Merlin functions as the imaginative and thoughtful side of Arthurian rule. Merlin and Arthur as separate figures represent a consciousness split between the thinking and doing parts of the human will, the meditative and the active sides of the personality. There is always a tension in the novels between the eager, impetuous activities of the young king and the cautious, rational plans of the old advisor. This undercurrent of dialectic is maintained throughout. Although the trilogy does not continue the story of Arthur's ultimate defeat, the failure of the sword without the sustaining power of the spirit is implicit in the role of Merlin and his relationship to the king.

Stewart's attitude toward her material as history and tragedy as well as fantasy also inspires both its successes and its shortcomings. In her desire to be historically authentic, she denies elements of magic; at the same time, in her choice of Merlin's single vision she imposes a sense of tragic loss which is historically pathetic, beyond the saving grace of magic which might have lifted the events out of the strictly temporal realm. Merlin's repeated denials of magical skills, however, refer to popular notions of trickery rather than to the deeper magic of creativity. The character of Merlin is an embodiment of the creative, transforming power of the imagination. In this sense he is a genuine wizard, an archetype of spirit.

The Wicked Day (1983) completes the Arthurian story, but more as historical novel than as fantasy. The focus is on Mordred, the incestuous child of Arthur and Morgause, at once victim and instrument of the fated tragedy of Arthur. Since Merlin is not present as a character, however, the fantasy element of magic is not present. Shortly before his death Arthur envisions his old mentor in a dream. Although well worth reading as a convincing version of the last stage of the Arthurian story, this work lacks the spirit of fantasy that characterizes the Merlin trilogy.

In the trilogy Merlin is depicted as the feminine side of the warrior-king Arthur. As the king's advisor he stresses the importance of relationships in balancing and moderating the urge to power. For himself he renounces power as a goal. Not a wonder-working magician, he is a seer, one whose remarkable insight is inspired by dreams and intuition. Contemplative rather than active, he understands human and earthly nature better than the king on his throne.

8

PATRICIA McKILLIP

PATRICIA McKILLIP'S DISTINCTIVE CONTRIBUTIONS to modern fantasy include one work about a female wizard with a living collection of mythic animals and a trilogy posited on a riddle game. Her first book, *Forgotten Beasts of Eld,* was the World Fantasy Award novel of 1975. Its unusual protagonist is Sybel, a youthful wizard who lives alone on a mountain with an array of mythic creatures whom she has summoned from the mysterious forest of Eld. Sybel is a descendant of wizards, all of whom have lived in isolation on the mountain, and while yet a child she finds herself alone but endowed with the magical power to summon the forgotten beasts. She has gathered into her little kingdom a prophetic boar, a guardian lion, a greedy dragon, a black swan, a sharp-eyed falcon, and a sly black cat, all of whom communicate with her in silent language. She lacks the fabled bird called the Liralen, which she tries intensely and incessantly to summon to her under her crystal dome. The solitary girl is interrupted in her summoning by the arrival of a young man with a baby, whom he insists on leaving in her care. What follows in the narrative is essentially her inward struggle between her wizardly power in isolation and her new involvement in the affairs of men, evoking two contradictory emotions, fear and love.

The wondrous world of Sybel gains a mythic allusiveness through McKillip's use of names. Most important is the protagonist whose name at first recalls the prophetess known as the Sybil. The reader soon suspects, however, from the iconography of her animals that the goddess Cybele is the more likely inspiration for the name.[1] The Phrygian Cybele was a mother goddess who had dominion over wild beasts, who formed her retinue. She was particularly associated with the lion, and in artistic representations she appears either with the lion or riding in a chariot drawn by lions. Sybel with her own lion, Gules, named from heraldry, becomes a mother figure during the course of the novel. Her other beasts are drawn from differing mythic traditions. Most interesting is the prophetic boar, Cyrin, heir to the sacred Celtic boar. Cyrin is also a riddler, whose wise, tantalizing riddles add much to the atmosphere of the book. The mythic dragon Gyld is individualized as a rather childlike creature who adores his gold. The falcon Ter is fierce and loyal, given to sardonic commentary. The Black Swan of Tirlith and the cat, Moriah, are much less individualized. In a sense all are childhood's imaginary companions, drawn deep from the unconscious, the forest of Eld.

Central to the imagistic and thematic meaning of the novel is the missing creature, the long-sought bird, the Liralen. Identified at first simply as the elusive white bird, it subsequently becomes identified with Sybel's inner self. She speaks of "deep within me where the white bird lives free" (p. 178), and at climactic points in the narrative her own state of mind is communicated by what happens to the Liralen. While she has been summoning the white bird, a very different creature has appeared in its stead, the terrifying Blammor. Described at first as a black mist, this shadow figure is clearly an object of fear. A deadly danger to most, the Blammor is less a threat to the innocent girl who has never known fear.

The introduction of humans into her life changes Sybel's idyllic existence. The baby so unexpectedly left in her care is not simply one more mythic beast in her loving, captive control but a complex creature creating a profound emotional relationship with her. One day she learns from Coren, the young man who brought the child Tam to her, that the youngster is actually the son of the ruling king and the object of political strife in the human society she has never known or wanted to know. Not only does Sybel's love for Tam involve her against her will in human squabbles, but she also falls in love with Coren, himself caught up in the power struggles of rival families living far below her peaceful mountain retreat. Tam wishes to join his father the king, and Coren persuades Sybel to become his wife. The literal descent from her mountain is for Sybel a symbolic descent as well, from wizardly power and aloofness to domesticity and turmoil. At home she is reduced to a domestic definition, and abroad she becomes a pawn in the power struggle beyond her control.

Sybel finds herself victimized both by the king, Dred, who wishes to reduce her to passivity, and by his wizard, Mithran, who tries both to seduce her body and to control her mind. Beset by confusion and feeling trapped by circumstances, Sybel dreams of the Liralen lying dead. Although she has to an extent weakened her power by agreeing to marry Coren and taking her wondrous menagerie to live in the confines of his family estate, she is nonetheless still capable of some wizardry. In the final scenes of the book, in which much happens suddenly, the narrative becomes too hurried. Although the author needs to maintain Sybel's point of view and must therefore rely on reported events, the reader finds the scene in which Sybel's freed animals win a battle in their own imaginative way simply too rushed. On the other hand, the chilling confrontation of Mithran and the Blammor is effectively sensuous and immediate.

Sybel's individuation eventually becomes clearly defined as a conflict between the Liralen and the Blammor. This psychological imagery is handled effectively as are descriptions of the mythic animals and certain episodes of wizardry. On the weak side must be included the dialogue, which occasionally becomes banal, and the precipitous wind up of the narrative. The growing-up theme as projected onto the mythic animals summoned from the forest of the unconscious, then onto the decline into domesticity and captivity redeemed by emotional fulfillment is brilliantly conceived if not completely worked out.

McKillip's potential is more fully realized in the *Riddle of the Stars* trilogy. In a highly original and convincing secondary world she weaves an intricate plot involving memorable characters, relying in part on the subtle adaptation of mythic materials but even more on her own provocative ideas and resonant images. The work is both satisfying and tantalizing, with its carefully resolved narrative leaving in its wake an abundance of haunting, imaginative motifs that drive the reader back to a prompt rereading. This time the dialogue rings true, with an added element of fine ironic wit missing in the earlier work. And this work stands beside Le Guin's in offering a metaphysical statement about life and art.

Riddles are the focal point of thought in this unnamed world. From the start the reader is drawn into the whirling philosophical and psychological currents of riddling as a way of life. Riddles are the object of all intellectual endeavor. The hero, Morgon, a farmer by descent and lifestyle but a scholar by temperament, is an advanced student at the College of Riddle Mastery. His talent for solving riddles is all the more remarkable as his native land of Hed, a country of pig-herders, is universally scorned for its lack of challenging riddles. But riddles are central to the entire world of which Hed is but a small part, and riddles are central to the meaning of the trilogy.

What is a riddle? Essentially a riddle is a metaphorical quest for identity. It asks "Who am I?" not as a direct question but through a series of metaphorical metamorphoses. One creature or object in a riddle is disguised in the garb of another. In Old English riddles, for example, the sun is a candle, the body a bone house, a glass of wine a temptress. There are two poles in this ontological game, the "I" of the riddler and the "I" of the creature or object. In projective riddles the narrative voice is that of the creature, saying "I am . . . , I was. . . ." In nonprojective riddles either the riddler reports "I saw . . ." or "I heard . . . ," or in some cases there is no reference to a riddler. Since the riddle itself is a metaphorical quest for identity, it provides a close analogue for the fantasy hero. As Craig Williamson explains in his edition of Old English riddles, "If the riddle solver is a quester thrust into the moment of metaphor, the hero is a solver whose riddle spins out before him in narrative time. He must leave home, confront the dream world of unreal shapes, recognize and be reconciled with the uncanny or kill it, and come home a conqueror or seed-king of worlds."[2] Morgon precisely fits this statement. He is a talented riddle solver yet the riddle of his own identity spins out before him in time. He must leave Hed, encounter shape-changers and other threats to his life, and he must ascertain the real nature of the mysterious harpist who accompanies him, a harpist named Deth. In his quest he pursues the elusive meaning of the three stars on his forehead, present from birth and the key to his identity.

Riddling is related to characterization in other ways. In their social context, riddles do not enhance amiability. The riddler seeks deliberately to confuse, to disconcert, to discomfit his adversary. Unlike proverbs with which they are often compared they tend to generate tension in an atmosphere of competition. In the cultural framework of the trilogy, where the riddle functions as an accepted convention, this tension takes on major significance. In this way Morgon is in direct contrast to Tolkien's hobbits as questers, for they rely on the proverb, the medium of folk wisdom, and succeed through cooperation. Morgon's riddling quest is a solitary one.

As hero Morgon is both riddle and riddler. As a riddle master he wins the crown of Peven, a king of five hundred years ago who still lives bound in his tower. Many have died through the centuries while challenging Peven, and Morgon is the first to defeat him. But the riddle of his own identity and destiny eludes his mastery. Morgon is also a divided man. On the one hand he is a farmer in love with the countryside of his native Hed, the object of his land rule. On the other he is a scholar, having studied at the College of Riddle Mastery but not yet able to take his final robes of mastery because of his need to assume duties at home. Temperamentally content to stay in Hed, raising pigs and making beer, he is forced to stir abroad and undertake a quest, but for him it is a destiny accepted with great reluctance. Furthermore, he wants to marry

Raederle, whom he loves and who has been promised to the man who wins the crown of Peven. Morgon's personal and political destinies in this case intersect.

Morgon asks both the projective and the nonprojective riddle. As a young man with three stars on his forehead he must ask "Who am I?" As a young man subjected to a series of threats to his life, he must also ask "Who is the High One?" for in his world the so-called High One is believed to be the supreme being in charge of the order of all things. Although this semimythic being seems in godlike fashion to weave a pattern to his own ends, quite beyond the understanding of men, he is perceived in human terms as one whose mind is the great web of all the minds of those in his realm. Some skeptics do not believe in his existence at all, regarding him as but a lie invented by the great wizards of old. Morgon's own belief in the High One is seemingly confirmed when he meets, as if by chance, the stranger who claims to be the High One's harpist, the stranger named Deth.

The notion of a High One as transcendental ruler representing a web of the other minds in his kingdom is conceptually related to McKillip's idea of land rule. Each of the separate portions of the realm has its own land ruler, who in turn has a land heir. Land rule is an internalized concept based on a mystical identification of the ruler with the actual land. When a given ruler dies, his heir instantly feels the change. When Morgon senses his father's death, he immediately sees every leaf, every seed, every root in Hed. He identifies with every newly planted seed. Somewhat later his brother Eliard feels the passage of land rule to himself, knowing thereby that Morgon must be either dead or out of control of his mind. Still later, when Morgon assumes the land rule of other kingdoms beyond Hed, he absorbs the nature of all of these lands until he is reeling with land rule. As Raederle puts it, the passage of land rule is "like suddenly growing an extra eye to see in the dark or an ear to hear things beneath the earth" (*HSF*, p. 91). The principle of rule is thus based not on ownership but on empathy.

Morgon's peaceful existence in his homeland comes to an abrupt end when he is shipwrecked on his sea voyage back to Hed after a visit to his brother at the college. The wreck leaves him unconscious, tossed up on a strange shore, and for a time without any memory. When he regains his memory he realizes that the three stars on his forehead are a threat not only to his life but to his friends and family as well. His own parents died in an unexplained shipwreck at sea, which he is now forced to investigate.

From this point on Morgon travels widely and has a series of lively adventures, but each time he answers a riddle a new and more challenging riddle takes it place. He finds an ancient harp with three stars on it which he is able to play although no one else ever has. His life is threatened again, and he narrowly escapes being killed by a shape-changer in the form of a white bird. One of the countries he visits is the realm of the Morgul, a woman ruler who is an old friend of Deth the harpist. Morgon learns that an earlier Morgul had died in an effort to learn the riddle of the three stars. The present Morgul's capital city is built in circles, with seven circular walls about it. Her own house is oval in shape. This country, Herun, has not accepted the masculine tradition of square dwellings and city structures. Morgon also visits Osterland, ruled by the Wolf-King Har, a shape-shifter and a riddle master. Har's court is enlivened by the presence of wild animals sitting about the fire in the hearth. Har teaches Morgon to transform himself into a vesta, one of a species somewhat like a reindeer but with purple eyes.

Journeying still further, Morgon visits Isig Mountain, ruled by Danan, who teaches him how to turn himself into a tree. There he also ventures deep underground, under the mountain, where he finds the Cave of the Lost Ones where the children of the Earth Masters who lived long ago have all turned to stone. There he finds a sword marked with three stars, obviously made and waiting for him. The children awake and address him as a man of peace.

All of these adventures are tantalizing restatements of the riddle of Morgon's identity and the destiny it implies. Morgon's mind is distinguished by its conflict between the part of him that simply wishes to stay home and be a farmer and the unknown part of him that must be awakened to face the challenge and danger implied in those three stars. He has no desire for power or fame and fights to remain an obscure farmer. In the climactic final scene of this first book the questions remain unanswered. The scene itself is a cliff-hanger, ending literally in mid-episode. The reader is advised to have the second volume close at hand.

The impatient reader, eager to find out what follows this startling conclusion, will be at first dismayed to find out that the second volume does not complete the dangling episode but instead shifts to an account of Morgon's fiancée Raederle and her adventures. The dismay will quickly give way, however, for this book is an equally exciting one. The reader knows that somehow Raederle will catch up with the missing Morgon eventually, but in the meantime the riddles, the shape-changing, the journeys to strange places continue in this volume but with a focus on female characters. Raederle is the most important, but she is joined in her quest for Morgon by his spunky younger sister, Tristan, only thirteen but determined to find her brother, and by Lyra, the Morgul's daughter, a lively young woman whose specialty is the spear. As a member of her mother's personal guard she is a sharpshooter, and she tends to think that all problems can be solved by throwing a spear at them. Hers is the code of the warrior. This is a work to delight feminists, with its range of resourceful, independent, capable and appealing female characters. In one delightful scene a sailor who makes the mistake of trying to steal a kiss from one of the Morgul's female guards finds himself pinned to the mast with an arrow through his sleeve. Essentially, however, this is Raederle's story, with her quest to find Morgon paralleled by her quest to find her own identity. She too has a strange destiny which frightens and puzzles her, but she courageously faces the need to learn what it is. Her fear, unlike Morgon's, does not concern the possible need to assume power over others but rather the potential powers within her own nature as heir of sea and fire.

Word has come that Morgon, after a year's unexplained absence, has died. His death has been perceived by his brother Eliard, who felt himself inherit the land rule. There is the possibility that instead of dying Morgon has lost his mind-control. At the same time the ancient wizards of the world have reappeared after an absence of centuries. One of them is acting as a pig-woman in Hel, Raederle's country. The Morgul considers the freeing of the wizards to take their own shape an act of Ohm, the master wizard, and related to the removal of the star-bearer. The riddle of Morgon's whereabouts, compounded by the reappearance of the wizards, drives Raederle over the realm in search of him. She sets out in a ship driven by her father's shipmaster, accompanied by Lyra and Tristan, in a journey fraught with dangers and discoveries.

She makes good use of the trickery taught her by the wizard pig-woman. Using a golden tangle of thread, she creates illusion to confuse her pursuers, and using a gemlike stone she blinds the warships on her trail. Along the way she discovers her ability to handle fire. She can carry and shape the flame in her hands. She also comes to realize that she inherits the shape-changer power in her ancestry. One of her ancestors, Ylon, was a shape-changer of the sea, from whom Raederle also inherits her ability to deal with the waters. Her quest for Morgon is thus also a quest for her own identity, revealing inner powers that frighten her. Like Morgon she would rather stay home and enjoy the peaceful country life, but she knows that she cannot do so until she learns what really happened to the star-bearer, whom she loves.

Raederle's climactic adventure is one of the most dramatic. In an attempt to gain protection for Morgon, whom she has learned is alive and traveling toward An, she arranges to bargain with a dead king. She offers him the return of his skull, presently sitting on the mantle of the victor's descendants, in exchange for the protection that he and his army of wraiths can offer to Morgon. She succeeds with the help of magic in effecting the bargain, but the king mistakenly protects Deth, also traveling toward An. Morgon in the meantime has sworn to kill Deth who he believes has betrayed him. In a final chilling scene Raederle, Deth, and Morgon confront one another together with the dead kings.

At last the heir of sea and fire has rejoined her beloved master of earth and winds, but the riddles remain unsolved.

The third and most complex volume is *Harpist in the Wind,* named for the enigmatic Deth. On several occasions Deth seems to die yet repeatedly reappears. More than ever the reader sees the harpist as a double-level characterization, both an individual and a concept. As an individual Deth suffers, pathetically appearing here with gnarled hands unable to play the harp and referring often to his own impending death. Yet he remains a riddle, as does the identity of the High One. Raederle suggests to Morgon that he seek the High One at the top of Wind Tower, which stands on the plain of the ruined city of the ancient Earth Masters. In a long ago catastrophic war the city and the Earth Masters were destroyed except for the stone children whom Morgon met under Isig Mountain. No one has ever climbed the Wind Tower before, but Morgon accepts the challenge.

In the literally whirlwind conclusion, Morgon learns the answers to the five riddles that have haunted him since he first learned them from the Wolf-King Har. Who is the star-bearer and what will he loose that is bound? What will one star call out of silence, one star out of darkness, and one star out of death? Who will come in the time's ending and what will he bring? Who will sound the Earth's harp, silent since the Beginning? Who will bear stars of fire and ice to the Ending of an Age? As star-bearer he both learns the answers to the riddles and fulfills the prophecies. At the top of Wind Tower Morgon has a final encounter with Deth, understanding at last the ironic complexity of their relationship in a stirring conclusion that each reader deserves to discover directly.

One strand of the many interwoven in this remarkable conclusion concerns Morgon's coming-of-age as master of earth and air. Morgon realizes at last that his journeys through the realm have prepared him to undertake a wider assumption of land rule. No longer a mere provincial pigherd from Hed, the star-bearer becomes land heir on a scale he had never dreamed of. Furthermore, it becomes his role to loosen the twelve winds that will in turn release the wild chaotic powers of the ancient Earth Masters. Morgon's job is to save the realm from this destructive force that must by prophecy be unleashed. While armies gather on Wind Plain to fight a hopeless final battle, Morgon acts to avert this appalling catastrophe. He renounces the way of aggression and instead drives the newly freed winds back into their own mountain, where he seals them forever. Thus the poised armies gathered to fight to the death are saved except for minor losses. Like Ged's pact with the dragon of Pendor Morgon's containment of the winds achieves a higher goal of peace through renunciation of aggressive action. The avoidance of fighting the last battle is also an inversion of the Arthurian legend which ends in a final battle, with death for both Arthur and Mordred. Peace and containment supplant the heroic code of battle to the death.

The trilogy is notable for its thematic materials as well as for its complex plotting. The ontology of the riddle is of course central, and closely related to it is the stricture, or lesson, attached to the riddle's correct answer. In retrospect the reader discovers that several of the philosophical points contained in these strictures have been demonstrated in the course of the narrative. One of the first strictures that Morgon learns is "turn forward into the unknown, rather than backward toward death" (*RH*, p. 89). Throughout the first few episodes he tries to turn backward to Hed, the safe familiar way of life he has always known, but he learns that death awaits him unless he turns toward the unknown. A closely related stricture plays on the double meaning of the harpist's name: "The man running from death must run first from himself" (*RH*, p. 35). For a time Morgon tries to run away from death and from his own identity as star-bearer, but Deth remains with him and he finds that he must seek himself. A similar stricture involving Deth/death asserts: "it is unwise to turn your back on death, since turning, you will only find it once more in front of you" (*HW*, p. 200). Again, it is true that Morgon tries to turn away from death only to find Deth in front of him. A stricture haunting Morgon is that "The wise man knows his own name" (*RH*, p. 70), for the young prince of Hed clearly does not. Finally, a stricture that might serve as thematic subtitle for the entire work occurs early: "Beware the unanswered riddle" (*RH*, p. 70).

Thematically, the magical transformations of the shape-changers are also related to riddling. The riddle assumes the fact of shape-changing in that the challenge of riddling is to perceive a person or an object in an unexpected form. It is not surprising that in the riddling world there are many shape-changers, both good and evil. Both Raederle and Morgon take on other shapes during the course of the narrative. Raederle is at first reluctant to try her power, fearing its consequences, but she eventually takes on the form of a crow and flies, as her father had often done. Morgon proves to be very adept, learning at first to become a vesta, then a tree, later a bird. (McKillip's lucent prose makes assuming the tree shape seem an ideal vacation, free from all anxiety and effort.) Several shape-changers are destructive, however, and in some cases they take on the shapes of the dead, adding a ghoulish element to the story. But whatever form it takes, shape-shifting is not an arbitrary mode of magic added to the plot for its own sake but an integral part of McKillip's riddling world.

Another important thematic feature is the subject of the four elements. The union, totality, balance, and control of the four elements— earth, air, fire, and water—represents wholeness in this world. (As indeed they did historically in the medieval and Renaissance vision of our own world.) Morgon as the land ruler of Hed is identified with earth from the start. Virtually an animating spirit of his own land, he knows every blade of grass and bit of soil in a symbiotic relationship which he eventually assumes over a much wider realm. In the process of discovering his own identity Morgon learns that the harp with three stars, made long ago for only him to play, was constructed by Yrth, another of McKillip's characters with an intriguing double-meaning name. Morgon also becomes associated with air in the form of winds. It is his job to answer the riddle of who will loose what is bound, i.e., the twelve winds. After the chaos of their loosing, which he achieves by climbing the Wind Tower, he directs them back to the mountain that will seal them within forever more. The land heir is thus also the wind master.

Raederle, on the other hand, is associated with water and fire. She is descended from a shape-changer born of seafoam and kelp. She feels completely at home on the sea, refusing to be daunted by Morgon's warnings about the danger of death by drowning. She is also a master of fire, with remarkable skill in shaping it in her hands. She can produce, control, and manipulate fire even as Morgon can the winds. The marriage of Morgon and Raederle is a union not only of male and female but of the four basic elements of creation.

McKillip also uses bird and animal imagery effectively. Raederle's family line has been adept at taking on the shape of crows. Early in the narrative her father flies off as a crow to investigate the fate of the missing Morgon. Later both Morgon and Raederle take the crow shape in their search for the High One. At one point they are joined by a falcon with intense eyes, whose earnest stare they later recognize in the wizard Yrth. The lovely animal called the vesta is the author's own creation. Somewhat like a reindeer, it is a horned animal capable of great speed and noted for its deep purple eyes. Pigs, too, are important, as they are in Celtic mythology. Early in the trilogy we learn about the ancient speaking pig Negids-Noon. In the middle volume Raederle expresses a wish that the pregnant boar will bear a speaking pig. At the end of the final volume comes the happy news that Negids-Noon has born a speaking pig. The myth nicely frames the narrative, which also includes a wildly funny pig stampede.

One of McKillip's original devices adding both drama and humor is the Great Shout. The reader first hears it from Raederle's brother at the College of Riddle Mastery. When he utters it, its power forces the locked books of the wizards to fly open. It is used once by the pig-woman, who dissipates her herd of pigs and disappears directly after giving it. Morgon catches on to the power of the shout which even in a casual use can bring devastating consequences. The Great Shout may be either a physical body-shout or a silent mind-shout. In either manifestation it can shatter structures in the immediate vicinity and cause unconsciousness in people within its range.

In addition to the intellectual appeal of the riddle quest and the original devices and images factored into the complex and suspenseful plot, the reader is impressed with the depth of its characterization. Morgon is a sympathetic hero in his frustrated desire to go home and raise pigs, leaving the outside world to solve its own problems. He is by no means the traditional self-demonstrative hero flexing his muscles and announcing his ambition to conquer the world. His gradual growth in awareness and acceptance of his destiny is very moving, and his internal conflict is poignantly presented. The female characters are also strong. Raederle, deeply in love with the destiny-haunted star-bearer, is in the grip of her own inner battle between the woman in love and the woman whose ancestry has conferred strange and frightening powers on her. The Morgul, with her gift of the Sight; her daughter Lyra, the soldierly spear-thrower; and Tristan, the kid sister who finds unexpected resources of heroism in her own adolescent willfulness are all convincing.

Above all, however, the ambivalent and ambiguous figure of Deth the harpist haunts the reader's imagination. Morgon's friend and enemy, servant and hero, leader and follower, mentor and betrayer, a mysterious man whose presence fills the books, Deth ultimately enables the youthful prince of Hed to assume his proper destiny as star-bearer. The ambiguity of the name is clearly recognized by Morgon, at first with amusement as he recalls his father's joke about Deth's playing at his wedding, and later with sudden profound insight as he directly addresses him at the top of Wind Tower as Death. Throughout this work Deth is both an individual and an idea, both a riddle and a stricture. In a real way Deth is the center of meaning in the trilogy. Somewhat like Ged's shadow, Deth is essential to the identity of the man who pursues him.

The harp offers clues to the meaning of Deth's role. Prominent in Celtic legend, and still appearing today on the Irish penny, the harp is rich in mythic content. The harp is symbolically related to the mystic ladder, acting as bridge between heaven and earth. In the Eddas the heroes wish to have their harps buried with them in their graves to facilitate their entrance into the otherworld. The tension in the harp strings is said to reflect the pangs of earthly life and the upward striving toward the spiritual. In a painting by Hieronymous Bosch, *The Garden of Earthly Delights*, a human figure hangs crucified on the strings of a harp. Since the harp suggests movement from earth to heaven through its continuing tension between two planes of existence, it is a fitting instrument to represent Deth/Death as the focal point between these two realms. As Death in the trilogy represents the ending of an epoch it also represents the beginning of a new one. "The king is dead, long live the king." Death provides the transformation from one order to another. McKillip thus exemplifies the theme of mortality vindicated. It is Morgon's proper and inescapable fate to begin the new era after the dissolution of the old, but this transformation is made possible by Deth, always with a harp.[3]

Deth's first appearance is strikingly simple, with a face "neither young nor old" and hair "a loose cap of silver" (*RH*, p. 14), with his black tunic bearing a chain of linked, stamped squares of silver. When Morgon decides to seek the High One in order to understand his own bizarre fate, Deth the harpist offers to accompany him. Morgon's response to the offer is ironic: "But will you mind traveling with a man tracked by death?" (*RH*, p. 81). As the young prince travels with the harpist, he recalls the several strictures referring to death. Throughout much of their journey toward the mountain seat of the High One, Deth is quiet, cryptic, yet subtly nagging Morgon to accept the burden of his unknown heritage tokened in the three stars on his forehead. Through Deth Morgon learns of the three-starred harp and sword supposedly made centuries ago for the man one day born to claim them. Deth admits that he lived a thousand years ago and knew Yrth, maker of both harp and sword, yet Morgon later learns that Yrth made the harp a century earlier than Deth's supposed birth date. Can Deth lie? The harpist asks simply that Morgon trust him "Beyond logic, beyond reason, beyond hope" (*RH*, p. 212). Only once on their journey to the mountain does Deth laugh. When Morgon practices the silent version of the Great Shout, which Deth has just taught him, and almost causes a landslide, he hears the sound of restrained laughter from the harpist. But this light moment is followed by the wild scene that climaxes the first volume. As a result of what he learns, Morgon concludes that Deth has betrayed him.

From this point the movement of the relationship between Morgon and Deth reverses direction. Deth had been following, but now Morgon begins to hunt for Deth. The narrative reversal suggests an analogy with Ged and his shadow in the Earthsea trilogy, for there, too, at mid-point Ged stops fleeing his shadow and begins hunting it. In the middle and final volumes Deth becomes more puzzling than ever. At times he is even pathetic, as when his scarred, broken hands struggle to play the harp.

Deth remains throughout an ambiguous character, and death the ultimate riddle. Even at the college for wizards they hold that one cannot turn one's back on death. Can Deth—or death—die? Or is it simply, as Morgon once suggests, replacing one mask with another? In any case it is clear that Deth is essential to Morgon's life. As companion and antagonist Deth leads the young man to fulfill the destiny of his own identity. The precise yet complex role that Deth has assumed in Morgon's life is not fully revealed until the last chapters of *Harpist in the Wind*, where it is described through image and event as well as through statement. As Morgon discovers, "Our lives were one constant, twisted riddle-game" (*HW*, p. 251).

McKillip's prose has a unique, painterly quality. Not a dramatic, fast-paced writer, she has a flare for the sharp unexpected simile—"like a fox looking up from a pile of chicken feathers"—but tends on the whole to visualize a scene detail by detail. Even the most exciting events tend not to be cited swiftly but spread out minutely, even to the gradual movement of a spear from one hand to the other. There is also considerable humor and irony, especially in the dialogue, features not common to most contemporary fantasies. Descriptions are poetically concrete: when Morgon assumes the land rule, "The more he understood, the deeper he drew himself into it: gazing at the moon out of a horned owl's eyes, melting with a wild cat through the bracken, twisting his thoughts even into the fragile angles of a spider's web, and into the endless, sinuous wind of ivy spiralling a tree trunk" (*HW*, p. 175-76); and when Raederle masters fire: "And deep within her, rousing out of a dormant, lawless heritage came the fiery, answering leap of understanding. The lucent, wordless knowledge of fire filled her; the soft rustlings became a language, the incessant weave a purpose, its color the color of the world, of her mind" (*HSF*, p. 123-4). The style thus sustains the artistic and intellectual integrity of the work.

McKillip's trilogy exemplifies the major feminist themes. The acceptance of death which is the vindication of mortality is portrayed by the role of Deth and through his relationship with Morgon. The renunciation of power is central to Morgon's own development, and his coming-of-age is marked by his triumphant averting of a battle. The depolarization of values is reflected in the marriage of Morgon and Raederle, as a union of the four elements, and in the pervasive recognition that nothing is evil of itself. The vision of harmony implicit in McKillip's world includes nature and animals as well as humans. Ecology is basic to the concept of land rule. In a world where life is a riddle-game and death is a harpist, male and female values are integrated, and people try out the life of a tree. Or a crow. Or a vesta.

Furthermore, McKillip utilizes circular structure as a feminine motif. As already mentioned, the woman ruler, the Morgul, not only lives in an oval house but also occupies a city surrounded by seven circular walls. Her vision of history in the trilogy is also circular and feminine. A prominent image of the past is the broken bowl. Morgon tries to ascertain both the mystery of his own identity and of the past by piecing together broken shards. The burial of the children of the early Earth Masters offers an appropriate comment on the anticyclical futility of war. These denizens of power had sacrificed their own children, and thus their own future, in their destructive quest for domination. In Morgon these children, now buried and turned to stone, see hope and stir to appeal to him as a man of peace. The natural cycle of birth, death, and renewal is restored in the final scenes following Morgon's ascent of the Wind Tower.

Perhaps McKillip is also slyly satirizing the established university system, essentially a masculine construct, in her College of Wizardry. A closed intellectual system, it relies on locked books and trained researchers. Imagination and intuition as modes of answering riddles are neglected in favor of arduous systematic research. But it is the "drop-out," Morgon, the man who did not stay for his degree, who is able to solve the riddle of Peven and win the crown. And it is ultimately the broken, the forgotten, and the dead who communicate what is important, not in books but through nonrational perceptions.

9

VERA CHAPMAN

VERA CHAPMAN SHOULD PROVE AN INSPIRATION to the writer who gets a late start. This remarkable Englishwoman published the first volume of her successful Arthurian trilogy at the age of seventy-five. In addition to completing the trilogy she has published more novels and short stories since that time. Her work has been entirely in the realm of fantasy and medieval adventure, including juvenile fantasies, one novel about the Wife of Bath, and several short stories about the Crusades. She regards herself as primarily an entertainer, hoping "to amuse and perhaps thrill with a few good stories, and to convey a little of the pleasure I myself have felt in life and literature."[1] Her lively *Three Damosels* trilogy certainly fulfills her own hopes for giving pleasure but goes beyond that modest aim by offering a feminist version of the Arthurian legend, modifying events as well as meanings. Each of the three books (*The Green Knight* [1975], *The King's Damosel* [1976], and *King Arthur's Daughter* [1976] is narrated by a female character, two of whom play minor roles in the original tales and one of whom is Chapman's own invention. Several feminine variations on the traditional medieval materials are introduced: the motif of the Grail is related to goddess worship; the individual chosen to find the Grail is not a pure knight but a fallen woman; Morgan le Fay becomes the negative side of the goddess whose positive manifestation is the Virgin Mary; Merlin has a daughter; and women are active on the battlefield both as warriors and messengers. Most important, however, is the central underlying theme of "the feminine line," i.e., direct inheritance through the matrilinear line rather than through the patrilinear name.

The Green Knight is structured in five parts, all recounted as first-person narratives, two by Vivian (wife of Bertilak), two by Gawain, and one by Merlin's assistant, Melior. The first half of the story follows the original romance of *Sir Gawain and the Green Knight* closely although the perspective is shifted since we see it first through the eyes of young Vivian, Bertilak's bride, then through Gawain's. The second half changes drastically, drawing on other legendary materials concerning the exploits of Gawain and also creating original episodes based on Celtic lore. A short book, it is packed with events heroic, romantic, and supernatural.

Vivian is Chapman's creation. The daughter of Vivian-Nimue, youngest of the three "witch" daughters of Igraine, she has been raised in the convent of Amesbury. Until the moment the story begins, she has never been abroad but has led an innocent, secluded existence. Her way of life is abruptly changed by the unexpected arrival of her aunt, Morgan le Fay, who takes her away from the peaceful confines of the sisterhood to face the challenge of a new life at the castle of Haut Desert. On the way to the castle, Vivian discovers some of the magical talents of her mysterious aunt who, while in the convent, never touched holy water or crossed herself. Morgan is skilled in the art of illusion. Although recognizing that her servants are illusory does not upset Vivian, discovering that the tempting banquet before her is illusion cruelly disappoints the hungry young woman. Morgan's own appearance is illusory in that she changes so radically and so often that no one knows what she really looks like. Vivian cannot be sure whether she is an old hag or a handsome, elegant woman of forty.

When Vivian arrives at the castle, she meets a handsome young man who attracts her romantically, but the apparent youth is suddenly transformed into the middle-aged Bertilak. Vivian then learns that he is completely dominated by Morgan who can transform him into an ugly beast or a giant green man. In his own shape he is essentially a kind man, so that Vivian is not completely dismayed to learn that she is to marry him. On her wedding night Bertilak informs her that their marriage will be Platonic, but she will be honored as mistress of the castle and serve as his hostess. Although her fleeting vision of the ideal lover seems lost forever, the youthful Vivian is not unhappy in her new role which preserves her virginity yet gains her authority and respect as Dame Bertilak. Meanwhile she also learns many arts from her sorceress aunt.

The reader then meets Gawain the Young, son of Gareth (not the Gawain who is Arthur's companion). This lad is also an innocent, narrating in the same breathless, naïve manner as Vivian's. Gawain is about to be knighted, but during his vigil he is sorely tempted both by

Mordred and by Morgan le Fay, who vainly try to distract him. Mordred also interferes with Gawain's performance during his tournament, so that when the young knight finally appears at Arthur's court he is embarrassed and dejected, regarding himself as a failure. Determined to redeem himself, he accepts the challenge of the Green Knight. As in the original, he strikes off the head of the giant visitor who calmly picks it up in front of the horrified spectators and agrees to meet him for a return blow at the Green Chapel a year later. What Chapman does is supply Gawain with a convincing motive.

Vivian, now a happy wife in name only and quite adept in the arts of transformation, is about to receive Gawain as a guest in her castle. Morgan, the wily manipulator, determined to undermine Arthur's court, plans to use Vivian to her own ends. She prepares a posset of milk and honey laced with her own drugs, under the influence of which Vivian is persuaded to tempt Gawain sexually. Again Chapman has supplied a motive where the original was lacking one. The three temptations, the three wagers, and the three strokes of the ax all follow the original, but Chapman changes the narrative by having Vivian choose to return to court with Gawain.

Gawain appears desolate as he returns to court after what he feels has been a humiliating experience. His depression and self-deprecation are intensified by the fever he has developed from the neglected neck wound inflicted by the Green Knight's ax. In this lamentable state he meets an old woman on horseback, who insists on accompanying him and who nurses him back to health. When a mysterious monk suddenly appears with a message for Gawain summoning him to Stonehenge, the young knight naïvely rides off, accepting the call and leaving his elderly companion behind, never suspecting that she is actually Vivian in disguise. At Stonehenge Gawain meets a man who calls himself Merlin, who asks him to sacrifice his life as the one chosen to die in the place of King Arthur. He agrees to become the sacrificial victim just as Vivian shows up in her own guise, offering to die with him. At the very last instant, and too late, Vivian suddenly recognizes that the supposed Merlin is a fake.

At this point the reader is thoroughly baffled not only because the original tale is left far behind, but also because Gawain does not appear in any of the medieval romances as a sacrifice at Stonehenge. The final section of the book clarifies Chapman's ingenious and wholly original plotting. The real Merlin, who is Vivian's grandfather, discovers in his visionary snakestone what is happening at Stonehenge and sets out on a rescue mission. He is delayed by a blinding snowstorm, by mists, by natural and supernatural intervention. He learns that his journey is being blocked by Bertilak, who protests that whenever he tries to arise out of his bestial state toward manhood he is thwarted by "she whom I obey."

He then appears in the shape of a bear on its hind legs. Merlin arrives at Stonehenge too late, but by performing an ancient and powerful ritual, using invocation, chanting, and evoking sensational lightning, he is able to resurrect the two bodies. The beast turns back into Bertilak as Merlin deals with his ultimate enemy, Morgan the deceiver, who now lies on the ground beside the altar stone. Gawain sets his foot on her but, following Merlin's orders, does not kill her. She shrivels and sinks from sight, but is not dead.

Merlin's powers are spent. Bertilak has been blinded by the lightning which was for him a vision of the Holy Mary. The four stand in four corners like four archangels facing in the four cardinal directions. Bertilak is now in the service of Mary rather than Morgan, and although Merlin dies, the line of Gawain and Vivian will save Britain in the future.

The Green Knight is obviously full of events. The pace is fast and the episodes varied. The style is sparse and economical, usually forceful and concrete as well, but occasionally the episodes are dispatched too abruptly. The scene of the sacrifice at Stonehenge tends to be melodrama since it lacks emotional preparation. Gawain's surrender is too hasty to be convincing. On the other hand, the repeated delays in Merlin's frantic efforts to rescue the victims are effectively handled. Partly because of style and partly as a result of the syncretic mingling of incidents from various sources, there are also a few loose ends. Gawain's vision of deflowering a maiden which disrupts his concentration during his knightly vigil is never followed up, and Merlin's implied return to Nimue at the end is never quite explained.

The characterization of Vivian and Gawain as innocents in a deceptive world challenging their survival is effective. Chapman makes their roles credible by providing motivation lacking in the original. Why does Gawain volunteer to take up the Green Knight's challenge? Why is he so diffident about himself in Arthur's court? Why does Vivian agree to tempt him? Why does Bertilak turn into the Green Knight? What is Morgan's purpose in masterminding the entire conspiracy? Providing psychologically convincing answers to these questions, Chapman offers a shy young knight, sorely tested during his vigil, and a naïve Vivian under the influence of her aunt's drugged potion. More complex is the characterization of Bertilak, who combines several elements. One dimension of his nature is the werewolf legend. He can be and often is transformed into a wild beast by Morgan. Bestiality is, however, but one layer of his being, for he wishes to rise through an upward evolutionary movement from the beast of the slime to the beast of the hills, then to the lower man and on to the higher man. The layered image of the human being as encompassing a vegetable, an animal, and a rational soul is of course sound medieval belief. What prevents Bertilak's rise is Morgan, "she whom I obey," the mysterious enchantress. When he observes

Merlin's magical restoration of Gawain and Vivian to life, his own life is totally changed. Blinded by lightning, he envisions the Virgin Mary. Just as he had wished to transform his own nature from bestial to human, so the goddess is for him transformed from the malicious witch Morgan to the spiritual Our Lady, who frees his higher nature by taking away his physical sight. This complex revisioning of Bertilak is brilliantly conceived but unfortunately too rushed in the actual narration for the reader to take it all in.

As in the original, Morgan is the central manipulator of the events, but here she is more fully developed. Referred to in a variety of negative epithets, such as the Great Deceiver, the Mistress of the Night, and the Witch-Queen, she is not wholly evil and therefore must not be wholly destroyed. As Merlin explains, she is also Dream, Fantasy, and Shaping, a potential source of power and wisdom but only if she is kept under one's feet. In this sense she is somewhat parallel to Le Guin's concept of the shadow in the Earthsea thrilogy, a potential source of creativity as well as of danger, needing to be controlled rather than rejected. Her characterization as witch also has a resemblance to C. S. Lewis's White Witch in the Narnia Chronicles. Her attempt to sacrifice the knight and lady on the stone table recalls the White Witch's sacrifice of Aslan, and Merlin's ability to resurrect her victims recalls the contrast that Lewis draws between deep magic from the dawn of time—the sacrificial—and magic from before the dawn of time—mercy and rebirth. The Christian interpretation is implicit in the transformation of Morgan le Fay into Our Lady.

Through the identification of Morgan and Mary as two dimensions of the goddess, Chapman introduces the feminist perspective of the matriarchal line. The idea is presented through Merlin who rejects the primacy of the patriarchal line based on the inheritance of the father's name. He foresees that Arthur will have no son (since Mordred is not to inherit the throne of Britain), and he knows that he has no son. But he has a daughter and granddaughter (whom he brings back from death), and Arthur will have a daughter (protagonist of a later book in the trilogy). Arthur's daughter will marry the son of Gawain and Vivian, carrying on the blood line. As Merlin points out, the maternal line has three threads to the father's one. The father's is wholly dependent on a son to maintain the name. The mother's line may, however, be carried on from mother to daughter, from father to daughter, and from mother to son. It carries on, as it were, underground: the name is forgotten, but the actual blood line is still there. It will thus work out that future ages will not even know that Arthur has a daughter, yet her blood will flow into the people of Britain from queens to commoners, and it will through history provide the very nerves and sinews of the land. Merlin too will live on through his granddaughter.

The events in *The King's Damosel,* middle volume of the trilogy, antedate those of *The Green Knight.* This is an eclectic work, not primarily retelling a single story like its predecessor but rather combining several different elements of medieval romance. Chapman's fondness for interweaving many strands from mythology, romance, history, and mysticism prompted her to remark that she has a "flypaper mind," a trait exemplified in this remarkably varied and colorful narrative.

The unifying factor is the title role, Chapman's most memorable characterization, Lynette. The story is told entirely from Lynette's point of view, partly through direct experience, partly through flashback, with her personality developed through her thoughts and feelings as well as through speech and actions. From her tomboy childhood through her mystic quest for the Grail, she emerges as a complex, delightful, totally engaging figure. She is introduced on the eve of an unwanted marriage, when a series of flashbacks informs the reader of her traumatic childhood experiences.

Lynette, which means "lion's cub," was brought up like a boy by her father. Her sister Leonie was very feminine, and their mother had died, so Lynette's tomboyish temperament conveniently substituted for the son her father could not have. She learned to ride, fish, and shoot, cutting her hair short at age eleven so she could wear a helmet. Unfortunately, at age thirteen, her boyish appearance and forward manner made exactly the wrong impression on an uncouth visitor at Lyonesse. This guest, named Bagdemus, gladly offered to take Lynette riding with him, treating her like a page, but then he raped her, threatening her life if she told anyone. Shocked, disillusioned, and desperately alone in her anguish, she was suddenly visited by Merlin, who consoled her and intimated that a great destiny awaited her. Loss of virginity might seem the end of the world for some women, but Lynette's future held greater promise than mere marriage and domesticity.

In another flashback, we learn of yet another crisis that occurred when Lynette was seventeen, shortly after the death of her father. At this time a coarse, violent knight named Sir Rubert sued for the hand of Leonie, threatening to occupy their castle until she agreed to marry him. The sisters managed to escape to the private part of the castle, leaving him besieged in the great hall, while Lynette, disguised as a kitchen scullery boy, slipped out to seek help. Lynette's aim was to go to Camelot and request the aid of one of Arthur's knights. Bravely daring the long journey through the dark forest at night, accompanied only by her hawk Jeanne, she reached Camelot in three days. Once there, however, she found herself pushed into a lineup of kitchen boys. When Sir Kay came to review the boys, she sharply rebuked him for his lack of knightly courtesy, revealing her own identity as a damsel in distress. At this point Lynette displays what becomes a major feature in her personality, her scolding tongue. Although Arthur is quite willing to offer her a champion, she takes offense that one of the kitchen boys volunteers to undertake the challenge. The lad, who turns out to be Gareth, is indeed a worthy champion, but on the ride back to the castle Lynette taunts and insults him all the way.

The gentle, mannerly Gareth bore these shrewish words without complaint, but now he is about to be married to Leonie while Lynette, who learned too late to appreciate her gentle champion, is to be married to his stupid, brutal brother, Gaheris. These are the thoughts of the unhappy young woman on her marriage eve, evoking sympathy from the reader for the outrages that marred the early years of this brave, spirited, but lonely woman.

Merlin's repeated visitations to Lynette in times of trouble clearly confirm her destiny to transcend the usual womanly roles. When her marriage is abruptly terminated by Gaheris, who walks out on their wedding night, rejecting her "like an unsavoury morsel, chewed and spat out" (p. 44), he appears again to console her with the promise of a special destiny. Her bitter words, turned at first against herself in frustrated rage, now turn against Merlin. His response to her anger and dejection goes beyond words, however, for he shows her a vision of her destiny in his magical crystal jewel. The vision is mystical, placing the incredulous young woman in the presence of the Holy Grail. Sharp-tongued Lynette dismisses it as absurd, for she is not a virgin, but Merlin suggests that charity is superior to chastity. For Lynette, who has vowed never to forgive her rapist, this distinction is meaningless. Charity is as far away for her as is her long-lost chastity. But a more immediate opportunity calls. Merlin sends Lynette to see King Arthur, who intends to make her his personal messenger to summon his knights all over the kingdom. In a ceremony similar to knighting, Arthur dubs the happy woman "The King's Damosel." Her mission as messenger will be to bring peace over the kingdom. Riding one of the king's giant chargers, accompanied by her dwarf and a contingent of four knights, four squires, and four men of arms who will provide protection if needed, she sets forth on the glorious mission. It is her charge to invite every knight in England to come and greet Arthur at Camelot on the feast of Whitsun two years hence.

The "falcon," as her accompanying knights fondly call her, has many adventures along the way, constituting a lively narrative. She proves her courage many times but also demonstrates her growing reputation for a shrewish tongue. The culmination of her mission poses a threat, for the last castle to be approached is that of Bagdemus, now a rebellious knight opposed to Arthur and calling himself king. In that squalid castle where she is tortured by Bagdemus's men, she seemingly forfeits her soul as she had fortfeited her honor years ago, for she is forced to lie under the pain of the thumbscrew and then swear that she told the truth. Eventually she is rescued by Lancelot who beheads the villainous Bagdemus at her request.

From this point on there is a shift in the tone of the narrative and in the outlook of the protagonist. Lynette's sharp words have been partly a matter of wit, partly a matter of overcompensation for a woman who wants to be treated as equal to a man. It begins to be clear, however, that they reflect within her a deeper bitterness, a hardness that savors revenge and scorns forgiveness. Lynette is haunted by Merlin's insistence that charity is better than chastity. As she rides back home with the head of her attacker secured in her saddlebag, she begins to feel less like a triumphant Judith and more like a guilty Salome. The adventures that she encounters on this return journey are more on the spiritual than the physical level. She and her attendants are repeatedly distracted and awed by several visions, including that of the Holy Grail. Supernatural visitations turn the homeward journey into a spiritual quest.

In one of these strange episodes when Lynette has been led astray by an illusion, she finds herself imprisoned in a dark cell with the head in the bag beside her. The head begins to glow in the dark, and the lamenting visage begs forgiveness, which she grants. In another, she falls into icy water but is saved by a young man dressed only in a loincloth. Totally blind, the young man is ironically named Lucius. Imprisoned underground long ago with his mother, who has since died, he now has an underground kingdom, a world of caves, streams, and tunnels in which he moves at will. His only contact with the upper world of light is a woman known as the Sybil, chosen by virtue of her gift of the Sight to serve the goddess, known as the White One.

Lynette is shown the white stone statue of the goddess which she finds ugly because of its exaggerated breasts and genitals. As Sybil explains, however, the goddess is neither beautiful nor foul, but simply that which is. Lynette's experience with the wise woman and the goddess is clearly part of her preparation for her destined quest for the Grail. It also seems inevitable that she fall in love with the gentle young blind man, so different from the sturdy, aggressive knights with whom she has always associated. He slightly resembles the soft-spoken Gareth, whom she drove away with her bitter mocking language. Above all, he is the antithesis of the vicious man who violated her. Their love hints at a tragic *Liebestod*, however, for his health has been ruined by years of deprivation. By now Lynette's character has been deeply modified. Not only is she a woman who can forgive but a woman who has been loved.

Chapman handles the climactic Grail scene effectively, following the medieval account closely. Lynette encounters the Fisher King in the Castle Carbonek where she sees the procession of four men carrying the four Hallows—sword, lance, cup, and platter—and a veiled maiden carrying the Grail. In keeping with Lynette's character to speak up and ask the questions most people would be afraid to, she now asks bluntly for whom the Grail is being served. The Fisher King whispers a name to her, then presents her with the Grail. In it lie two wafers, like consecrated hosts, one of which she offers to the ailing Fisher King who is then promptly restored to health.

The event is familiar, but what is strikingly original is the person of Lynette as the blessed individual chosen to find the precious Grail. A woman, not even a virgin, she is antithetical to the medieval ideal of the pure knight Galahad. Knighthood as a concept was based on standards of conduct unavailable to women: battle prowess, courtesy to and protection of women. The knight chosen to find the Grail was expected to transcend the military definition of the order by surrendering worldly vanities, specifically by being sexually pure. Lynette as a violated woman moves from the lowest level of object, i.e., of knightly protection, to the highest level of subject, the spiritual heir to the holy vessel. She is qualified for this supreme honor through charity, not chastity.

In a further deviation from the original tale, she is then permitted to carry the Grail back with her to her blind lover, Lucius, who may ask of it one boon. Will he ask for his sight to be restored so that he may see his beloved? Or will he ask for longer life in order to share it with her? These and other questions are answered for the reader in an ending that seems somewhat hurried after the intensity of all that precedes it.

Lynette represents a feminist ideal in her vocation as Arthur's messenger. The king clearly states that his goal is peace and that communication among his various knights is essential to that aim. It is Lynette's task to achieve a network of communication throughout the kingdom. It should also be noted as part of the feminist vision of the book that Lucius does not conform to the knightly ideals of valor and loyalty to king and God. Lucius, victim of cruelty on the part of an aggressor, is himself a gentle person and his worship is of the goddess whom he accepts as the mother of all.

King Arthur's Daughter features a completely original Chapman character, the "forgotten" daughter of the king, Ursulet, or "little bear." The dying Arthur, determined not to lose what he has achieved in unifying his country and establishing peace, prepares a document establishing his daughter as his lawful successor. Mordred, who has sworn lifelong fidelity to Arthur's enemy, Morgan le Fay, plots to take over the kingdom for himself, not hesitating at murder in order to do so.

Meanwhile, the young son of Gawain and Vivian, Ambris, dreams of becoming a knight and rescuing a princess. Obviously Merlin's predictions from the first book are about to come true.

Ursulet has been reared in a convent for the sake of her own safety, but pillaging Saxons put an abrupt end to that hope. When they raid and loot the convent, raping the nuns, Ursulet escapes, running off into the woods alone, wet, hungry and desolate. In a dream vision a beautiful woman offers her help in exchange for an oath of loyalty which she refuses to give. When she awakes, her gold cross has been replaced by a silver chain with a pendant pentagram, with its middle point downward. Alone and on the run, she comes to a primitive Jutish settlement where she offers to do menial chores. A Jutish midwife calls her pentagram a witches' star.

Ambris, in the meantime, has reached the age of eighteen and is duly knighted, with his aunt Lynette in attendance. Just as Gawain had been taunted during his vigil, young Ambris is tempted during his by Morgan, who tries to persuade him to turn around and look behind him, a forbidden gesture. In spite of her alluring perfume and seductive voice, he manages to resist until the cock crows at dawn, releasing him from his vow.

The thrust of the narrative movement at this point is to bring the knight and the princess together. Ursulet, however, after six years of servitude to the Jutes, has been sold into slavery to a Saxon who tries to rape her but is stopped by fear when he sees the reversed pentagram around her neck. Although she is able to run away one more time, now it is with a chain and slave ring on her neck. In his determined search for her, Ambris finally succeeds by discovering her lost gold cross, and they set forth together through a strange forest fraught with wonders.

Some of Chapman's most imaginative writing occurs in this book, where the narrative is not hurried as it was in its predecessors. In one episode an ethereally beautiful unicorn appears to protect Ursulet as she sleeps in the forest. In another, Ursulet and Ambris meet an eerie cold drake, the opposite of the more typical fire drake. Passing him is a chilling experience psychologically as well as physically. Together they also have an otherworldly encounter with the sleeping knights of the Round Table in an underground cave.

The conflict is developed on several levels. Politically, Arthur is opposed by Mordred, who wishes to seize control of the kingdom. Magically, the wizard Merlin is opposed by the witch Morgan le Fay. Both of these figures appear frequently and mysteriously, intervening in their own separate ways in order to advance and protect their favorites. Symbolically, the cross is opposed by the pentagram, which portends evil only when the center point is downward. Thematically, the conflict also develops between the patriarchal line which Mordred is eager to maintain, and the matriarchal, which Merlin favors and which Arthur recognizes as his own best hope for the future of his country.

A wild battle provides an exciting conclusion to this lively trilogy. The feminine element emerges heroically, with Ursulet leading her own army, moving far beyond the timidity of her secluded upbringing and fighting with a sword as well as providing spirited leadership. Lynette, who has been in all of Arthur's battles, is scornful of staying behind and busies herself with healing, carrying water and messages, and being absolutely indispensable. There is a touch of humor about the battle, for the Saxons are so astonished at the sight of women fighting that they become convinced that the Valkyries have appeared.

The perspective of the maternal line is most clearly expressed in this final volume of the trilogy. Although the mother's name is forgotten, her line is always there. Mother to daughter, millions will be born—"here a soldier, there a poet, there a traveler in strange places, a priest, a sage," (p. 95), all will carry the fire, the light, that is the spirit of Britain. The hieratic voice of Merlin proclaims the feminine view of heredity: "By [the] line, but not by [the] name. By blood, but not by bloodshed. By the distaff, not by the sword" (p. 122).

Not merely an entertaining story, the Damosel trilogy is rich in its admixture of fantasy, mythology, folklore, mysticism, and philosophy. A retelling of the Arthurian legend from the points of view of several strong female characters, it adds a whole new dimension to the familiar material. Lynette, the king's messenger, more important than his warriors, is an unforgettable character. As the King's "Damosel" she gains the honor and respect due a knight but for a career consisting not of battles but of aiding the wounded and maintaining communications throughout the kingdom. Ultimately she even attains the Holy Grail. For a woman to achieve the Grail is, I believe, a unique event in the enormous body of literature dealing with the Arthurian legend. And all of those other "daughters," including Arthur's own Ursulet, generally neglected in the medieval versions, suddenly become central to the meaning of the whole tale.

10

GILLIAN BRADSHAW

GILLIAN BRADSHAW IS THE NEWEST AND YOUNGEST of the women fantasists discussed in this book. Like so many other contemporary fantasy writers, she turned to the Arthurian mythos for inspiration in her trilogy, consisting of *Hawk of May* (1980), *Kingdom of Summer* (1981), and *In Winter's Shadow* (1982). Unlike the others, indeed unlike most writers, she received an award for her first novel while still a senior in college. *Hawk of May* was the recipient of the Jule and Avery Hopwood Award for Major Fiction from the University of Michigan in 1977 and was subsequently reviewed in the *New York Times Book Review*. No doubt the award was influential, but one likes to think that a promising fantasy writer in the 1980s is less likely to be automatically relegated to the fanzines than a similar writer in the 1970s.

The trilogy is exquisitely written, with a controlled blend of fantasy and historical detail. Although the works offer much in the way of action, the emphasis is on character and theme. The first two novels are focused on Gwalchmai (Gawain) and Gwynhwyfar (Guenevere). All are concerned with the conflict of Light and Dark, a theme manifested on several levels, from personal to mythological, from numinously symbolic to physically literal. The conflict is also handled philosophically, with a solid background in medieval philosophy and theology. The overall tone is that of classical high tragedy. An ironic Sophoclean vision of life is inherent in the tragically doomed efforts of Arthur to achieve a peaceful and just realm based on the loving loyalty of his personal followers, the

Family. Unfortunately the very love which makes it all possible also destroys it. This is a vitally serious and moving account of the great Arthurian story, not mere sword and sorcery. As one reviewer put it, "not the bright, shiny stuff of medieval romance but the sweat-stained remnant of an older, almost forgotten tapestry."[1]

Hawk of May is a first-person narrative, related by Gwalchmai, beginning with his childhood experiences in the Orcades, kingdom of his father Lot. A quiet, sensitive boy who likes to be alone, a skilled harpist and eager student, he is not at all like his older brother, Agravain, a fighter. Their father Lot, himself a warrior king, naturally prefers Agravain, but their mother Morgawse, reputedly a witch, delights in Gwalchmai's intellectual leanings and tutors him in Latin. A third child, Medraut, is not Lot's son, but he is desirous of joining the learning sessions shared by his mother and brother. What the boys soon discover is that their study of the *Aenead*, which they enjoy, is but preparation for the study of sorcery. Morgawse's offer of Power through alliance with the Dark appeals to both boys, but Gwalchmai is troubled by it, remembering the line from the *Aenead* that warns that although the descent to Avernus is easy, the climb up from it and out into the air is extremely hard. One night when Gwalchmai is but fourteen his mother invites him to participate in a horrifying ritual of human sacrifice. Medraut is a willing accomplice, but Gwalchmai rebels, first deftly throwing a dagger at the throat of the intended victim, giving him a quick merciful death, then running away, riding his horse as swiftly and as far as he can before being overcome by exhaustion. Gwalchmai's first moral choice is thus made on the side of Light, when he perceives his mother not as a glamorous mistress of sorcery, but as a queen of darkness, a hideous creature wholly transformed by evil. From this point on, his conflict will always be presented in terms of Light vs. Dark, but the nature of these opposites will never again be as clear as in this early confrontation. The warning line from the *Aenead* about the difficult ascent from Avernus will become a persistent and recurring motif but much harder to apply to real-life situations.

The next stage in Gwalchmai's development is depicted in an otherworldly episode set in the Isles of the Blessed, where he stays until he is seventeen years old. Drifting there in a boat apparently sent by magic, he finds himself in the presence of the sun god Lugh. Gawain as an Arthurian knight is a solar figure, whose strength waxes at noon and declines with the sun. The climactic event of his maturation experience here is drawing the sword Caledvwlch, a weapon that burns with power to fight the Dark. He swears on it the threefold oath to defend the Light: "[I]f I break faith with you, may the sea rise up and drown me and the sky break and fall on me, and the earth open and swallow me" (p. 79). In this episode the basic conflict is clearly delineated, with Lugh as sun god and the supreme representative of the Light and Morgawse, Gwalchmai's sorceress mother, the epitome of the Dark. But this profound moral conflict is not reduced to the simplified image of a battle to be lost or won. Gwalchmai learns that the Dark will never be destroyed even if its specific manifestations are defeated. Furthermore, in the world of ordinary men and women these polarities coexist in everyone.

After leaving the otherworldly Isles and returning to his own realm, Gwalchmai finds himself in thrall to Cerdic, a Saxon warrior who admires the lad's skills in both harping and horsemanship. His harsh existence with the Saxon fighters is brightened by the unexpected appearance of a horse from the Blessed Isles, Ceingaled, whom Cerdic cannot manage but who achieves instant rapport with Gwalchmai. The otherworldly horse eventually becomes his means of escape from thralldom. From this point, it becomes the young man's aim in life to join the Family of King Arthur, whom he sees as the leader in the cause of the Light.

Many trials afflict Gwalchmai, including the malign appearance of a demonic shadow sent by Morgawse to destroy him. He retains his belief in the Light, however, and eventually, after proving himself in battle and gaining the respect of Arthur's other followers, he offers his services to the king. To his dismay and astonishment, he is rejected. In spite of his heroic deeds and his obvious fidelity to Arthur's ideals, the king stubbornly refuses to accept his nephew into the Family of knights. Arthur's reluctance is based on his fear of his sister Morgawse, whose sorcery he suspects may have infected her son. Eventually Arthur comes to accept Gwalchmai's loyalty, not on the basis of his battle prowess but because of his kindness to a dying man. Already the young hero is discovering the validity of Lugh's warning that there are no easy victories or simple solutions.

The first-person narrative reveals Gwalchmai as a sensitive, idealistic but diffident young man. Not a fighter he nonetheless goes mad in battle only when riding the otherworldly horse Ceingaled. The boy who preferred harping to fighting and who learned to throw a spear only from horseback becomes an adult warrior only when carried by the steed of the Sidhe. Even then, after the battle he forgets his performance during it.

When Gwalchmai finally becomes one of the Family, one of his best friends is Bedwyr, a learned man as well as a follower of the Light. Unlike the fighting men, Lot and Agravain, the more imaginative Bedwyr is willing to believe Gwalchmai's account of his journey to the Isles of the Blessed. On one occasion Bedwyr reports to Gwalchmai a philosophical conversation he had with Arthur, during which each man considered the nature of good and evil. Bedwyr cites the beliefs of

Victorinus, but Arthur is an Augustinian, believing that evil is not a substance but rather an absence or denial of the good. Arthur concludes from this that the highest good is action rather than meditation. For Arthur the active quest for the highest good takes the form of restoring the Roman Empire for the sake of preserving civilization. He prefers well-intended action, even if unsuccessful, over silent virtue. "[T]o act with a desire for good, even if we may act wrongly, is better than not to act at all" (p. 177). His fervor persuades Bedwyr, the contemplative man, to become a warrior in the service of Arthur, the active man.

Throughout the novel, the theme of evil as deprivation of the good is carefully interwoven with the theme of the difficult ascent from Avernus. Gwalchmai's struggle for maturity, his moral choices, his frustrating efforts to receive acceptance by Arthur, all represent for him the difficult path upward out of darkness. Since darkness may be defined as the absence of light, the Virgilian image combines with the Augustinian theology quite gracefully. But the actual struggle is by no means easy. As Gwalchmai discovers, "[T]he world of men is mixed, good and evil together, and there was no clear and simple struggle" (p. 172). In his dreams a sharp image clarifies the nature of the battle, as he sees Lugh the sun god standing opposite Morgawse the witch, "holding his arm above the island so that the queen could not touch it" (p. 194). But in the world of empirical experience Arthur's refusal to accept him painfully demonstrates the continuing clash of reality with the abstracted image.

Although middle volumes in trilogies tend to sag under the weight of their transitional nature, *Kingdom of Summer* maintains its pace and intensity as if there were no break from the first volume. The major change is in point of view, for this book is narrated by Gwalchmai's devoted follower, Rhys. The reader benefits from seeing the hero through the eyes of a companion, a man who knows him intimately and loves him, yet who is far removed from him by social class and personal nature. Our subjective knowledge of Gwalchmai is heightened by this objective view of him.

As narrator Rhys is an interesting and appealing character in his own right. He is the son of a farmer, Sion, who offers Gwalchmai lodging while on his quest for a lady whom he has dishonored. Rhys is much taken with Gwalchmai and wishes to serve him. Although his father sensibly observes that Arthur's knights have too much darkness in themselves to fight against the darkness, he reluctantly agrees to his son's accepting the call to serve one of them. Rhys's practical knowledge and shrewd bargaining skills are helpful to the brave but socially naïve warrior as the two set forth on their travels. Quite unaware, they are pursued by the malice of Morgawse, who succeeds in capturing Rhys in an effort to bewitch him. The unfortunate victim is rescued from this dangerous predicament by the queen's serving girl, Eivlin, a pert Irish lass who takes a fancy to him. Eivlin is a spunky, lively girl with a delightful sense of humor, and the growing love between her and Rhys provides a romantic and comic subplot to the heroic adventures of the Family. They eventually marry, have children, enjoy farming, but along the way suffer contrapuntal interludes of demonic enchantment. On one occasion when Eivlin has been attacked by a demon-shadow, only Gwalchmai's prayer spoken over her while holding a sword from the Blessed Isles is spiritually strong enough to save her.

Rhys's point of view as narrator is important in other ways than directing reader response to the hero. His homely philosophy also provides objective commentary on the Arthurian ideals, which seem doomed to tragic failure. "The world's a mixture, and something always goes wrong" (p. 229), he reflects, echoing Gwalchmai's realization of the inevitable mingling of good and evil. He is a plain country man but inexorably involved in the military and political complications of more ambitious men. He prefers his farm, the fields, the hearth of his home, to the glories of battle. "These vast conflicts were too absolute and lofty and remote from the texture of my life" (p. 204). But as always in fiction and life, he is drawn into those vast conflicts through no desire of his own. But at least by the end of this volume, he and Eivlin determine to start their own home in Camlan, where Rhys can at the same time continue to help his lord fight for the Light. For a fleeting moment it seems that the joys of marriage, family, and the simple life can coexist with the struggle against the onslaught of the Dark.

Rhys inadvertently accomplishes the goal of Gwalchmai's quest. Rhys discovers that the nun Elidan, who lives in a convent where he and Eivlin have taken refuge, is actually the woman whom the knight dishonored and whom he has been desperately seeking in order to ask her forgiveness. Elidan has a young son, Gwyn, whose father is Gwalchmai, although the warrior has no knowledge of it. Elidan speaks out against warriors in general and against the Arthurian Family in particular since she associates her betrayal with them and with their apparent hypocrisy concerning the ideals they so aggressively assert. Although Gwyn admires the knights, Elidan is fiercely determined that he become a priest, not a fighter.

The outward forces of the Dark are still concentrated in the malign person of Morgawse, who murders Lot by means of a magic spell. She argues passionately for the supreme reality of the Dark, reversing the Augustinian position that dark is the absence of light. "All things begin in Darkness, and all things will return to Darkness, though you may struggle your brief moment on the edge of the abyss. . . . Light is illusion; Darkness alone is true and strong" (p. 200). But she is struck down by Agravain, who revenges his father's death by killing her with his sword. This proud warrior suffers the stain of matricide. Violent and moody, yet brave and honest, Agravain will be destroyed by the Dark that he has destroyed.

The end of the book is double-edged as its transitional nature demands. Although Morgawse is dead, Medraut survives; although Gwalchmai will fight for Arthur, Medraut will try to destroy the king; although Rhys and Eivlin will try to continue life domestically, the winds of war will sweep away their happiness; although Gwalchmai makes his peace with Elidan, young Gwyn will become a pawn of fate through no fault of his own. The world is indeed mixed, and the darkness within the knights will collaborate with the Dark forces without, for the way up from Avernus is hard.

As its seasonal title suggests, *In Winter's Shadow* gives the tragic conclusion to this tale. This time the narrator and center of consciousness is the queen, Gwynhwyfar. A sad and deeply moving book, this work achieves the depth of high tragedy in its presentation of the concluding episodes in the Arthurian myth. It also offers a remarkable portrait of the queen, sympathetic, complex, convincing, fully human, a woman commanding both compassion and admiration. Effective as the final volume in a fantasy trilogy, it also stands on its own as an excellent novel.

Highly educated by her father but socially isolated on their country estate, Gwynhwyfar meets Arthur when she is twenty-one and marries him a year later. From the beginning of their marriage she is faced with both hard work and challenging problems. While Arthur is away fighting, which is most of the time, she is left in charge of trying to get supplies for his armies as well as managing Camlan. Supplies are always short and extremely difficult to acquire. Adding to her troubles is Medraut, now twenty-six, continuously stirring up trouble. He lies viciously in order to create enmity and factionalism. He spreads the false rumor that it was actually Gwalchmai who killed Morgawse, and he poisons Agravain. Buffeted by his efforts to undermine the Family, Gwynhwyfar finds joy only in the happy family life of Rhys and Eivlin, now with children. But Rhys, who still acts as occasional commentator, laments that in spite of all good intentions in this world, "all goes wrong" (p. 227).

Arthur's perfect knight, the philosopher-warrior Bedwyr, who is the equivalent of Lancelot in the well-known episode of the queen's adultery, figures prominently in this work. Overworked and almost overwrought with problems, the queen finds solace in Bedwyr, a sensitive, reflective, understanding man. On one occasion when she sees him reading the *Aenead,* her weariness and his compassion, combined with their mutual attraction and loneliness, lead them reluctantly but inevitably into the guilty act of love. At first Gwynhwyfar is filled with contradictory emotions, "my longing, his kindness, Arthur's pain." But she soon realizes that she does in fact love Bedwyr with a passion "bitter-sweet, irresistible. And adulterous, treacherous, ruinous" (p. 69). The reference to the *Aenead* is doubly significant. It reiterates the warning about the difficult ascent from Avernus. It also reminds the reader of the Paolo and Francesco episode in Dante's *Inferno*, where the lovers attribute their fall into sin to their reading about the love of Dido and Aeneas in Virgil's epic.

The adulterous relationship between the struggling queen and the deeply divided knight is depicted both movingly and sympathetically. The intensely loyal and hard-working queen suffers the frustration of childlessness, the threats of Medraut, and the burden of inordinate responsibility for the well-being of the kingdom in her husband's absence. She drifts into the hopeless adulterous love through no real fault of her own. Both lovers, equally drawn by their devotion to each other and to Arthur, suffer intensely. Rhys rightly notes that the best intentions do not do any good in this world beset by darkness. Even Arthur is driven to ask, "Why must we love the Light so much when we are bound to work its destruction?" (p. 138).

Gwalchmai's destiny adds yet another tragic dimension. When he learns that Gwyn is his son, he feels a rush of fatherly feeling for him and helps him to realize his ambition to serve Arthur at Camlan. At fourteen Gwyn swears the triple oath of allegiance to Arthur and is given his own set of arms. Although Elidan had always intended him for the priesthood, Gwyn is happy because he had always wanted to be a knight. His dark destiny dooms his happiness, however, when the lad becomes an innocent victim of the queen's adultery. Arthur has banished Bedwyr to Less Britain and sent Gwynhwyfar back to her family. When Gwyn tries to deliver a message to the queen, he is caught in a sudden fight that flares between Bedwyr and another knight and is inadvertently killed by Bedwyr's spear. This is the ultimate senseless tragedy, confirming Rhys's conviction that they are all under a curse. Gwalchmai is stunned by grief; Bedwyr is overcome and almost suicidal with guilt; Arthur is dismayed because he had wanted Gwyn to be his successor. Gwalchmai dies shortly after. No longer the hopeful young hawk of May, the dying warrior is bitter over the death of his son and depressed over the apparent triumph of the Dark. The otherworld of the Blessed Isles now seems remote from earth, for here "even the best of intentions of those devoted to the Light can create Darkness" (p. 235).

The tragic irony of these events is climaxed in the last battle. Bradshaw's effective version is realistic without either the heroism or the supernatural usually associated with the scene. Both Arthur and Medraut are killed, but the king's body is never found. For a time

Gwynhwyfar tries to hope but soon realizes that his survival would not be possible. She is kept busy caring for the wounded and, as usual, seeing to supplies. When someone suggests that Arthur may be dead, she responds with a fitting gesture; she closes her inventory book. There is no romanticism or sense of glory in her curt remark that even if she looked for his body on the battlefield she would not recognize it, for the charge went over the dead, mutilating them beyond recognition. In this version of the last battle there is no barge waiting to take the dying king to Avalon. There is only Gwynhwyfar closing out her inventory.

In the final scene the queen's pent-up anger finally explodes when the bard Taliessin announces that he will sing of Arthur's glorious career, giving his ideals immortality in song. Not at all consoled, the queen rejects such immortality and cries that the Arthurian ideals are lost because of the weaknesses of the Family who fought for them. Gwynhwyfar retires to a convent. Her last words are written as an old woman when she is again in charge, responsible for the well-being of a hundred people, once more ordering supplies.

These final events are sad and catastrophic, but in Bradshaw's artful telling there is neither sentimentality nor melodrama. The queen's bitterness toward the bard as he tries to salvage the broken dreams as at least a heroic song eliminates the pathos inherent in the situation. The failure to find Arthur's body removes both the mythic mists of the original story, with its focus on immortality in Avalon, and the melodramatic possibilities of dealing with a dead king in any other way. The battles are what battles have always been for the queen, a struggle between emotional exhaustion and endurance, making endless demands for meaningless details. Gwynhwyfar is a woman who has learned to cope. When the battle is over, she calls for ink to write the necessary letters of explanation. Writing to Bedwyr, now in Less Britain, is but one more item on her interminable list of chores. Ironically, when we see Gwynhwyfar in the epilogue, years later, she is still occupied with lists, with administrative details, with coping. In this way the queen is a prototype of the active modern woman, balancing the demands of home and career, with the characteristic emphasis on keeping lists.

Bradshaw's rewriting of the Arthurian legend from the feminine point of view in *In Winter's Shadow* thus stresses the major feminist themes of modern fantasy. The Arthurian quest for power based on absolutist ideals is exposed as hollow and essentially inhumane. The desire for glory and immortality loses its lustre in the context of the human loss, pain, suffering and death it causes. Light and Dark are personified ideas in the sun god Lugh and the sorceress Morgawse, but they are not isolated in individual humans. In fact, it is the virtual identity of good intentions and evil consequences that turns the Arthurian ideal into a tragic failure. The queen and Bedwyr are guilty of the act of adultery but not a deliberate betrayal. Bedwyr is guilty of the act of killing Gwyn, but there was no malice in the accidental deed. Arthur was guilty of the incestuous act that produced Medraut, but he was unaware of it at the time it occurred. Even the malicious intentions of Medraut, the fatal thorn in the garden of the Family, succeed largely from the good will of those who try to follow the Light.

Rhys expresses the tragic vision inherent in these stories when he says that they all live under a curse. But the ending is by no means negative. "Our failure will not put out the sun," writes the queen, putting the Light/Dark struggle in its widest perspective. Although human virtue is paradoxical, its achievements have value. Camlan did not last, but it did happen. Mortal achievement is more important than immortal reputation. And the monks, without even being aware of Rome or of the Arthurian ideal, are converting the Saxons to Christianity, thereby fulfilling one of Arthur's goals.

The seasonal flow of death and renewal is central to the narrative movement. The child Gwalchmai is the hawk of May, whose quest leads him to the kingdom of summer. The Family of Arthur move with him through the desolation of the last battle to the winter of defeat. The last words of the last novel, however, speak of Easter, the time of rebirth. There are elements of both fantasy and the supernatural in this mythic level of meaning. Gwalchmai's trip to the Isles of the Blessed is a significant fantasy dimension in the story. The role of Christianity, although not emphasized in the tale, becomes important in the end as Easter represents a spiritual spring.

The feminist perspective is communicated through Eivlin and Elidan as well as the queen. The Arthurian ideals of order and authority, of obedience and hierarchy, represent the code of the warrior, but the women express a negative point of view on both war and politics. This conflict is demonstrated in an exchange between Eivlin and her father-in-law after the death of her husband Rhys in battle. The father accepts his son's death as in a good cause, the empire. Eivlin, however, vehemently protests the death of the man she loves who is the father of her three children. What does the ideal of empire mean to her and to them in their loss? The queen, hearing the exchange, suddenly feels at one with the woman who has lost her beloved husband. The two women embrace, momentarily alienated from the world of men about them.

Bradshaw's treatment of the Arthurian legend is thus distinctive in several ways. Although it is a fantasy trilogy with significant elements of fantasy, such as the Celtic otherworld, magic is minimized. Merlin does not appear, and Taliessin is a bard, not a magician. Arthur's death does not involve either magic or mysticism, and the Grail is never mentioned. The trilogy also deemphasizes the heroic and romantic dimensions of the mythic material. The heroism of the warriors in battle is not glorified, and warfare is deemed useless as well as destructive. The knights who defeat the Saxons cannot defeat their own weaknesses. Bradshaw internalizes the tragic outcome of the Arthurian quest for empire through the first-person points of view, first of a young hero who prefers harping to fighting, then of an ordinary young man who wants to farm and raise a family, and finally of a woman who as queen finds herself thrust into the role of accomplice in fulfilling someone else's ambitions.

Just as Bradshaw's tragic vision of the legend stresses the internal causes for failure, her vision of the Middle Ages is internalized through emphasis on the ideas and beliefs of the time rather than on external details. Her medieval world incorporates the philosophy of Augustine and Victorinus and the poetry of the *Aenead*. It is neither the austere primitive world of Stewart's fifth-century Merlin trilogy nor the dashing chivalric world of Chapman's *Damosel* trilogy. Rather it is the intellectual world of the Middle Ages, with its many conflicting ideologies concretized through its vivid characters.

11.

MARION ZIMMER BRADLEY

COLORFULLY DETAILED AS A MEDIEVAL TAPESTRY, *The Mists of Avalon* (1984) is probably the most ambitious retelling of the Arthurian legend in the twentieth century.[1] Indeed Marion Zimmer Bradley's substantial novel is much more than a retelling. Unlike Walton's retelling of the *Mabinogion,* which fleshed out the original narrative by means of added details, *The Mists of Avalon* is a profound revisioning. Imaginatively conceived, intricately structured, and richly peopled, it offers a brilliant reinterpretation of the traditional material from the point of view of the major female characters.

Unlike Chapman and Bradshaw, who focus on a few chosen episodes and perspectives, Bradley includes virtually the entire career of Arthur from his mysterious conception to his magical departure for Avalon. The long cast of characters includes minor figures, like Bors and Accolon, as well as the major, like Launcelot and Mordred. And the vivid world of the historical Arthur is offered in a superb recreation of fifth-century Britain, pagan, enchanted, tumultuous, torn by bitter conflict between the old religion of the mother goddess and the new dispensation of Christ. Most importantly, however, the events, characters, and setting are narrated primarily from the perspectives of three women: Igraine, Viviane, and Morgaine.

There are minor changes in plot and emphasis as well as in the identity and relationship of a few characters. The familiar Round Table and sword in the stone, for example, are referred to but not elaborated.

Merlin is presented as "the" Merlin, a role of wise advisor rather than a proper name, held at first by the bard Taliessin but later conferred on a successor. Nimue, Niniane, and Viviane are depicted as three separate characters. Morgaine le Fay is simply Morgaine, Arthur's sister, who bears their incestuous son, Gwydion, later called Mordred. The major change, however, is not in plot but in meaning. The perceptions of the three women, especially Morgaine who is the dominant voice in the narrative, create a moving, vivid account of the Arthurian legend with its spiritual meaning deeply rooted in the religious struggle between matriarchal worship of the goddess and the patriarchal institution of Christianity, between what Bradley calls "the cauldron and the cross."

The narrative point of view is initially that of Igraine, then it moves to Viviane. Finally it becomes that of Morgaine, the most important character in the book, whose words begin and end the story and whose ambivalent role in the tragic web of events arouses both pity and fear in the reader. Igraine, Viviane, and Morgause are introduced as sisters, all daughters of the former priestess of the Holy Isle of Avalon but with different fathers. Viviane as the oldest has inherited the mantle of priestess and is known as the Lady of the Lake. Igraine is married to Gorlois, by whom she bears Morgaine as her first child. Morgause is soon to be married to Lot, King of Orkney. Viviane notes the resemblance of the four women to aspects of the triple goddess whom they worship: Viviane herself as wise woman, Igraine as mother, Morgaine as maiden, and Morgause as the dark, hidden, ominous fourth side.

The goddess of ancient Britain, like the goddess in most ancient matriarchal cultures, bears a resemblance to the feminine quaternity in Jungian psychology.[2] In Jungian terms there are four dimensions in the feminine psyche: mother and maiden at opposite poles and wise woman and warrior at opposite poles. Every woman to a certain extent participates in each of these four cardinal dimensions, but most women tend to favor one aspect over the others. Some women, for example, are primarily maternal in their behavior and attitudes towards life, while others are more individually oriented toward achievement, i.e., the "warrior" or simply "hero" dimension. Each of these four types can be manifested in either a positive or a negative way. The mother may be the Great Mother, nurturing and caring, or the Terrible Mother, devouring and destructive. Similarly, the wise woman may be helpful and redemptive in her wisdom or she may be a witch.

Bradley informs each of her major female figures with a dimension of the goddess. The characterization functions on a double level, endowing the individual with archetypal depth. As readers become engrossed in the highly individualized personalities of Igraine, Morgause, and Morgaine, they also participate in the archetypally perceived nature of the feminine. To read this book is to encounter the goddess manifested in convincingly realistic female roles.

Igraine initiates the narrative. As a daughter of the holy Isle of Avalon, she possesses limited skills in sorcery and the Sight, but given as bride to Gorlois, a Romanized Christian leader, when only fifteen and a mother at sixteen, she has lost her close ties with her spiritual heritage. She learns from Viviane, however, that it is her destiny to bear the Great King who will one day unify Britain. Viviane's plan is to combine the ancient blood line of Avalon, descended from the fairy folk, with the native British through wedding Igraine to the leader of the Britons, Uther Pendragon.

When the youthful and still somewhat naïve Igraine first sees Uther, she considers him a clumsy, hulking man, fair-haired and uncouth, with an unsavory reputation for wenching. In spite of her negative impression, she finds him a congenial conversationalist and rouses Gorlois's jealousy by engaging with him in religious discussion. More importantly, Igraine has a dream-vision in which she encounters Uther in an earlier life. Belief in rebirth was one of the central tenets of goddess worship, and one of the many points of contention with Christianity. In this vision Igraine learns that Uther was once a priest of Atlantis, long before the drowning of that land, one who had shared the mysteries with her as closely as if he were the other side of her soul. They stand together at the site of Stonehenge and bind themselves to each other and to the land of Britain. Unknown to her at the time, Uther shares this dream. Shortly after this shared visionary experience, Igraine learns of her husband's planned treachery toward Uther. She taps her dormant skills in sorcery and sends her spirit to him with a warning message. Saved by her magical intervention, Uther subsequently appears at her house dressed in the garments of Gorlois and wearing the Duke's ring. It is midwinter night, a propitious time for conceiving the future High King, and apart from Igraine, no one notices that the returning warrior is not her husband.

When news follows directly of the duke's death in battle, Igraine and Uther marry. In the years that follow, they enjoy a close marital relationship, so much so that she neglects her two children, Morgaine and Arthur. Young Arthur is turned over to Morgaine for care until she is old enough to be sent to Avalon for priestly training and Arthur is sent to Sir Ectorious. Always wearing her moonstone pendant, Igraine never forsakes the goddess although at Tintagel and later at Camelot she follows Christian customs for political reasons. A loyal and supportive wife, as a mother she is ambivalent. Although she bears and nurses her infants, she does not undertake their training as children. Late in life, after the death of Uther, she retires to a convent where she dies denouncing the Christian ways she reluctantly conformed to during her marriage. At the time of her death she regrets that Morgaine, who should know about her dying through means of the Sight, does not come to see her.

Whereas Igraine is a mother, Viviane is the wise-woman dimension of the triple goddess. Dark-haired and slight of build, she is nevertheless a priestess who commands authority. With her symbolic sickle knife at her belt and a blue crescent moon dyed on her brow, she is an impressive holy presence. She has also been a natural mother twice. While quite young she bore a son, Balan, after her ritual union with the Horned One in a ceremony celebrating Beltane in the spring. Annually a young man is chosen to mate with the Virgin Huntress after proving his bravery in bringing down the King Stag. Balan has been fostered by a close friend, Priscilla, who bore her own son Balin at about the same time. During the course of the book Viviane bears another son, Galahad, at the advanced age of thirty-nine. This boy, later renamed Lancelot, is fostered in the court of Arthur. Viviane has fulfilled her maternal feeling more through Morgaine, whom she has treated as her protégée.

Viviane's primary function, however, is to represent the ancient mystery of the goddess. She is a wise woman, with the gift of the Sight to an extraordinary degree, seeing both future and distant present, and she is capable of performing sacred acts of magic. It is also part of her role as wise woman to interpret the will of the goddess to others. Her complex plans involve the manipulation of many destinies. Through the birth of Arthur she hopes to unify Britain. She provides Arthur with the sword Excalibur, made of precious meteorite, and arranges for Morgaine to weave him a magic scabbard which will prevent any wound from being mortal. She also plans the sacred union between Arthur and Morgaine for the sake of insuring the heritage through the birth of their child, since Gwenhwyfar is doomed to barrenness. This carefully planned event has far-reaching and tragic consequences.

As the priestess of Avalon, Viviane represents opposite sides of the goddess, birth and death. When Priscilla is near death, suffering great pain, Viviane takes on the death-crone guise and eases her passing with carefully chosen herbs. Unfortunately, her son Balin suspects her of hastening his mother's death and vows to take vengeance on her.

Viviane senses impending failure of her grand strategy when she realizes that Arthur has broken his oath to the goddess. When Arthur became High King, she presented him with the magically endowed sword and showed him the other items of the Sacred Regalia of the Druids, the spear, cup, and platter.[3] In the presence of these holy things she asked Arthur to swear as king to deal fairly with both Druids and Christians and to be guided by the sacred magic of those who set him on the throne. Although Arthur swears accordingly, now that he is king he has begun to slight his oath under the influence of Gwenhwyfar. He carried the banner of the Virgin at the battle of Mt. Badon, putting aside the dragon banner. Much worse, he has permitted his priests to ban Beltane rites and despoil the sacred groves. Furthermore, he has put the order of knighthood into the church as one of the sacraments.

Viviane goes to Arthur's court on the day of the king's Pentecostal feast for the purpose of petitioning him to reaffirm his oath. Pentecost is the occasion when the king invites all his subjects to make requests involving matters of justice. As Viviane initiates her own request, Balin immediately rushes forward from the crowd, seizes an ax left leaning against the throne by another petitioner, and cleaves her head in a murderous blow.

The remarkable scene of Viviane's death is one of the most dramatic in the book. The stage is set for festivity at Camelot. Banners are flying in the courtyard, the halls and pavilions decorated with flowers, lists set up for games with a chest of sumptuous prizes awaiting the winners, and people of all rank are flooding in, bright in their holiday garb. The Companions of the Round Table are in fine clothing with weapons gleaming; the common folk play at dice and drink the wine set out for them. As the petitioners approach Arthur with their problems of local justice, the reader is somewhat reminded of the scene in Spenser's *The Faerie Queene* when Una requests the service of a knight to rescue her parents from the dragon. A petty squabble between two country bumpkins provides a moment of comedy. Then as the proud Lady of the Lake asks to be heard, stunning the court with her glamorous appearance—white hair artfully braided high on her head, her sickle knife and crescent moon announcing the goddess—her clear, low, but resonant voice scarcely begins its plea before the mad violence of the vengeful Balin turns the festive court into an infamous site of blood sacrifice. After the initial screams and shouts, a heavy silence comes over the horrified crowd, and only the mournful sound of the harpist's dirge is heard as the gaily decked hall is slowly emptied, and the cloaked body of the murdered priestess carried out.

Viviane's spiritual heir is Morgaine. Seen at first as the maiden side of the goddess, she eventually becomes mother and priestess as well. Her point of view is the most central and pervasive, and she represents the most drastically revisioned of the traditional roles. This complex and largely sympathetic character is a far cry from the evil manipulator portrayed in such tales as *Sir Gawain and the Green Knight*. Here she is both fate and the fated (Morgana Fata), both the fairy enchantress (Morgan le Fay) and the embattled human, subject to pressures from within her own nature and from the world without. Above all, she is Woman, an image of the Female in all her roles.

The reader first sees Morgaine as a child, devoted to her infant brother Arthur but resentful of her apparently neglectful mother. Later, the reader learns of her training on the magical Isle of Avalon, where she discovers that it will be her fate to mate with the Horned One in the annual fertility ritual of the stag hunt. Morgaine is at first shocked to learn that the winner of the hunt is her own brother whom she has not seen in years and who does not recognize her. The act of sex and the fact of birth are sacred to the goddess, however, and the moral rejection of incest by Christianity is essentially irrelevant to the nature of the mother goddess. Morgaine leaves Avalon, preferring to give birth in the household of Morgause, now living in Orkney, married to Lot and herself the mother of four sons.

After this crucial event, which no one knows about, Morgaine continues as the dominant voice in the narrative. She leaves her son Gwydion to be fostered by Morgause and returns to the court of Arthur. Through her we learn about the major figures in the courtly circle, including the new queen, Gwenhwyfar. Morgaine has a frustrating relationship with Lancelot. She loves him, but she recognizes the futility of her passion for this knight who is hopelessly enamored of the king's wife. Morgaine, always sensitive to the ironies of life, notes bitterly that she has born a son to Arthur which the queen would give anything to achieve while the queen has the love of Lancelot for which Morgaine would give her soul.

Morgaine falls in love a second time, with even more ironic consequences. At the age of thirty-four she meets Accalon, the young son of King Uriens of North Wales, who is visiting Camelot. They are sexually attracted, and Accolon wears the symbol of Avalon on his wrists. When Arthur then proposes a match between his unmarried sister and the visitor, Morgaine assumes that he refers to the attractive young son only to learn to her dismay that he means the elderly father, in want of a well-born companion to share his home and rule. She accepts her fate, publicly maintaining her passive pose as always in Christian Camelot, but feels inwardly betrayed.

Morgaine plays her role as wife and queen effectively. She cares for her elderly husband, catering to his needs and acting as nursemaid to his ills. She also treats his young son Uwaine with kindness and affection. At court she is generally respected and liked. As priestess she has developed skills in healing, and she is also talented in singing and playing the harp. Unlike most Christian women of the time she has clerical skills, including knowledge of Latin and Greek. She is possessed of a mordant wit and endowed with political ability. In this stage of her life as queen Morgaine acts out the warrior-hero-achiever side of the triple goddess.

Moving through her roles as mother, wise woman, and heroic achiever, Morgaine in her later years takes on the death-crone aspect of each of these more and more. Since Viviane's death she has become increasingly concerned with Arthur's failure to keep his oath and decides that in order to save Avalon she must destroy the king. Her first step is to regain the Sacred Regalia, which the king has profaned. In order to do so she persuades her lover Accolon, whose child she carries, to challenge Arthur to a duel. The outcome is the death of the young challenger, followed shortly by the death through miscarriage of his child.

As in the original, then, Gwenhwyfar is a major cause of Arthur's downfall but for a different reason. It is not her adulterous affair with Lancelot but her dogmatic imposition of Christianity that alienates the king and drives the supporters of the goddess to plot his death. In this sense Gwenhwyfar, like Morgaine, becomes both victim and instrument of the deity she worships.

The characterization of all these female figures from Arthurian legend is inextricably bound up in the religion and culture of a matriarchal world. Goddess worship is focused on nature and fecundity, with a close connection between human and vegetal fertility. From this perspective the Christian rejection of sex as sinful seemed outrageous and unnatural. The ideal of priestly abstinence also conflicted directly with the priestess's function to mate with the king and bear his child.

The attitudes toward sexuality inevitably influenced the attitudes toward women. In this matriarchal world the role of women was central to life and to worship. The institution of fatherhood had not been recognized. In this moon-centered world woman was revered as a triple goddess in terms of the lunar cycle: new moon as virgin, full moon as woman, and waning moon as old crone. Women were in charge of birth and death. Woman was creator but also destroyer, symbolized in turn by the crescent moon and the sickle knife.

As in Walton's retelling of the *Mabinogion*, the Bradley novel stresses the concept of rebirth as believed in by the Celtic world. Bradley specifically associates the cauldron of rebirth with the goddess Ceridwen, an enchantress who granted poetic inspiration as well as fertility. Her cauldron of inspiration, plenty, and rebirth was ultimately transformed into the Holy Grail in Christian myth. Since she also had a semidivine son, Gwion, her image became easily attached to that of the Virgin in early Christianity.

In Bradley's world, however, the struggle between the cauldron and the cross is profoundly tragic. As the figure of Christ personally challenged the power and prestige of the goddess, so organized Christianity threatened the sanctity of women and nature. Although serious, the conflict is presented with touches of humor. To Morgaine the Christian god seems like an elderly chaperone who goes around at night peeking into bedroom windows in order to see who is sleeping with whom. Her devotion to the goddess as a sexual being leads her to scorn this god who has such a prurient interest in everyone's sex habits. Even Gwenhwyfar as a Christian has moments of doubt about the new male god, for she strongly suspects that he does not like women.

The struggle between the cauldron and the cross is effective not merely as authentic background but as intrinsic to the whole meaning of the Arthurian story. It is because Arthur breaks his oath to protect the worship of the goddess that Morgaine determines to destroy his kingship. Arthur forgets that he is the King Stag as well as the Christian leader. The loss of Arthur also means the loss of Avalon to the world of men. It will disappear into the mists of the summer sea.

The one ecumenical figure who tries unsuccessfully to mediate the contrary worship is the Merlin, who argues for the natural practices of ritual and festival yet at the same time respects the views of the Christian leaders. He defends the existence of many truths and many gods, and is alienated by the exclusiveness and intolerance of Christianity. Although deeply rooted in nature, he also represents reason and tolerance. His primary attribute as "the" Merlin is wisdom.

In her authentication of background, Bradley is revisioning medieval life from the feminine point of view. Like Kurtz, she is rewriting medieval history only from the point of view of social customs. Daily life in this period is marked by extreme contrasts of vividness and drabness. Winters are devastating for the women, who are housebound, unable to go anywhere. Racked by boredom, they spend most of their time spinning and weaving. Morgaine, with her unusual sensitivity, finds that the endless task of spinning does more than simply bore her. It puts her into a trance from which she has to be awakened. The fires are easy to tend during the daytime, but at night the women must get up, fill the pan with hot coals, then feed the coals with bits of tinder to the hearth fire. To sleep soundly and neglect the fire pan would be to freeze infants in their sleep. Even in the long winter, however, the houses have their amenities. Hot bannock and honey, and apples baked in cream tantalize the appetite, and the horn of wine ingratiates the thirst. For the festive occasions, clothing may be quite elegant, dyed saffron for holiday dresses, in contrast to the undyed wool for everyday wear. Personal effects may be things of beauty—mirrors of silver and combs of carved horn. Always welcome in the winter is the traveler, especially the blue-robed bard and harpist, popular for his songs and stories. In warmer weather travel outward is a psychological as well as physical necessity, especially to fairs and markets in cities like Londinium, offering spices, cloth, and other household items. While the men were away for long periods of time in the winter, the huge, canopied and curtained bed typically held three women and a child. The same bed, scene of sex, birth, warmth, and death, came to symbolize the continuity of life and death.

Although Bradley's major characters are female, and although the perspectives of daily life, history, and religion are also feminine, the significant male characters from Arthurian legend are definitely in the cast of the novel. Bradley's technique, however, is to characterize the males only externally. Whereas the women are internalized, so that we know their thoughts, their innermost concerns and fears and desires, we learn about the men only from their language, their outward appearance, and their deeds. Arthur, Taliessin, Uther, Lancelot, and others emerge as strong personalities but alike in the mode of presentation from externals, and from the point of view of women.

Uther is described as a blond, hulking warrior, clumsy in movement yet a respected leader of men. Igraine learns through a dream that he was a priest of Atlantis in a former life, but we learn it from her. We do not see it from within his own consciousness of it. Similarly, we see Gorlois primarily through Igraine's eyes and partly through interaction with others. We see him as a contradictory man, at once kind and cruel to his youthful wife. But we do not know why he is either kind or cruel, and we do not know which side of this double behavior pattern is closest to his own deepest sense of self. We only see and hear what he says and does.

Arthur is the most complexly characterized of the male roles, but even his portrayal is not internalized. As the young stag in the ritual hunt he is stunned by guilt when he realizes that he has committed incest. As king he is torn by conflict between his love for Gwenhwyfar and his profound desire for an heir, which she seems unable to give him. And he is divided between his love for his wife and his love for his friend Lancelot. The many conflicts within this divided character are not explored, however, but rather cited and exemplified in actions.

Rather the opposite of Arthur, his son Gwydion is not at all soldierly but of a political cast of mind. Both shrewd and observant, he sees everything. He is also an outsider. When all of the other knights decide to go on a quest to recover the Grail, he decides to stay behind at court. Sinister and cynical, he evokes little sympathy. Throughout the narrative he expresses feeling for no one except Gareth and Morgause. He senses the destruction of Arthur as his inevitable destiny but feels neither qualms nor doubts. Cold and unemotional, although given to outbursts of violent anger, Gwydion comes through as a disturbed and disturbing man.

Some readers may feel disappointed at the absence of an archetypal wizard called Merlin. The two characters who occupy the role of "the" Merlin are quite different. The initial Merlin is the bard Taliessin, who has lived many lives. A scholar and wise man, he is the spiritual advisor to the ruler, in effect the spiritual father to all Britain. He is a prophet and a universally admired figure. His chosen successor is a young harpist, Kevin, who as a boy was seriously injured in a Saxon raid on his house. Since that event, which he scarcely survived, he has had a misshapen body and twisted hands. Ugly, physically unappealing, he is gentle, lyrical, and, at one point, the lover of Morgaine, who takes pity on him. It is his fate, however, to betray Avalon, an act he pays for with his life.

The many characters in the novel, although memorable, are but parts of a whole. For the reader that whole is a complex reading experience wherein the many-faceted Arthurian legend is transformed through a new, feminist perspective. The legend, while never failing to be treated as fantasy, is ultimately perceived as a tragedy, as it was by Bradshaw. The sense of the inexorable tragic fate is interwoven into the events, the historical setting, and the principal participants. It is a tragedy of social history, of a clash of religions, of a mingling of peoples. The retreat of the Celtic culture and the disappearance of goddess worship were inevitable under Roman and Christian dominance, but Bradley presents the loss as a tragic one nonetheless.

But the loss of the Celtic world with its worship of the sacred mother is redeemed through the feminine vision it bequeathed. Although the goddess may not be actually worshipped in the modern world, we are now more aware than ever before of the nature of the feminine which the goddess represents. This profound awareness permeates the book. To read this novel is to imbibe the nature of womanhood, of being a mother, of loving a man, of being violated, of being adored, of being both a victim and a beneficiary of that very nature of femaleness. Through the character of Morgaine the reader encounters the complete circle of feminine experience; birth and death, love and hate, attack and surrender, nurture and killing. Morgaine's social passivity and private activism is an image that modern women may easily identify with. And, as both Morgaine and Viviane in turn see themselves as the "death crone," that image evokes the experience of the aging woman, so rarely presented in fiction, either realism or fantasy. Abandoned by her son and betrayed by her lover, haunted by erotic memories, a woman of tremendous skill and power yet essentially alone and helpless, Morgaine contains within her the image of the mature woman's plight.

Such mundane and hypothetical concerns as the psychological needs and problems of women may seem the prerogative of realistic fiction rather than of fantasy, but this is not the case. Bradley's novel is indeed fantasy, depicting a secondary world in which magic is operative. As in many other fantasies, her secondary world is the Arthurian fifth century. But Bradley's symbolic quest for identity through the creative transformation of magic is entirely focused on the feminine.

The moving description of the dying Arthur in the arms of his sister recalls the *Pieta*, with Morgaine as surrogate mother. After the death of Arthur, Morgaine visits the convent and realizes for the first time, kneeling before the statue of the Mother Mary, that the goddess is in this world as well as in Avalon. Her work is not a failure any more than Arthur's was. He brought civilization to Britain, and she brought the goddess. Avalon will never be seen again, for it has drifted far away into the mists, but the spirit of the goddess and of the Grail are part of our world now. The Virgin Mary is but another incarnation of the goddess, reconciling the contrary images of the cross and the cauldron.

Bradley's novel is thus the most centrally and pervasively feminine fantasy we have discussed. She revisions one of the most powerfully masculine legends of all time from the viewpoint of its major female characters. It shifts the focus of the events from the battlefield to the domestic scene. It also radically shifts the supreme betrayal: Mordred's betrayal of his king and father is less significant than Arthur's betrayal of Avalon and the goddess. While portraying a matriarchal society, Bradley also incorporates the themes of renunciation of power, vindication of mortality, and depolarization of values. She suggests a world view committed to the sanctity of the goddess and of all women as her manifestation. Above all *The Mists of Avalon* addresses the woman reader as the goddess incarnate.

12.

CONCLUSION

CONTEMPORARY WOMEN WRITERS have not only produced many excellent fantasy novels, but they have also carved out a distinctively feminine domain in this area of fiction so long dominated by male writers. They have in fact modified fantasy fiction in ways that are not only unconventional but subversive. Their message is "change." It is important to realize that the highly imaginative elements in these novels have reference to real societies as well as to real psyches. As Jack Zipes comments in his study of the fairy tale, the fantasy world offers hope to "alienated individuals that imagination can pierce the administered walls of their existence and illuminate the path toward a utopia within humankind's grasp."[1] Although Tolkien's Middle Earth fantasy was both progressive and subversive in offering such hope to the alienated, it was reactionary in slighting the role of women in that utopian vision. The enchanted quest for contemporary women writers is a quest for change on the social as well as individual level, and it is a distinctively feminine quest.

One change is in gender roles. These novels feature strong female protagonists in what are conventionally masculine roles, including those of warriors and wizards. Casting women as heroes, as masters of magic and wielders of weapons, however, is but a part of a larger revisioning of gender. Even as the stereotypical roles of women as damsels in distress or paragons of domesticity are rejected, so are the equally stereotyped perceptions of men as aggressive, lustful, and insensitive. Gender differences are explored in a number of ways as shifting cultural constructs. Norton's witches are idealized women with occult powers; Walton's hero Pryderi wins the goddess as his wife when he stops pursuing her and instead politely asks; Chapman's Lynette, Arthur's female messenger, possesses all the knightly virtues and achieves the Grail even though she is not a maid, having been raped; Stewart's Merlin represents the feminine side of King Arthur; Kurtz's Deryni are a race, male and female, with feminine intuitive and healing powers, feared and repressed by the patriarchal society that dominates them. Correspondingly, a new concept of heroism emerges in these works. Bradshaw's Gwalchmai is a fierce fighter who is not accepted by Arthur for his battle prowess but because he stops fighting to comfort a dying soldier. In Bradley's Arthurian novel the heroism that sustains life is that of the women at home, not the men riding to battle. Their heroism is not limited to nurturing the young and maintaining the household but reaches outward to include planning and managing, establishing communication, dealing with the unknown and the unexpected.

The change in the concept of heroism is related to the changes in traditional values. Only a few of these writers (Norton, Walton, Bradley) actually posit a matriarchal world, but all consider a reevaluation of societal goals. Probably most central is the renunciation of the drive for power and domination. Whereas the traditional fantasy quest stresses the achievement of a power-oriented goal—kingship, empire, treasure—the feminine quest favors the quality and continuity of life and the vitality of relationships over mere victory, whether military or political. Closely allied to power as a goal is the desire for fame and glory, for an immortal name. The female protagonists are concerned with the moment over eternity, with being rather than becoming, and with the cyclical nature of life rather than the linear nature of ambition. In Bradshaw's novel the body of King Arthur is never found, and it would not be recognizable if it were. The bard Taliessin's attempt to console Gwynhwyfar with the idea of the king's continuing fame through poetry about his deeds fails completely. For the queen the simple renewal of life in the spring is more important. Cooper's youthful hero, Bran, the new Pendragon, rejects the offer of sharing immortality with his father Arthur in favor of living and dying with the country folk who brought him up and whose loving bonds he reveres. In Le Guin's Earthsea one sorcerer's attempt to achieve personal immortality upsets the balance of nature, taking the joy out of life altogether. And in McKillip's world the powerful Earth Masters of old succeeded in conquest but thereby destroyed their own children and their own future. The hero who brings peace to that world is a young pig-herder with no ambitions beyond his desire to get married and to pursue his favorite intellectual pastime of solving riddles, and who reluctantly accepts his destiny to act.

Also significant in these fantasy novels by women is a pervasive tendency to depolarize values. The traditional dualisms have historically designated women as Other. In this fiction, whether the Other is posited as gender, race, or ideology, the aim is not to destroy it or to convert its nature but to accept and integrate it. Norton's Witch World boasts many rational races in nonhuman form, all of which are respected as equals. On the social level Kurtz's gifted sorcerers and Le Guin's wise dragons are Others who deserve to be integrated, not repelled. When the polarized conflict takes the form of Feminine vs. Masculine, the resolution is often through androgyny. The cult of virginity among Norton's witches gives way to marriage. In McKillip the union of male and female signifies the totality of the four elements, with Morgon as earth and air, and Raederle as fire and water. In this depolarization of opposites, the conventional conflict of good and evil also tends to give way. For Le Guin the concepts are irrelevant to the more fundamental issue of balance in nature, of the equal importance of dark and light. Even for writers like Cooper and Bradshaw who deal with a polarity of dark and light, these concepts are seen as extrahuman, with the force of the light just as negative and blinding as that of the dark. On the human plane the stress is on ambiguity and ambivalence. For Bradley this moral dualism represents the destructive intrusion of Christianity as a patriarchal religion, which heedlessly despoils the environment and arbitrarily condemns the natural freedom of sexuality.

Several of these women writers have also effectively undermined the authority of male discourse concerning one of the major myths of the Western world, i.e., the legends of King Arthur and the knights of the Round Table. In the traditional Arthurian material the major figures are the king, his advisor Merlin, and several of his knightly followers. Most of the female roles are either passive or negative. Particularly villainous are Guenevere, guilty of betraying Arthur through her adultery with Lancelot, and Morgan le Fay, an evil sorceress determined to bring about the fall of Arthur by any means. In the fantasy novels, however, the whole myth is revisioned from a feminine perspective and the female roles are presented in a new light. Stewart gives us a sympathetic Guenevere, while Bradshaw's portrayal of the queen is not only sympathetic but both heroic and tragic. Even more striking is Bradley's portrayal of Morgan le Fay (called simply Morgaine) as a complex and admirable figure, at once narrator and protagonist, and ultimately an embodiment of the goddess as Everywoman—maiden, mother, warrior, and wise woman. These writers choose as their setting the dark, barbarous Britain of the fifth century, not the glamorous chivalric era of the late Middle Ages. And they shift the traditional Arthurian goals of empire, legitimacy, and the Grail away from their patriarchal base. Chapman gives Arthur a daughter to carry on the line, but not the name, and Bradley has Morgaine see in Mother Mary the continuity of the sacred goddess, whom Arthur threatened to destroy.

In keeping with the emphasis on continuity and renewal over achievement, these fantasy novels by women tend to exhibit a circular rather than a linear narrative structure. "To go is to return" is a recurring motif in Le Guin, and Stewart's Merlin retires to the same cave where he was conceived. McKillip's trilogy has a complexly circular structure, ending with a beginning and a disarming lack of closure. Cooper interweaves past and present episodes for a circular view of history.

Not the least of the changes signified in these fantasy novels is a change in the canon. Le Guin once asked why Philip Dick is not shelved next to Dickens. I wish to ask why is Le Guin not taught in modern novel courses? Presumably for the same reason that McKillip is reviewed only in children's journals. Is it not time for revisioning a canon that categorically excludes contemporary fantasy although it is firmly based on such great fantasies of the past as *Beowulf, Sir Gawain and the Green Knight, The Faerie Queene, Paradise Lost,* and *Gulliver's Travels?*

If it is indeed valid that creative art induces what is not yet conscious (unfulfilled and repressed wishes, dreams, and needs) to become conscious, then fantasy fiction, with its focus on magic as metaphor for the transforming power of the imagination, may indeed change the world. The enchanted feminine quest, with its dragons and unicorns, shape-shifters and spells, speaks directly to the wishes and dreams of us all.

APPENDIX:
OTHER WOMEN FANTASISTS

FOR THE GENERAL READER my purposes would not be fulfilled without some reference to several other women fantasy writers on the current scene.

Joy Chant's first fantasy novel, *Red Moon and Black Mountain* (1970), has become a classic. It concerns three English children who find themselves enchanted into the world of Vandarei, where they become involved in conflict with the Black Enchanter. Each of the three must fulfill a quest, but the focus is on the oldest boy, whose dangerous quest brings him to manhood. The secondary world is original and convincing, and several mythic figures, including a mother goddess, are vividly drawn. The second novel, *Gray Mane of Morning* (1977), is a "prequel," set in Vandarei centuries earlier. Less of a fantasy, this work resembles lost-world fiction in its depiction of the nomadic life of the Horse People on the plains. The fantasy elements are concerned primarily with the religious beliefs and practices of the characters.

Nancy Kress introduced a comic vein in her fantasy *The Prince of Morning Bells* (1981), with the adventures of the Princess Kirila and her purple dog Chessie among the Kingdom of the Quirks and other delightful people and places. Its two successors are more sombre. The *Golden Grove* (1984) is based on the legend of Arachne. As goddess she is disturbed by the loss of power in her enchanted grove, where spiders spin silken webs and her devotees experience a mystical state of being. The declining magic functions as a metaphor of the restricted world of women. Less dark but also moving is *The White Pipes* (1985), a medieval-style quest with an esoteric conflict between the gifted storytellers and the evil soul-besetters who use their power to dominate others. The titular white pipes are the goal of the quest for both groups.

Megan Lindholm has a feminist focus in her trilogy beginning with *Harpy's Flight* (1984). This novel is set in a magical, pretechnological world with several coexisting sentient species. Although influenced by Norton, the work shows much originality. *Windsingers* (1984) continues the adventures of the same hero and heroine while introducing the theme of feminist social principles. The final novel in the series is *The Lembreth Gate* (1984).

Roberta A. McAvoy won the John W. Campbell Award for her delightfully different fantasy, *Tea With the Black Dragon* (1984). An ancient Chinese dragon in human form helps an eccentric, middle-aged American woman save her daughter from becoming a victim of a vast computer fraud scheme. The mixture of fantasy, science, mystery, and humor combines well, and the unusual quest results in a most unusual romantic ending. More ambitious and even more eclectic, with witches, angels, and devils for good measure is MacAvoy's trilogy set in fourteenth-century Europe. *Damiano* (1983) and *Damiano's Lute* (1984) focus on the adventures of a talented young lutist whose music teacher is an archangel, and the final volume, *Raphael,* features the archangel who suffers demotion to human form. Along with such fantasy conventions as talking animals these books offer a supernatural crowd and theological twists in an authentic medieval setting. Her most recent fantasy, *The Book of Kells* (1985), is set in Ireland, both ancient and modern, with a weak artistic hero, somewhat like Damiano, and a supernatural visitation from Saint Bridget. From a tenth-century battle with Vikings to a street scene in twentieth-century Dublin, the far-ranging events focus on the Book of Kells, housed in a medieval abbey.

Elizabeth Scarborough's hallmark in her fantasy trilogy is humor. *Song of Sorcery* (1982), *Unicorn Creed* (1983), and *Bronwyn's Bane* (1983) bring to women's fantasy rare elements of punning and playfulness. Language, character, and situation range from comic to ironic in this account of the child giantess who is cursed so that she can only tell lies. The hearthwitch Maggie also adds humor with her unlikely friends, a lovesick dragon and an enchanted bear. The fantasy world is Argonia, a wildly unforgettable place.

Nancy Springer's trilogy is based on Celtic myth and folklore, particularly the *Mabinogion. The White Hart* (1979) deals centrally with the destruction of the cauldron of rebirth, which has been stolen by a tyrant who uses it to revive the bodies of the dead for his own vicious purposes. In this work as in the sequels, *The Silver Sun* (1980) and *The Sable Moon* (1981), the feminist perspective is focused in the impressive

and pervasive figure of the goddess, who appears in many manifestations, including chaste maiden, seductress, sorceress, and seeress. In the
final volume the relationship between the hero and his double, an earth-
child made of twigs and leaves, adds a psychological dimension to the
narrative.

Robin McKinley's fantasies accomplish for Grimm's fairy tales what
Walton does for the *Mabinogion*. She deepens the characters,
strengthens the plots, and adds much emotional and aesthetic
heightening through her lyrical style. Her first book, *Beauty* (1978), is a
sensitive handling of the tale of beauty and the beast. In *Door in the
Hedge* (1981) and *The Blue Sword* (1983) she deals with more traditional
tales, incorporating contemporary perspectives as well as the structural
and stylistic refinements exhibited in the earlier work.

Not only is the figure of the goddess variously manifested in these
fantasies, but the themes already discussed, such as the renunciation of
power and the integration of the Other are much in evidence. Not only
are women writing fantasies of high literary quality, but they are also
offering a subtle criticism of many traditional Western values. Not only
are these female fantasists creating original secondary worlds, but they
are also transforming our primary world through the creative power of
their imagination.

NOTES

PREFACE

1. The critical ambivalence has been noted in many recent studies; see Ann Swinfen, *In Defence of Fantasy* (London: Routledge and Kegan Paul, 1984), which attributes this "curiously ambivalent position" of modern fantasy in part to critics and academics who "condemn the whole genre with a passion which seems to have its roots in emotion rather than objective critical standards" (p. 1).

2. Tolkien's word "subcreation" is from his essay, "On Fairy Stories," reprinted in *The Tolkien Reader* (New York: Ballantine, 1966).

3. Brian Attebury, *The Fantasy Tradition in American Literature* (Bloomington: Indiana University Press, 1980), p. 185.

4. Ursula K. Le Guin, "Why Are Americans Afraid of Dragons?" in *Language of the Night* (New York: G. P. Putnam's, 1979), pp. 39-45.

5. Attebery, p. 1.

1. FANTASY AND THE FEMININE

1. Harvey Cox, *The Feast of Fools* (Cambridge, Mass.: Harvard University Press, 1969; New York: Harper and Row, 1970); Tzvetan Todorov, *The Fantastic: A Structural Approach to a Literary Genre,* trans. Richard Howard (Cleveland, Ohio: Case Western Reserve University, 1973).

2. W. R. Irwin, *The Game of the Impossible: The Rhetoric of Fantasy* (Urbana: University of Illinois, 1976); Eric Rabkin, *The Fantastic in Literature* (Princeton, N.J.: Princeton University Press, 1976).

3. Colin Manlove, "On the Nature of Fantasy," in *The Aesthetics of Fantasy Literature and Art,* ed. Roger C. Schlobin (Notre Dame, Ind.: University of Notre Dame, 1982), p. 27.

4. Ibid., p. 16. The definition appeared earlier in Colin Manlove, *Modern Fantasy: Five Studies* (Cambridge: Cambridge University Press, 1975).

5. Charlotte Spivack, "The Perilous Realm: Phantasy as Literature," *Centennial Review* 25 (1981): 133-149

6. Ursula K. Le Guin, "The Child and the Shadow," in *Language of the Night*, p. 63.

7. Plato's distinction between the faculties of fantasy and the imagination is considered in *The Republic* as well as in other dialogues.

8. Jane Mobley, "Toward a Definition of Fantasy Fiction," *Extrapolation* 15 (1974): 117-128.

9. Ibid., p. 120.

10. Ursula K. Le Guin, "Dreams Must Explain Themselves," in *Language of the Night*, p. 53.

11. Carolly Erickson, *The Medieval Vision* (New York: Oxford University Press, 1976), p. 27.

12. The split in Western consciousness during the late Renaissance has become commonplace among historians and critics. Probably its most famous formulation is T. S. Eliot's phrase "the dissociation of sensibility" applied to early seventeenth-century poetry.

13. Rosemary Jackson, *Fantasy: The Literature of Subversion* (London and New York: Methuen, 1981).

14. For a comparative study of Arthurian fantasy see Raymond H. Thompson, *The Return From Avalon* (Westport, Conn.: Greenwood Press, 1985).

15. In *Modern Fantasy: Five Studies* Manlove notes that Tolkien represented passive resistance and idealism for American youth during the Vietnam period.

16. For an interesting study of the circular plot as used by a male writer, see Colin Manlove, "Circularity in Fantasy," *The Impulse to Fantasy* (Kent, Ohio: Kent State University, 1983), pp. 70-92.

17. The concept of "To go is to return" is not limited to Le Guin's fantasy but is also central to her major science-fiction novels, *The Dispossessed* and *The Left Hand of Darkness*.

18. For a discussion of the feminist emphasis on the second half of the hero journey, see Linda Olds, *Fully Human* (Englewood Cliffs, N. J.: Prentice-Hall, 1981), pp. 179 ff.

19. Butor is quoted in Jack Zipes, *Breaking the Magic Spell* (Austin: University of Texas Press, 1979; New York: Methuen, 1984), p. 30. Zipes also notes that the impulse to magic is "rooted in a historically explicable desire to overcome oppression and change society" (p. 30).

20. Terry Eagleton, *Literary Theory* (Minneaspolis: University of Minnesota Press, 1983), p. 150.

2. ANDRE NORTON

1. See Roger C. Schlobin, *Andre Norton: A Primary and Secondary Bibliography* (Boston: G. K. Hall, 1980), pp. xiii-xv.

2. Paul Walker, *Speaking of Science Fiction: The Paul Walker Interviews* (Oradell, N. J.: Luna Publications, 1978), p. 265.

3. Ibid., p. 268. "I firmly believe that a too-quick expansion of 'science' in the past century is at the root of many of our present ills."

4. Sandra Miesel, "Introduction," *Witch World*, by Andre Norton (Boston: Gregg Press, 1977), p. xxiv.

3. SUSAN COOPER

1. Her rich use of Celtic myth is worthy of a separate study.

4. URSULA K. LE GUIN

1. The Earthsea trilogy has received extensive critical attention. The reader is referred to my annotated bibliography in *Ursula K. Le Guin* (Boston: G. K. Hall), 1984.

2. Ursula K. Le Guin, "The Child and the Shadow," in *The Language of the Night* (New York: G. P. Putnam's, 1979), p. 65.

3. Ibid., p. 64.

4. The bird is symbolic of the soul in folklore the world over, as attested to extensive evidence in Frazer's *Golden Bough*. The moment of death was symbolized in medieval French drama by the release of a caged bird.

5. In ancient times bactyllic stones, or meteorites, were held to be sacred.

6. See John Pfeiffer, "But Dragons Have Keen Ears: On Hearing Earthsea with Recollections of Beowulf," in *Ursula K. Le Guin: Voyager to Inner Lands and Outer Space*, ed. Joe de Bolt (Port Washington, N.Y.: Kennikat Press, 1979), pp. 115-127.

7. Le Guin, "Dreams Must Explain Themselves," in *Language of the Night*, p. 55.

8. See Erich Neumann, *The Great Mother* (Princeton, N.J.: Princeton University Press, 1963).

9. Ibid.

10. For a discussion of the labyrinth, see John Layard, *The Lady with the Hare* (London: Faber and Faber, 1944).

11. Rollin A. Lassiter, "Four Letters About Le Guin," *Le Guin: Voyager*, p. 100.

12. Le Guin, "Dreams Must Explain Themselves," in *Language of the Night*, p. 55.

13. For a discussion of the cosmic tree and the world axis, see Mircea Eliade, *Patterns of Comparative Religion* (New York: Sheed and Ward, 1958).

14. The analogy with Shakespeare's Prospero (*The Tempest*) is worth noting. Prospero, however, discards his wand deliberately.

5. EVANGELINE WALTON

1. The four traditional tales treated by Walton are actually a subgroup of the *Mabinogion* called the Four Branches. For the reader who wishes to compare Walton's version with a translation of the original Four Branches, the following are recommended: Jeffrey Gantz, *The Mabinogion* (Harmondsworth, Eng.: Penguin Books, 1976); Patrick K. Ford, *The Mabinogi* (Berkeley, Los Angeles, and London: University of California Press, 1977).

2. Celtic beliefs concerning the otherworld(s) are discussed in Proinsias MacCana, *Celtic Mythology* (London: Hamlyn, 1970).

3. Quoted from an interview in *Fantasy Review* (March 1984): 7-10.

6. KATHERINE KURTZ

1. For an interesting interview with Katherine Kurtz, see "Tapestries of Medieval Wonder," *Fantasy Newsletter* (May 1980): 16-21; (June 1980): 12-17, 31.

7. MARY STEWART

1. For the reader who wishes to compare Stewart's handling of the Arthurian legendary material with others, see Raymond H. Thompson, *The Return from Avalon* (Westport, Conn.: Greenwood Press, 1985). For a specific comparison of Stewart's Merlin trilogy with T. H. White's *The Once and Future King,* see "Camelot Revisited," *Philological Quarterly* 56 (1977): 258-265.

2. For accounts of Merlin's life as a wild man in the woods, see the following study: Roger Loomis, *Development of Arthurian Romance* (London: Harper & Row, 1964).

3. Harold J. Herman, "The Women in Mary Stewart's Merlin Trilogy," *Arthurian Interpretations* (1984): 101-114.

8. PATRICIA McKILLIP

1. Cybele, along with her attendant animals, is the subject of a recent study: Maarten J. Vermaseren, *Cybele and Attis: The Myth and the Cult* (London: Thames and Hudson, 1977).

2. Craig Williamson, *A Feast of Creatures* (Philadelphia: University of Pennsylvania Press, 1982), p. 39.

3. J. E. Cirlot, *A Dictionary of Symbols* (New York: Philosophical Library, 1962).

9. VERA CHAPMAN

1. *Contemporary Authors* 81-84 (Detroit: Gale Research, 1979), p. 86.

10. GILLIAN BRADSHAW

1. *School Library Journal* (September 1981): 144.

11. MARION ZIMMER BRADLEY

1. See Chapter 7, note 1, for reference to comparative information on the Arthurian legend in fiction.

2. For a detailed discussion of Jung's theory of the four-sided feminine psyche, see the following: Nor Hall, *The Moon and the Virgin* (New York: Harper and Row, 1980); Ann Belford Ulanov, *The Feminine in Jungian Psychology and in Christian Theology* (Evanston: Northwestern University, 1971).

3. Descriptions of the Holy Grail and of the four items constituting the Holy Regalia (spear, lance, chalice, platter) that are part of the legendary quest are to be found in several studies, including Emma Jung and Marie-Louise von Franz, *The Grail Legend* (London: Hodder and Stoughton, 1971; New York: G. P.

Putnam's, 1970); Roger Loomis, *The Grail: From Celtic Myth to Christian Symbol* (Cardiff: University of Wales Press; New York: Columbia University Press, 1963); and John Matthews, *The Grail: Quest for Eternal Life* (London: Thames and Hudson, 1981; New York: Crossroads, 1981).

12. CONCLUSION

1. Jack Zipes, *Breaking the Magic Spell* (New York: Methuen, 1984), p. 157.

BIBLIOGRAPHY

PRIMARY SOURCES

Bradley, Marion Zimmer. *The Mists of Avalon*. New York: Alfred A. Knopf, 1983.

Bradshaw, Gillian. *Hawk of May*. New York: Simon and Schuster, 1980; New York: NAL, 1981.

_____. *Kingdom of Summer*. New York: Simon and Schuster, 1981; New York: NAL, 1982.

_____. *In Winter's Shadow*. New York: Simon and Schuster, 1982; New York, NAL, 1983.

Chant, Joy. *Red Moon and Black Mountain*. London: Allen and Unwin, 1970; New York: Dutton, 1976.

_____. *The Grey Mane of Morning*. London: Allen and Unwin, 1977.

Chapman, Vera. *The Green Knight*. London: Collings, 1975; New York: Avon, 1978.

_____. *The King's Damosel*. London: Collings, 1976; New York: Avon, 1978.

_____. *King Arthur's Daughter*. London: Collings, 1976; New York: Avon, 1978.

Cooper, Susan. *The Dark Is Rising*. New York: Atheneum, 1973; New York: Aladdin, 1976.

_____. *Greenwitch*. New York: Atheneum, 1974; New York: Aladdin, 1977.

_____. *The Grey King*. New York: Atheneum, 1975; New York: Aladdin, 1978.

_____. *Over Sea, Under Stone*. New York: Harcourt, 1976.

_____. *Silver on the Tree*. New York: Atheneum, 1977; New York: Aladdin, 1977.

Kress, Nancy. *The Prince of Morning Bells*. New York: Pocket Books, 1981.

_____. *The Golden Grove*. New York: Pocket Books, 1984.

_____. *The White Pipes*. New York: Pocket Books, 1985.

Kurtz, Katherine. *Deryni Rising*. New York: Ballantine, 1970.

———. *Deryni Checkmate*. New York: Ballantine, 1972.

———. *High Deryni*. New York: Ballantine, 1973.

———. *Camber of Culdi*. New York: Ballantine, 1976; New York: Del Rey, 1979.

———. *Saint Camber*. New York: Del Rey, 1978.

———. *Camber the Heretic*. New York: Del Rey, 1981.

Le Guin, Ursula K. *A Wizard of Earthsea*. Berkeley: Parnassus, 1968; New York: Bantam, 1975.

———. *The Tombs of Atuan*. New York: Atheneum, 1971; New York: Bantam, 1975.

———. *The Farthest Shore*. New York: Atheneum, 1972; New York: Bantam, 1975.

Lindholm, Megan. *Harpy's Flight*. New York: Ace, 1984.

———. *Windsinger*. New York: Ace, 1984.

———. *The Lembreth Gate*. New York: Ace, 1984.

McAvoy, Roberta A. *Tea With the Black Dragon*. New York: Bantam, 1983.

———. *Damiano*. New York: Bantam, 1984.

———. *Damiano's Lute*. New York: Bantam, 1984.

———. *Raphael*. New York: Bantam, 1984.

———. *The Book of Kells*. New York; Bantam, 1985.

McKillip, Patricia A. *The Forgotten Beasts of Eld*. New York: Berkeley, 1974.

———. *The Riddlemaster of Hed*. New York: Ballantine, 1976.

———. *Heir of Sea and Fire*. New York: Ballantine, 1977.

———. *Harpist in the Wind*. New York; Ballantine, 1979.

McKinley, Robin. *Beauty*. New York: Harper & Row, 1978.

———. *Door in the Hedge*. New York: Ace, 1981.

———. *The Blue Sword*. New York: Berkeley, 1983.

Norton, Andre. *Witch World*. New York: Ace, 1963; Boston: Gregg, 1977.

———. *Web of the Witch World*. New York: Ace, 1964; Boston: Gregg, 1977.

———. *Three Against the Witch World*. New York: Ace, 1965; Boston: Gregg, 1977.

———. *Steel Magic*. Cleveland: World, 1965.

———. *The Year of the Unicorn*. New York: Ace, 1965.

———. *Octagon Magic*. New York: Pocket Books, 1967.

———. *Warlock of the Witch World*. New York: Ace, 1967; Boston: Gregg, 1977.

———. *Sorceress of the Witch World*. New York: Ace, 1968; Boston: Gregg, 1977.

———. *Fur Magic*. New York: Pocket Books, 1968.

———. *Dragon Magic*. New York: Ace, 1972.

———. *The Crystal Gryphon*. New York: Atheneum, 1972.

———. *The Jargoon Pard*. New York: Atheneum, 1974; New York: Fawcett, 1975.

———. *Lavender-Green Magic*. New York: Ace, 1974.

———. *Merlin's Mirror*. New York: Daw, 1975.

———. *Red Hart Magic*. New York: Ace, 1976.

———. *Gryphon in Glory*. New York; Atheneum, 1981.

Scarborough, Elizabeth. *Song of Sorcery*. New York: Bantam, 1982.

———. *The Unicorn Creed*. New York: Bantam, 1983.

———. *Bronwyn's Bane*. New York; Bantam, 1983.

Springer, Nancy. *The White Hart*. New York: Pocket Books, 1979.

_____. *The Silver Sun*. New York: Pocket Books, 1980.

_____. *The Sable Moon*. New York: Pocket Books, 1981.

Stewart, Mary. *The Crystal Cave*. New York: Morrow, 1970; New York: Fawcett, 1978.

_____. *The Hollow Hills*. New York: Morrow, 1973; New York: Fawcett, 1978.

_____. *The Last Enchantment*. New York: Morrow, 1979; New York: Fawcett, 1981.

_____. *The Wicked Day*. New York: Morrow, 1983.

Walton, Evangeline. *The Children of Llyr*. New York: Ballantine, 1971; New York: Del Ray, 1978.

_____. *The Prince of Annwn*. New York: Ballantine, 1974; New York: Del Rey, 1978.

_____. *The Island of the Mighty*. New York: Ballantine, 1970; New York: Del Rey, 1979. (Originally published as *The Virgin and the Swine*. Chicago: Willett, Clark, 1936).

_____. *The Song of Rhiannon*. New York: Ballantine, 1972; New York: Del Rey, 1979.

SECONDARY SOURCES

Attebury, Brian. *The Fantasy Tradition in American Literature*. Bloomington: Indiana University Press, 1980.

Collins, Bob. "Evangeline Walton: An Appreciation." *Fantasy Review* (March 1985): 6.

Cox, Harvey. *The Feast of Fools*. Cambridge, Mass.: Harvard University Press, 1969.

Crossley, Robert. "Education and Fantasy." *College English* 37 (1975): 281-93.

Elliot, Jeffrey. "Tapestries of Medieval Wonder." *Fantasy Newsletter* (May 1980): 16-21; (June 1980): 12-17, 31.

Evans, W.D. Emrys. "The Welsh Mabinogion: Tellings and Retellings." *Children's Literature in Education* 1 (1978): 17-33.

Fredericks, S. C. "Problems of Fantasy." *Science-Fiction Studies* 5 (1978): 33-44.

Fries, Maureen. "Camelot Revisited." *Philological Quarterly* 56 (1977): 258-265.

Godwin, Parke. "The Road to Camelot." *Fantasy Review* (April 1984): 6-9.

Irwin, W. R. *The Game of the Impossible: The Rhetoric of Fantasy*. Urbana: University of Illinois, 1976.

Jackson, Rosemary. *Fantasy: The Literature of Subversion*. New York and London: Methuen, 1981.

Jameson, Frederic. "Magical Narratives." *New Literary History* (1975): 136-63.

Manlove, Colin. *Modern Fantasy: Five Studies*. Cambridge: Cambridge University Press, 1975.

_____. *The Impulse to Fantasy*. Kent, Ohio: Kent State University, 1983.

Miesel, Sandra. Introduction to *Witch World,* by Andre Norton. Boston: Gregg Press, 1977.

Mobley, Jane. "Toward a Definition of Fantasy." *Extrapolation* 15 (1974): 117-128.

Prickett, Stephen. *Victorian Fantasy*. Bloomington: Indiana University Press, 1970.

Rabkin, Eric. *The Fantastic in Literature*. Princeton, N.J.: Princeton University Press, 1976.

Schlobin, Roger C., ed. *The Aesthetics of Fantasy Literature and Art*. Notre Dame, Ind.: University of Notre Dame Press and Harvester Press, 1982.

Spencer, Paul. "Evangeline Walton: An Interview." *Fantasy Review* (March 1985): 7-10.

Spivack, Charlotte. "Merlin Redivivus: The Celtic Wizard in Modern Literature." *Centennial Review* (Spring 1978): 164-179.

_____. "The Perilous Realm: Phantasy as Literature." *Centennial Review* 25 (1981): 133-149.

_____. *Ursula K. Le Guin*. Boston: G. K. Hall, 1984.

Swinfen, Ann. *In Defence of Fantasy*. London and Boston: Routledge and Kegan Paul, 1984.

Thompson, Raymond H. *The Return from Avalon*. Westport, Conn.: Greenwood Press, 1985.

Todorov, Tzvetan. *Fantasy: A Structural Approach to a Literary Genre*. Translated by Richard Howard. Cleveland: Case Western Reserve University, 1973.

Walker, Paul. *Speaking of Science Fiction: The Paul Walker Interviews*. Oradell, N. J.: Luna Publications, 1978.

Wolfe, Gary. "Symbolic Fantasy." *Genre* 8 (1975): 194-209.

Yoke, Carl. *Proponents of Individualism: Roger Zelasny and Andre Norton*. Kent, Ohio: Kent State University Press, 1979.

Zipes, Jack. *Breaking the Magic Spell*. Austin: University of Texas Press, 1979; New York: Methuen, 1984.

REFERENCE WORKS

Cogell, Elizabeth Cummins. *Ursula K. Le Guin: A Primary and Secondary Bibliography*. Boston: G. K. Hall, 1983.

Schlobin, Roger C. *Andre Norton: A Primary and Secondary Bibliography*. Boston: G. K. Hall, 1980.

Schlobin, Roger C. *The Literature of Fantasy: A Comprehensive, Annotated Bibliography of Modern Fantasy Fiction*. New York: Garland, 1979.

Tymn, Marshall B.; Zahorski, Kenneth J.; and Boyer, Robert H. *Fantasy Literature: A Core Collection and Reference Guide*. New York: R.R. Bowker, 1979.

INDEX

About the Author

CHARLOTTE SPIVAK is Professor of English at the University of Massachusetts. She is the author of *George Chapman, The Comedy of Evil on Shakespear's Stage,* and *Ursula K. Le Guin.* Her many articles have appeared in such publications as *Centennial Review, Journal of Women's Studies in Literature,* and *Critical Survey of Poetry.*